EVERYDAY UTOPIAS

EVERYDAY UTOPIAS

THE CONCEPTUAL LIFE OF PROMISING SPACES

DAVINA COOPER

Duke University Press Durham and London 2014

© 2014 Duke University Press
All rights reserved
Printed in the United States of America on acid-free paper ∞
Designed by Heather Hensley
Typeset in Whitman by Tseng Information Systems, Inc.

Library of Congress Cataloging-in-Publication Data
Cooper, Davina.
Everyday Utopias : the conceptual life of promising spaces /
Davina Cooper.
pages cm
Includes bibliographical references and index.
ISBN 978-0-8223-5555-7 (cloth : alk. paper)
ISBN 978-0-8223-5569-4 (pbk. : alk. paper)
1. Utopias — Political aspects. 2. Utopias —
Social aspects. I. Title.
HX806.c668 2014
335′.02 — dc23   2013025249

FOR YVONNE AND PETER

CONTENTS

ACKNOWLEDGMENTS

This book started life as a research project on prefigurative community spaces. Funded by the Leverhulme Trust, its inception and development were deeply shadowed by the deaths of two people in November 2001 whose work and attitude to life were hugely formative for this project's imagining: my father, Charles Cooper, and my close friend the Canadian scholar Marlee Kline.

In the twelve years since, the development of this book has benefited from the time, generosity, and reflections of many colleagues, family, and friends. I want to thank those who variously answered my calls for help in finding relevant texts, inspired my thinking with their thoughts and suggestions, discussed ideas over coffee, meals, and walks, and gave me feedback on draft chapters: Lucy Sargisson, Reina Lewis, John Clarke, Janet Newman, David Bell, Alan Norrie, Jon Goldberg-Hiller, Stewart Motha, John Roberts, Morag McDermont, Toni Williams, Iain Ramsay, Shona Hunter, Marilyn Strathern, Fleur Johns, Susan Boyd, Rosemary Auchmuty, Jon Binnie, Vikki Bell, Miranda Joseph, Judy Fudge, Lisa Herman, Chris Newfield, Avery Gordon, Wendy Larner, Gail Mason, Yvette Taylor, Brenna Bhandar, Lisa Adkins, Kitty Cooper, Sue Cooper, Adi Cooper, Ruth Barcan, Christine Cocker, Alan Kanter, Vivi Lachs, Yvonne Lawrence, Peter Levine, Eleanor Curran, Maria Drakopoulou, Kal Michael, Antu Sorainen, Miriam David, Bonnie Honig, Ian Stronach, Chris Beasley, Pam Alldred, Brenda Cossman, Jamie Heckert, and, the late Nina Klowden Herman. A big thank you also goes to Eve Darian-Smith and Philip McCarty for the use of their lovely house in Santa Barbara, a good place to finish a book on everyday utopias.

Many lines of thought have been significantly influenced by the doctoral students I worked with during the book's progression. I am grateful to Toni Johnson for her work on the imaginary domain; Sarah Lamble got me thinking further about the dynamic and processual character of knowledge generation in conditions of conflict; I learned a lot from Sarah Keenan's work on space and property, and from Emily Grabham's work on the body. Suhraiya Jivraj, Ryoko Matsuno, Toni Johnson, Sarah Lamble, Stacy Douglas, Jenny Smith, Lucy Barnes, and Achala Chandani Abeysekara also all provided excellent research assistance at different points during the project.

I was very lucky to have four excellent readers—Margaret Davies, Mariana Valverde, Kate Bedford, and Emily Grabham—who generously gave feedback on different parts of the book in various early forms. Their comments, suggestions, and insights have shaped the text in many places. The book also benefited considerably from being workshopped shortly before its completion. Margaret Denike, Doris Buss, Kim Brooks, Vrinda Narain, Carissima Mathen, Robert Leckey, and Shauna Van Praagh generously gave their time to reading and discussing the manuscript in ways that helped me to sharpen the book's core and to tie up some of its loose threads.

I want to thank Ruth Levitas. Her influence on the content of this book is profound, and I am particularly grateful for her encouragement in its latter stages. I am also very grateful to the anonymous readers for Duke University Press, whose excellent suggestions, at different stages of development, made for a much improved book. My editor at Duke University Press, Courtney Berger, gave thoughtful feedback that was always spot on. Christine Choi, also at Duke, provided considerable help and advice, especially with the images used in this book.

Many chapters in this book are based on interviews. I am grateful to the Leverhulme Trust, the Arts and Humanities Research Council, and Kent Law School for funding the necessary research. These chapters, however, could not have been written without the willingness, tolerance, and kindness shown by actors in many of the everyday utopias studied, as they answered questions, sent me materials, and introduced me to other people willing to reflect on the sites in which they were involved. In this respect, I especially want to thank Carlyle Jansen, Zoe Readhead,

Michael Newman, Jason Preater, Gordon Rhead, Sarah Spencer, Moira Dustin, Karen Jochelson, and Heiko Khoo.

Finally, thanks go to my partner, Didi Herman, for her incisive questions and efforts to draw from me cogent responses, for reading and commenting on countless drafts, and for modeling how to make completing a book look effortless (a modeling I singularly failed to live up to)—in other words, for everything . . . and for everything else.

Some of the material included in this book has appeared in earlier form elsewhere. An earlier version of chapter 3 was published as "Reading the State as a Multi-Identity Formation: The Touch and Feel of Equality Governance," *Feminist Legal Studies* 19 (2011): 3–25. A previous version of chapter 6 was published as "Time against Time: Normative Temporalities and the Failure of Community Labour in Local Exchange Trading Schemes," *Time and Society* 22 (2013): 31–54. Sections of chapters 4 and 7 were published in earlier form in "Theorising Nudist Equality: An Encounter between Political Fantasy and Public Appearance," *Antipode* 43 (2011): 326–57, and in "Opening up Ownership: Community Belonging, Belongings and the Productive Life of Property," *Law and Social Inquiry* 32 (2007): 625–64.

CHAPTER 1

INTRODUCTION

In 1995 Florence joined a Local Exchange Trading Scheme (LETS) in England's West Midlands.[1] She joined to meet people like herself, left-wing alternative kinds of people, and to be able to trade without using pounds. Through her LETS, she got to know people and made friends. She produced homemade bread and jams, offered some decorating and gardening, and bought other people's produce and services, including a ride to the airport, dog care, and house sitting. Samantha joined a North London LETS a couple of years later, attracted too by the idea of exchanging skills without official money. She gave people lifts, offered word-processing, and gained a cleaner. Eventually she left because few people took up her services, and the main thing she wanted, house repairs, was unavailable on a scheme dominated by, in her words, alternative therapies, arts, and crafts.

Meanwhile, across the Atlantic, another experimental social space was in full swing. In 1998 a group of Canadians, dissatisfied with the lack of casual sex spaces for women, started a bathhouse. Inspired by the agentic sexual openness of men's bathhouses, while seeking to develop something that was community-based, feminist, and progressive, Pussy Palace was born. It aimed to create a space where women and subsequently transgendered people could develop erotic confidence and a more raunchy sexual culture. Bathhouse volunteers offered a practical education in anal sex, finding your g-spot, lap dancing, and breast play. Carla volunteered to lap-dance at a bathhouse event, the first time she'd ever done such a thing. She described the venue as warren-like, dark, confusing, and exciting. It seemed like a place of incredible opportunity, a place to meet people and to be sexually visible in new and unanticipated ways.

Far older than LETS or the Toronto bathhouse is Speakers' Corner in London's Hyde Park. There, for over a century, people have come to orate, to gather in throngs to discuss current affairs, and to listen. An unusual space, in the sense that you can join unknown others in conversation about politics and religion, stand on a stepladder and lecture into the air, heckle, tease, and make fun of speakers or audience, Speakers' Corner continues to be a place that is especially attractive to those excluded from mainstream discursive fora. Charles is a regular, attending most Sundays to listen to speakers and enjoy their boisterous dialogue with the crowds. But he also goes to meet Corner friends, other regulars he has come to know. They will ask how he is doing and about his week. With them he can express life's daily frustrations and get a sympathetic response.

Sites such as these are everyday utopias—networks and spaces that perform regular daily life, in the global North,[2] in a radically different fashion. Everyday utopias don't focus on campaigning or advocacy. They don't place their energy on pressuring mainstream institutions to change, on winning votes, or on taking over dominant social structures. Rather they work by creating the change they wish to encounter, building and forging new ways of experiencing social and political life.[3] Because their focus is on building alternatives to dominant practices, everyday utopias have faced both disregard and disdain from those on the left who judge this strategy to be misplaced. However, at a time of considerable pessimism and uncertainty among radicals about the character and accomplishment of wholesale change, what it entails, and how it can be brought about, interest has risen in the transformative potential of initiatives that pursue in a more open, partial, and contingent way the building of another world.

This book focuses on six everyday utopian sites. Alongside LETS, Speakers' Corner, and the Toronto bathhouse, they are public nudism, equality governance, and Summerhill School. These are sites involved in the daily practice of trading, public speaking, having sex, appearing in public, governing, learning, and living in community with others. They are also sites that vary hugely—in their form, scale, duration, and relationship to mainstream life. Given the very obvious and considerable differences between public nudism and state equality governance, for instance, it may be hard to see what these sites have in common, particularly what they have *significantly* in common. The premise of this book is that what these very different sites share is captured by the paradoxical articulation of the utopian and the everyday.[4] Over the next few pages, I want to map the main contours of this articulation and then cut through to the heart of this book, which concerns the potential of everyday utopias to contribute to a transformative politics specifically through the concepts they actualize and imaginatively invoke.

Since its early identification as an impossible kind of good space, the utopian has led to a range of literary representations, as well as to other kinds of materialization in music, art, urban design, and community living. Interest in the utopian has also generated a growing field of academic scholarship. While much of this work focuses on utopian "objects"—including novels, buildings, and planned communities (e.g., Kraftl 2007; Kumar 1987; Sargisson 2012; Sargisson and Sargent 2004)—increasing attention has been paid to the utopian as an orientation or form of attunement, a *way* of engaging with spaces, objects, and practices that is oriented to the hope, desire, and belief in the possibility of other, better worlds (e.g., Levitas 2013). This orientation can take a conservative or reactionary form; however, within utopian studies it has largely been tuned to the possibility of more egalitarian, democratic, and emancipatory ways of living.

For Ruth Levitas, one of the leading scholars in utopian studies, social dreaming, longing, and desire for change are key dimensions of the utopian, along with the hope — or, perhaps more accurately, the belief—that more egalitarian, freer ways of living are possible. Levitas's work builds on the influential utopian Marxist Ernst Bloch. While Bloch (1986) finds glimpses of the utopian in a wide array of different social practices, including daydreaming and storytelling, he also emphasizes the limitations of what he calls "abstract utopias," compensatory fantasies invested in so that the present world can be made livable. Bloch argues instead for "concrete utopias," which anticipate and reach forward toward a real possible future. While abstract utopias are wishful, concrete utopias are deliberate and determined (also Levitas 1990). "Concrete utopia can be understood both as latency and as tendency. It is present historically, as an element in human culture which Bloch seeks to recover; and it refers

forward to the emergent future . . . a praxis-oriented category characterized by 'militant optimism'" (Levitas 1997: 70). The everyday utopias of
this book form a kind of concrete utopia. While Bloch focused more on
the *latencies* of the present and the horizon of future possibility, everyday utopias share his emphasis on what is doable and viable given the
conditions of the present. Yet everyday utopias also capture a sense of
hope and potential, in that they anticipate something more, something
beyond and other to what they can currently realize.

The dynamic quality of everyday utopias is an important aspect of
what it is to be a contemporary utopian space. While none of the sites
discussed is entirely spontaneous and most are planned or designed to
some degree, they are not the realization of a blueprint. Moving away
from an interest in blueprints has been a significant dimension of modern utopian studies.[5] While many generations of scholars, politicians,
activists, and writers have criticized the utopian for relying on a static
notion of the perfect society that can be imagined and then executed
(e.g., Bauman 2003b; Shklar 1994), contemporary scholarship and writing is far more interested in the utopian as an ethos or complex process, whose failure and struggles are as important as success (e.g., see
Levitas 2007; Moylan 1986; Sargisson 2007). In the case of everyday
utopias, the materialization of a plan or idea is never a final putting into
effect; instead it involves constant adaptation and change. This may be
in order to keep as close as possible to the original vision, as witnessed
at Summerhill School in seeking to sustain Neill's original vision in the
face of ongoing challenges. But it can also be a way of responding to new
desires and wants, as with the Toronto bathhouse and British equality
governance.

At the same time, despite the reforms and evolution that highlight
their temporal contingency, everyday utopias share continuities with an
older utopian tradition in their ambition and confidence. Trading without "real" money, going about one's business naked, running a school in
which children don't have to go to class, all challenge basic presumptions
about how things should work. Many everyday utopias are dismissed as
bizarre and ludicrous, for they take regular activities beyond their conventional parameters. Against the assumption that anything outside the
"normal" is impossible, everyday utopias reveal their possibility. Indeed
it may be the everyday aspect of the activities that most intensifies perceptions of them as strange and unsettling as they offer an alternative

model for doing the things people take for granted as necessary to do. Everyday utopias do so with confidence, refusing to view their activities as the "outside" world does. For participants, the practices engaged in are normal and right. Yet these feelings and perceptions of normality don't necessarily predate participation; they often come from immersion. In this sense, everyday utopias don't simply enact new practices, responding to participants' prior interests and sense of how things should be. Everyday utopias also bring about (or seek to bring about) new forms of normalization, desire,[6] and subjectivity—from the self-regulating children of Summerhill School to the active erotic agents of the Toronto bathhouse.

In ways that resonate with utopian studies and utopian literature, everyday utopias are oriented toward a better world.[7] At the same time, the movement toward the world that is sought does not take shape only in attempts to prefigure it. A key theme in discussions of the utopian is the place it makes available from which to critique the world as it currently is. By creating a world at a (temporal or spatial) distance from their own, utopian creators de-familiarize the world they know and inhabit; in the process they enable taken-for-granted aspects to be questioned and rethought. *Everyday* utopias also offer sites of judgment, even though this is not an *explicit* feature of most of the sites I discuss. Like literary utopias, everyday utopias largely oppose *indirectly* what exists and what is coming into being, by creating other, better ways.[8] So Local Exchange Trading Schemes expose capitalist societies' seemingly unproductive dependence on scarce monies and fruitless drive to accumulate and Speakers' Corner exposes the inequalities of an inaccessible, corporate-owned mass media, but neither site focuses its time and energies on opposing what is. Rather critique depends on everyday utopias' ability to pose a more desirable but also *viable* alternative.

Critique through establishing something new lies, however, in a complex relationship with the notion of utopia as an impossible space—the "no place" as well as the "good place" that the word *utopia* puns on. What it means to be impossible varies. For the sites I discuss, impossibility does not mean a lack of existence, for the sites are very clearly up and running. Rather everyday utopias are impossible in the way a liberal government promoting equality may seem engaged in an impossible—because paradoxical—pursuit (see chapter 3), impossible in the sense of nonviable (as I explore with LETS in chapter 6), or impossible in the sense of unimaginable (as with the women's casual sex space, discussed in chapter 5). It is because of this apparently impossible character that the sites discussed remain largely (although not entirely or evenly) absent from imaginings of their sector. In a sense, everyday utopias are social black holes, absorbing those who enter but missing from prevailing maps of their field, whether this concerns the field of state governance,[9] schooling, appearing in public, or having sex. Of course, one reason for their erasure may be that of scale: the sites are simply too small to be noticed. Yet, on their own terms, many of the sites—Summerhill School, nudism, Speakers' Corner, for instance—have acquired fame or notoriety. Still, on the school-scape, clothes-scape, or discursive-scape, where one might expect to find them, everyday utopias' relative singularity—their lack of intelligible, institutionalized, or visible connections and relationships to other practices and institutions within their sector—leaves them unseen and unrecognized.

In *Cultural Studies in the Future Tense*, Lawrence Grossberg (2010: 278) writes, "Everyday life . . . refers to the uncatalogued, habitual, and often routinized nature of day-to-day living, what we don't think about while we're living it; it encompasses all those activities whose temporality goes unnoticed." As the tissue of life socially lived, the everyday is something people and institutions (elite and nonelite) routinely and habitually co-create—forging routines and responding to recurrent needs through times of calm as well as times of social crisis.[10] How do these dimensions of the routinized and organized everyday cohere with the ambitious, impossible, critical domain of utopian social dreaming?

Within utopian novels, extension into the everyday is commonplace as utopian inhabitants go about their daily lives. In this book, by contrast, a focus on the everyday extends into utopia. Here prosaic dimensions of regular life — sex, trading, teaching, politics, public appearance, and speech—are performed in innovative and socially ambitious ways that, by challenging, simultaneously *reveal* prevailing norms, ideologies, and practices. But it isn't just the character of the activities that makes these utopias everyday. It also lies in their routines, rules, and commonplace concerns; their embeddedness within wider social life; their "here and now" ethos; and in the way they open up the terrain of the everyday to deliberate refashioning.

Accounts of the utopian in music, painting, and other arts often imply a mysterious, magical, tantalizing quality—a world that is glimpsed but not fully apparent (Levitas 2013). While similar claims have been made about the everyday,[11] there is also a sense in which the everyday confronts, nonsentimentally and unromantically, the mechanics and operation of regular, sometimes boring existence. This ethos of maintenance, of digging in and getting things done, is apparent in many if not all of the sites I discuss. It is a pragmatism oriented to survival and to doing the best one can; of establishing, promoting, and maintaining internal rules, systems, adjudicative structures, and etiquette conventions.[12] Such pragmatism undercuts any notion of perfection still residing within the utopian; as such it echoes the work of utopian scholars and creators who emphasize the dynamic, improvised, often flawed quality of many utopian spaces. As H. G. Wells ([1905] 2005: 176) wrote more than a hundred years ago, "In a modern Utopia there will, indeed, be no perfection; in Utopia there must also be friction, conflicts and waste, but the waste will be enormously less than in our world."[13]

What makes the everyday, with its rules, procedures, challenges, pleasures, and anxieties, so striking in the spaces I discuss is the way such an everyday folds into the utopian. To take one example, interviewing volunteer sexual service providers at the Toronto bathhouse, I was struck by the commonplace character of their concerns. These women were engaged in unusual practices, in the sense of providing (mainly women) with free sexual services and experiences, yet their concerns, for the most part, were intensely quotidian: how to deal with poor client hygiene without causing offense; how to make sure they kept to time so queues didn't build outside their door; how to end an encounter with an inexperienced client who thought she had found a date for the night (see chapter 5).[14]

The deployment of rules and routines indicates something of the isomorphic character of everyday utopias. While they may ambitiously seek to actualize counterhegemonic practices, they draw on many aspects of mainstream culture. The embedding of everyday utopias within wider social life is important too in other respects. In their work on intentional communities in New Zealand, Lucy Sargisson and Lyman Tower Sargent (2004) suggest that proximity and connection to the world outside are vital for sustaining alternative residential communities' well-being and influence. In everyday utopias, the importance of this connection is also evident. I suggested earlier that everyday utopias may be absent or missed from their wider scapes, even as they can prove utterly immersing for participants. But while everyday utopias demand and absorb the attention of those involved, they aren't totalizing lifelong places. In this sense, they differ from many intentional communities, where people live out (or plan to live out) significant chunks of their life. Most of the sites discussed in this book are entered or engaged for discrete periods: a fortnight's holiday rambling naked or relaxing at a naturist resort; carving out time to sell homemade cakes to other LETS members; the office-day advancement of equality governance by state officials; occasional evenings spent at a bathhouse. Nudism, LETS trading, promoting equality, and casual sex can, of course, extend beyond such time-limited slots. However, in the main, the cases discussed in this book concern lives lived only partially, transiently, or momentarily within everyday utopias. Even in the case of a residential site, such as Summerhill School, where people eat, sleep, study, socialize, and play in the same complex of buildings, what we have is an intentionally temporary dwelling (to the extent that it functions as school children's primary home). And even when living at the school, young Summerhillians regularly leave its grounds to go into town, to go home during the holidays, or to take part in school trips.

Such movement between everyday utopias and the wider world requires physical proximity. Literary utopias may involve complex journeys or temporal-spatial warps that deposit the traveler somewhere else, but the sites discussed here lie close to people's doorsteps. Certainly some travel is involved, whether for the children who attend Summerhill School from Japan, South Korea, and the United States or the far-flung international visitors who come to Speakers' Corner. Yet, for the most part, the quotidian character of everyday utopias depends on being nearby; regulars can participate because the site (practice or network) is easy to reach.[15] Indeed a repeated complaint from LETS participants, particularly (but not only) from those who had to cross rural counties in order to trade, was the time, effort, and transportation costs involved.

Participative ease, of course, is not limited to physical proximity. While in practice ease is not always possible or evident, the ethos and symbolic character of everyday utopias suggest access should be unexceptional—that sites are open, available, or touched by a broad public and that modes of entry or membership are straightforward. Regularity and durability are important here also. LETS, for instance, cannot provide a meaningful trading alternative if exchanges occur only annually.

Equality governance seems doomed to fail if policies are ad hoc and sporadic. This doesn't mean everyday utopias necessarily *achieve* a systematic regularity. However, in the case of LETS and the Toronto bathhouse, lack of trading, on the one hand, and ad hoc infrequent events, on the other, were identified by participants as major impediments to the site's more complete realization.

The movement of members between everyday utopias and a wide array of other sites—indeed the interwoven character of the sites themselves in their multiple entangled relationships to other places and processes—highlights a crucial dimension of everyday utopias. Far from offering totalizing expressions of what an ideal self-sufficient life could be, everyday utopias are more akin to hot spots of innovative practice, instantiating something like the utopian strands Jeffrey Alexander (2001) discusses, engaged in the work of "civil repair." While my focus is not on everyday utopias' *extroverted* activities (with the exception of equality governance), the "critical proximity" of everyday utopias to mainstream social forces and processes is centrally important. Scholars in utopian studies often focus on the importance of distance, the estrangement or de-familiarization that comes from observing one's own world from a place that is very definitely someplace else.[16] Everyday utopias, as I discuss, also provide this estrangement. Yet as proximate everyday sites, they offer a critical form of closeness as well. Critical proximity here works in several ways: the productive disjuncture of inappropriately placed activities (such as being naked in public nonnudist spaces); the pressure that political and social contiguity can exert and the channels it can open up (the hope of state-based equality governance and LETS); and the knowledge of mainstream practices that comes from being close at hand (crucial to Speakers' Corner as a critical, deliberative space).

In this way the contiguity associated with the everyday identifies the productive potential of these sites as well as their prosaic character. But the productivity of everyday utopias doesn't pertain just to the quality of being proximate. What the everyday also opens up is the possibility of enacting and performing the tissue of daily life differently. For the everyday is not uniform or homogeneous. While its general form transcends the particularities of any specific social formation, the characteristics it takes on in any given context are shaped and colored by that formation. To what extent, then, can collective actors *choose* to enact the everyday in ways that counter or confront mainstream rhythms and systems? One example of such an attempt — in the sense of being forged as a reversal (even as its terms are also generated by dominant, socioeconomic conditions) — is the slow-food movement (Leitch 2003). Developed in Italy in the late 1980s, although swiftly spreading farther, slow food sought to transform the everyday experience of culinary production, exchange, and consumption. Contesting late capitalism's industrialization of food production and cooking, slow food sought to build social economies around more attentive, locally embedded, culinary encounters. In ways that resonate with other utopian norms, slow food aimed to educate taste, to make visible (rather than obscure) the links between production and consumption, and to revalue pleasure and well-being alongside a more general respect for nature, producers, and consumers (Leitch 2003; Parkins 2004; Petrini 2001; Pietrykowski 2004). I don't want to romanticize slow food, which has also been associated with cultural commodification, the strengthening of geopolitical identities, and various forms of national and economic protectionism (see Leitch 2003; Pietrykowski 2004).[17] However, along with the slow-city movement, which sought to encourage calmer, less polluted urban environments, attentive to a local sense of place, and to supporting local crafts and produce (see Knox 2005), slow food stands as an intervention in the enactment of everyday life, a deliberate attempt to construct or encourage alternative forms of culinary performance.

While not discussed further in this book, slow food as a way of reconstituting everyday life shares many of the aspirations (as well as some of the problems) of LETS, a networked site I do discuss. In LETS, trading, work, and exchange were deliberately articulated to community, locality, sociability, and pleasure in opposition to the exploitation, waste, and alienation associated with contemporary global economies (see chapter 6). Somewhat differently, Speakers' Corner stands as a counter to the commodification of speech apparent in mainstream communicative and media forums (see chapter 8). By demonstrating the emotional and intellectual power of open-air public speech and dialogue, Speakers' Corner challenges the privatization and commercialization of the deliberative public sphere.

Speakers' Corner differs from LETS and slow food in many respects. However, one quality they share is an apparent nostalgia for earlier modes of social engagement and consumption against modern forms of institutionally mediated and managed large-scale production.[18] But everyday utopias do not invariably face backward. Several sites discussed in this book provide a reworking of the everyday that, more explicitly, projects *forward* to new kinds of social relations: from the imagined environment of nondiscrimination toward which equality governance beckons to the new gendered modes of sexual expression and performance witnessed at the Toronto bathhouse.

The Conceptual Force of Promising Spaces

Radical sites and other experiments in living have been approached from different angles. Drawing on a variety of terms to capture their innovative, socially promising character,[19] scholars have explored the ethos, conventions, and norms of counterhegemonic practices, the activities they develop, the challenges and obstacles they face, and the relationships they form. In this book I want to complement existing work by taking a different approach. While it shares a concern with the contribution alternative sites make and might make to a socially transformative politics oriented to more egalitarian, democratic, and liberatory social worlds, the focus of this book is on the *conceptual* life and potential of everyday utopias.

This focus is driven by two interlocking claims. First, as conceptually potent, innovative sites, everyday utopias can revitalize progressive and radical politics through their capacity to put everyday concepts, such as property, care, markets, work, and equality, into practice in counternormative ways. This does not necessarily mean that everyday utopias invert status quo concepts. While some sites may identify such inversions in their original planning or design, as, for instance, in the education pioneer A. S. Neill's objectives in establishing Summerhill School, the practical experiment of keeping an everyday utopia going over many years means the relationship between the way concepts are actualized within such sites and the status quo becomes more multifaceted and complex. Consequently, and this is the book's second claim, everyday utopias, as nondominant "minor stream" social sites, are hugely fruitful places from which to *think* differently and imaginatively about concepts, particularly when such thinking is oriented to a socially transformative politics.

Underpinning these two claims is a particular understanding of concepts. This book works from the premise that concepts are not ideas or mental constructs through which social life appears but the oscillating movement between imagining and actualization. Approaching concepts in this way generates a range of questions: How does the movement between imagining and actualization take place? What happens when these two 'forms' diverge or grow apart so that the way a concept is imagined has no relationship to how it is manifested? And how does conceptual development within an everyday utopia relate to worlds outside?

I address these questions through a utopian framework, which is explored in more detail in chapter 2. Utopianism is often charged with idealism: that it treats the imagination as an autonomous domain out of which new ways of living can and will emerge. While utopian approaches are generally more complex, central to the conceptual framework developed in this book is the importance of *material* practices and spaces. For it is in these differently forged ways of doing things that everyday concepts become both actualized and imagined otherwise. Everyday utopias condition participants to think, feel, hope, imagine, and experience life differently; at the same time, as I have discussed, they are not sealed-off, autonomous sites. Through the movement of people and processes, everyday utopian practice can incite nonmembers also to imagine concepts differently. So visitors can be inspired by what they see and learn, allowing their brief incursion into a more utopian world to reframe the way they experience and think about a life largely lived elsewhere.

The modeling and inspiration that alternative spaces can provide has been explored in relation to various spaces, including Sasha Roseneil's (1995) groundbreaking work on the Greenham Common Women's Peace Camp of the 1980s. There, in a makeshift camp snaking the perimeter of a U.S. military base in southern England, women experienced life along feminist, antihierarchical lines. Those who left took with them lessons learned about participatory democracy, lesbian sexualities, living independently, and protest. But how did these lessons learned relate to what was experienced at Greenham in terms of its practice? Did Greenham women understand democracy differently as a result of participating in its successful realization at the camp, or did their thinking about democracy emerge from the camp's expressed ideals combined with its practical failure to accomplish them?

The complex and uneven relationship between how concepts are imagined and how they are actualized lies at the heart of this book, as I explore in some detail in chapter 2. A conventional approach to innovative spaces or experiments in living tends to focus on stable local concepts, where imaginings and actualization cohere. These are often the dimensions of a space or practice that receive the most attention (public and academic). In the case of this book's sites, this could mean addressing the way freedom is understood and expressed at Summerhill, or in relation to nudism, casual sex, or speech acts at Speakers' Corner. Of course, in any of these contexts, actualization may fall short, but the relationship between how freedom is imagined and practiced is presumed to be a clear and straightforward one in which both forms can be known and identified; indeed that is how we can know that actualization has fallen short or diverged from freedom's imagining. Stable conceptual lines, where what is done and what is imagined are *seen* to cohere,[20] are important, generating and shoring up the distinctive identity and recognized value of particular sites. But while such conceptualizations help to secure the site's existence, making visible what it stands for, attracting participants, and indeed signaling what the site can model to those who participate and then move on (or to those who continue to inhabit other worlds as well), they are not the conceptual lines on which this book dwells.

Rather I am interested in those more oblique, what one might even call "queer" lines. These are the lines that emerge when particular sites are considered in relation to unexpected concepts—property, for instance, rather than freedom at Summerhill School; touch rather than discrimination in the context of equality governance. They are also the lines that emerge when actualization and imagining don't do what is expected, producing complex relationships of nonresemblance. This failure to converge does not necessarily depend on unexpected couplings. It can also occur when mainstream imaginings, such as of care or equality, meet community practices they cannot adequately recognize; when community imaginings of particular concepts acquire, in their operational pursuit, an undesired or unsought practical shape; or when concepts are manifested in ways that differ significantly from the expressed imaginings of participants.

In a book that is concerned with everyday utopias' contribution to a transformative politics, why focus on these oblique, queer, or circuitous lines? Two reasons stand out, which I explore in more detail in chapter 2. First, such lines illuminate the sites in question in new, valuable ways. Exploring the Toronto bathhouse in relation to care and ethics rather than sex or bodies, for instance, fleshes out aspects of the site that remain less familiar despite the cluster of writing on the Toronto site. Likewise considering equality governance through the concept of touch rather than in relation to more commonly applied concepts draws attention to oft-neglected questions about the form and normative implications of state contact, feeling, and proximity. The value of this illumination goes beyond simply understanding particular sites better. Because it draws attention to the manifold things such sites do, beyond their headline contribution, it demonstrates what they can bring to different kinds of social politics. So Speakers' Corner can contribute to reimagining markets through the multiple ways it practically articulates markets to play, as well as doing what it is famous for: instantiating a symbolic domain of "free" speech.

Second, instances where the actualization and imagining of concepts fail to converge in simple, linear ways identify political pressure points. Everyday utopias' practical manifestation of concepts, such as property or markets, for instance, can support new conceptual lines that lead to different forms of imagining. While this may be based on the way concepts are materialized within everyday utopias, it can extend further to unsettle wider commonsense assumptions about what concepts mean and how they operate, providing resources for reimagining in other contexts. Focusing on less developed or less traveled conceptual lines, where imagining and actualization do not converge, also identifies those lines that are most dynamic and in formation. These less settled lines hold out the most potential to develop in multiple, new ways.

The conceptual richness of innovative social spaces is a dimension of utopian epistemology that has received little attention. But if a reason for exploring this richness lies in the relationship of everyday utopias to social transformation, how should we understand this relationship? The question of how change occurs has been given both a temporal and a spatial configuration within utopian studies. Yet while the tendency has been to see change through the lens of nostalgia or hope, the material presence of everyday utopias—as something more than imagined spaces—begs important questions about the place of the present. While the present can provide the terrain in which seeds of the future flourish or where traces, ghosts, and longings for the past lie, it can also be a time in which utopian actors find themselves utterly captivated by the texture and demands of what is now. In this sense, everyday utopias might contribute to a transformative politics by sustaining what *is*, including through the concepts they actualize and invoke. I return to these themes in my concluding chapter.

A Visitor in Another Land

Utopias, for the most part, are peopled spaces, and the visitor is an important figure within much utopian writing, the bridge between the world that is left and the imaginary idealized world (or *nomos*), of some other time or place, that is entered. Heuristically it is through the visitor's journey and growing acceptance of the new world that the one (temporarily) left behind becomes ever more problematized and estranged. This process and relationship are also central to this book's unfolding. Researching different spaces and practices, I too had hosts, people who answered my questions, took responsibility for my presence, and introduced me to others. Yet while visitors to literary utopias may start out hostile or skeptical before coming to see the benefits of their new temporary home, this was not my relationship to the sites I researched. While the sites selected were chosen for their significance—in terms of their ambition, scale, or longevity—they were also sites that were in some way familiar. I was not a member or participant in any, but I came to the sites with some prior knowledge: stories about Summerhill School told to me as a child by my father, my occasional teenage visits to Speakers' Corner, some know-how about equality governance gleaned from my years as an elected member of a radical local council, family friends' involvement in LETS and, to a lesser degree, nudism, and my friends' involvement with the Toronto bathhouse.

Yet unlike the visitor who temporarily becomes part of a new world, my aim wasn't immersion; also unlike the visitor of many utopian novels, my stays in everyday utopias often proved short—a few days at a time at Summerhill, a number of Sundays over the course of eight years at Speakers' Corner. For other sites, where entry largely took place through phone conversations, my inhabiting was also less richly embodied (or perhaps differently embodied in ways that could combine drinking tea in my kitchen while considering the challenges of LETS trading or late-night bathhouse sex). Keen to avoid the exoticization that can come from a traveler encountering striking new ways of performing familiar activities, I also did not want the sites to become too familiar, to lose the particular intellectual, ethical, sensory, and affective traction that came from an interchange between inside and out. Paramount in being a visitor in this context is the movement (virtual and actual) between different spaces, the process of crossing as much as the practices within any given space, the sensory experience of entering from the outside, of trying to act appropriately, and of dwelling on what rightly should be given in return. I return to this relationship later, but first let me say something about my sources and data.

While anchoring my conceptual analysis in an understanding of the different sites' practices was essential, this book does not provide an ethnographic account of everyday utopias. For many of the sites, ethnographic or at least richly detailed accounts are already available. Consequently the descriptions offered in the chapters that follow are brief and purposive, intended to give readers a sense of the different sites and of the relationship the concepts explored have to them, rather than full, textured accounts of places and practices (even as I have tried to avoid easy conceptualizations that come from ignoring the complex, multifaceted character of the sites concerned). With the exception of public nudism, where the material used is exclusively textual, interviews took place with participants in all the sites discussed, and over the course of a decade I interviewed about 150 people.[21] Given the diversity of participants in each setting, my approach to identifying and selecting interviewees varied. But for the most part, I sought to interview people with different levels of involvement—key actors as well as more casual participants or one-time players. I also sought to interview people differently located in terms of age, gender, class, education, ethnicity, and sexuality. Most interviews were one-time events, but some participants—particularly those playing key roles in the organizations I researched—were interviewed on several occasions over a number of years. In this way, most clearly with the Toronto bathhouse, Summerhill School, and LETS, I was able to develop an impression of the site or initiative as it evolved and changed over the course of a decade.

Different approaches to generating data have different strengths and weaknesses, and some of the approaches adopted reflected what was practically possible rather than necessarily preferred. I would have liked, for instance, to visit the Toronto bathhouse, but I was never able to fly to Canada to attend on the one or two occasions a year the bathhouse took place. At the same time, not having my own personal experience to place against the recollections of others perhaps had some benefits (or at least shaped the research process) in that I listened in a different way to stories told, unable to select between them according to my own perception of how the bathhouse functioned. Observation of organizations as a researcher is clearly partial; not everything is on view, and perceptions of places can be unduly influenced by the conditions dominating one's visits. At the same time, interviews are not any more transparent. I was acutely aware of this during bathhouse interviews, since those volunteering to talk were predominantly participants who had had a good time. Few people told me stories of disastrous or even difficult experiences, whether their own or those of others attending that they knew. Thus I am conscious that my narrative is based on the stories of those who enjoyed themselves or who were stimulated by the event, as it is also based on the choices interviewees made about what to relate to an outsider, choices which, perhaps inevitably, focused on interesting moments or episodes. Whether these stories exaggerated the sexual buzz, tension, and experimentation of the bathhouse is hard to gauge. A few women told me stories of disappointment, how the sexual excitement they had anticipated and hoped for never arose; some interviewees described an erotic fading away over the course of the bathhouse's life span. But for the most part, different people's narratives coalesced around an image of a sensual, erotically charged, sexually experimental space.

The political choices involved in responding to interview questions shaped interviewee accounts from other sites also, and the promotional work of bathhouse participants was evident elsewhere—hardly surprising given that I, as an outsider, was interviewing people involved in often controversial places. Summerhill children were striking in their advocacy and desire to protect their school from unnecessary exposure and critique. Officials working in the field of equality governance, if for somewhat different reasons, were also guarded, or at least careful in the ways they discussed organizational practice. If interviewees were unsurprisingly protective of their site—apart from the occasional critic—documents were equally so, particularly those produced by the official bodies that equality governance brought forth.[22] Media stories, mainly drawn on in my public nudism chapter, may have revealed different agenda but certainly were far from transparent in their often sensationalistic accounts of "improperly" naked happenings.

In using different data sources, I have sought to create accounts that resonate with participants' experiences and perceptions. At the same time, my focus on concepts—how they were actualized and the discrepancies between actualization and imagining among participants and outsiders—means this book is not primarily an "insider" account, in the sense of focusing on what concepts meant to utopian members. Rather it offers one visitor's interpretation, anchored in the stimulation and experience that comes from entering, attending to, and thinking about places and practices beyond one's own domain, from being conditionally and temporarily welcomed and then leaving. In this way the conceptual lines followed are ones that cross and recross different spaces and practices. They are lines that move between external imaginings (mainstream and dissident), the conceptual imaginings of site participants as these were communicated through texts, speech, and other kinds of conscious enactment, and the ways concepts were practically manifested: how care and property, for instance, were done, as well as talked about. Exploring these conceptual lines, which are also in a sense my own lines, is not intended as a solipsistic endeavor.[23] Nor is it my claim that these lines are better or truer than those generated by others. Oriented to a politics of social transformation and to the active place of everyday utopias within such a project, these lines offer one set of conceptual reflections crafted through a particular intellectual and practical history grown from left politics, academic traditions of Marxism, feminism, and poststructuralism, the renewed interest in materiality and the senses, and the particular interdisciplinary inflections of sociolegal studies, sociopolitical analysis, normative theory, and utopian scholarship. Other mediations, academic or otherwise, would undoubtedly produce other conceptual lines, and it is the relationship with these other lines, as well as the value of encouraging interaction across them (rather than their forced convergence or silo-ization), that drives this book.[24]

Everyday utopias are places *from* which to think and *about* which to think. Yet one thing to emphasize, in the light of the chapters that follow, is that the attitude adopted by this book for the most part side-steps normative critique. Perhaps surprisingly, given the growing interest in equivocal, critical, and reflexive utopias (Levitas 2013; Moylan 1986), this book works from the premise that the sites explored have something progressive to offer and, for the most part, it does not interrogate this premise by critically assessing or pulling apart the aspirations or projects of the sites and activities discussed. Certainly none of the sites claimed to be perfect or, for that matter, to be utopias, and I do not wish to hold them up to, or evaluate their departure from, a standard they never sought or promised. The problem of academic research adopting such a perfectionist orientation was clearly and challengingly spelled out in my very first interview with a LETS activist in 2001. Deeply frustrated with academic interest in LETS at that time, he remarked that academics got drawn excitedly to LETS politics and promise, but having conducted their research—having exploited the energies and taken advantage of the time of LETS activists—they then reverted to being academics and proceeded to intellectually dismantle the sites studied. Whether this is a fair comment about LETS research I am not sure; however, the gist of his annoyance returned to me many times over the decade as I found myself more critically contemplating the politics and values of various sites.

My decision to decenter normative critique does not only come, however, from a disinclination to hold the sites up to an excessively high, impossible, and perhaps fundamentally undesirable moral standard. It is also a response to their varied and hybrid political ideologies. The six everyday utopias I discuss span a variety of politics, from social democratic to queer feminist, egalitarian, communitarian, localist, and libertarian. Thus it would be too simple to say that the sites speak to my own political commitments and values. In different ways, for different sites, moments of connection and common ground sit alongside moments of intense unease. For while these sites reveal commitments to certain kinds of democracy, freedom, and equality, they also display in different ways relations of hierarchy, exclusion, repression, and inequality. These dimensions are important to understanding the sites as multidimensional networked practices, complexly entwined with the wider world of which they are part. However, because the book's aim is to develop lines of conceptualizing anchored in the *progressive* possibilities of the practices addressed, it is this which I center. Certainly I have not avoided critique altogether. Chapter 3 does address more critically the kind of touch equality governance procures; chapter 4 comments on the troubled relationship between nudism and other equality politics; and in chapter 6 I explore why LETS failed to pull off their project of community labor (an examination that despite its constructive intentions may fall within the scope of my early interviewee's objections). But even as this book does address the challenges facing particular sites and the problems that proximity to mainstream social practices can generate, for the most part I have steered away from assessing the dreams and values around which these sites were organized.

I want to close this chapter by briefly setting out the main themes of the rest of the book. Chapter 2 takes up the question of a utopian conceptual attitude. For, if we want to understand the conceptual contribution of everyday utopias to a transformative politics, we need a framework that is attentive to the creativity, imagination, hopefulness, and challenges that innovative conceptual developments face. We also need a framework that is attentive to practice and materiality. Against a conventional approach to concepts, which treats concepts as ideas that explicitly or implicitly relate to mainstream life and dominant social relations, the chapter explores what it would mean to approach concepts as the oscillating movement between imagining and actualization, a movement that can create new conceptual lines through (and from) everyday utopian spaces. In the six chapters that follow, I go on to explore different dimensions of this framework, working through six different site-concept couplings. Loosely divided into two clusters, the first cluster, chapters 3 to 5, focuses on the questions and challenges arising from progressive scholarship's interest in equality, care, ethics, and pleasure.

Chapter 3 addresses the everyday utopia of "casting equality," a governmental project intent on advancing social equality through statutory and bureaucratic means. In the light of a wider literature that has very profitably drawn on the senses, and especially sight, to understand state governance, this chapter takes touch as its lens in order to explore the forms of touch that casting equality expressly imagines and deploys. Touch is a way of governing and of understanding governance, but what are the limits of touch as a social democratic means of rule in neoliberal times? Can we imagine (and perhaps even find) more radical forms of governmental touch—of a state, for instance, that feels and feels its way? Yet imagining a more sensitive form of governmental touch immediately comes up against the problematic of the state. Critical scholarship has long been wary of the proximity and intrusion that a touching-feeling state might engender, but does this mean states should be kept at a distance? Adopting a utopian attitude, can states touch differently? Building on the conceptual framework established in chapter 2, I seek to create a conceptual line between the state that is actualized in equality governance and progressive modes of state reimagining in order to explore the political strategies that this might make available for advancing different kinds of state contact and proximity.

The construction of new possibilities as a result of reframing how concepts are understood provides a central axis for chapter 4. While chapter 3 takes its primary concept, touch, as a relatively stable lens through which to look in order to see the state, in chapter 4 the analytical relationship is reversed. Here the main concept, equality, is what is in flux, animated and shaped by the social terrain through which it is explored. This chapter also continues with the theme of equality explored in chapter 3. However, instead of approaching equality as an elaborately expressed governmental program, equality here takes shape as a set of normative principles within the far less organized, grassroots terrain of public nudism. At the heart of this chapter is the question of presence. How can equality exist in a context where it is neither uttered nor socially operational (given the extensive discrimination nudists and nudism face)? Moreover, even if we can find equality present, what form can it take given the conservative norms that also structure its realization? Journeying through different manifestations of public nudism (from public spheres to public appearances) and different conceptions of equality (from equal allocation of spaces to the insignificance of differences), this chapter explores how public nudism expresses equality as both a presupposition and as potential. Focusing on what equality can come to mean, the chapter explores how practices, such as public nudism, can open up ways of thinking about concepts beyond the limits of their past and present form.

Public nudism demonstrates how bodily sensation, pleasure, and freedom can intersect the orderly calculating orientation of equality. This intersection is explored further in chapter 5, which addresses the relationship between feminist care ethics and a women's sexual bathhouse. While the bathhouse, as a queer feminist space, manifests certain accepted elements of ethical care, it also reveals the limitations and risks endemic to the exercise of importing normative conceptual frameworks from other, more mainstream contexts. Approaching ethical care through the bathhouse (rather than imposing care ethics on the bathhouse) foregrounds other ways of imagining both care and ethics, grounded in attentiveness, sensation, and the multiple ways in which dilemmas about what to do are experienced and perceived. Yet exploring how a women's bathhouse generates other conceptual lines when it comes to care and ethics is not intended to displace feminist care ethics. Rather it gestures to the importance of approaching concepts in ways that avoid the monolithic investments of much normative conceptualizing.

Chapters 3 to 5 focus on concepts that critical and progressive commentators have tended to avow (namely equality, care, and touch). Chapters 6 through 8, by contrast, turn to concepts (trading, property, and markets) about which the left has conventionally been more ambivalent. Drawing on contemporary scholarship within economic sociology and sociolegal studies, these three chapters address the challenges involved in reimagining and reactualizing relations of exchange, attachment, and selection. Chapter 6 centers on the effort and struggle to put new, community-based forms of trade into effect. Specifically, it focuses on the difficulties LETS encountered in attempting to establish a virtuous cycle in which economic transactions and community development would build and augment each other. The chapter asks why this failed to happen. Why was such a powerful and sustained imagining unable to be put into effect, or put into effect in ways so different from what was sought? While several explanations can be identified, this discussion focuses on time—not just in its insufficiency but in the presence and force of incompatible temporalities, namely of labor time and community time. Exploring why these were unable to cohere, the chapter considers the pressure exerted by three material factors: the limits of LETS design, the individualization of responsibility, and the difficulties arising from LETS' proximity to mainstream labor markets.

Community labor proved a concept that, in the case of LETS, could not move from imagining to actualization, at least not in ways governed by the logic of resemblance; chapter 7 explores the movement in reverse. It addresses how actualization can provide an impetus to new forms of imagining when established imaginings prove unable to make sense of the innovative practices they are supposed to represent. As with other forms of movement between imagining and actualization, this process requires mediators (academics, community members, activists, policymakers) working through the relationship between what is practiced and what is elsewhere imagined to create new conceptual lines. Drawing on community perceptions and academic scholarship on ownership, this chapter pursues a way of thinking about property, anchored in the work property performs at Summerhill School. Specifically it explores how property, organized around an axis of belonging (and not just belongings), worked to sustain a variegated residential community in which public, intimate, and boundary-crossing practices could comfortably coexist.

Chapter 8 also focuses on the work a particular concept can do. But here, rather than taking a single conceptual line, as with property in chapter 7, it explores how two concepts can simultaneously be actualized in multiple ways, with very different implications for a transformative politics. My focus is Speakers' Corner as a place of market play. Through the mediating work of four cultural formations—carnival, tasting, contact zones, and edgework (or risky play)—the chapter explores how the articulation of market play provides a tool for leveraging and for holding an audience; works to redefine markets as pleasurable, exploratory, *nontrading* spaces; and provides a playful structure through which neoliberal market relations can be parodied and critiqued. Thus this chapter works with the conceptual plasticity of the marketplace to supplement critiques of market capitalism. Its aim is not to recuperate the market as a beneficial and delightful sensory structure, but to explore what can be gained and learned from the variegated conceptual lines a space such as Speakers' Corner opens up.

Over the course of these six case studies, this book advances in two directions (which, given the nature of utopian epistemology, is often the same direction): toward a utopian understanding of concepts (as *concepts*), on the one hand, and toward the conceptual pathways and openings that might contribute to a transformative politics, on the other. I indicated earlier that this book approaches such a politics as oriented to more egalitarian, freer, and democratic ways of living. But how do the conceptual pathways of everyday utopias in fact contribute to this? In the final chapter, I turn to this question of politics and change. While utopian thinking conventionally places change in some future time, contemporary theoretical and political developments have cast doubt on change's arrow. In this last chapter, then, I consider the transformative temporality of everyday utopias' conceptual lives and consider the extent to which change is past or present rather than to come.

CHAPTER 2

TOWARD A UTOPIAN CONCEPTUAL ATTITUDE

If utopia is . . . philosophically, a method rather than a state, it cannot be realized or not realized—it can only be applied.

Suvin 1979: 52

The conceptual lines of everyday utopias contribute to a transformative politics, but what does this mean, and how does it happen? In this book I explore this relationship and its promise from different angles working through a series of sites and concepts. Since the book takes a somewhat idiosyncratic approach to particular concepts as well as to the notion of the concept in general, this chapter establishes some core building blocks, explaining what I mean by concepts, exploring their dynamic character, where we find them, what they look like, and what it is that concepts actually do.

To develop a way of approaching everyday utopias' conceptual life and promise that may also prove useful for other conceptual projects, I turn to utopian studies.[1] This turn has a necessarily improvised quality since, while utopian studies offers a rich and vibrant body of scholarship, it has not, for the most part, developed a distinctive conceptual framework. Nevertheless, as I explore in more detail below, its methods, debates, and general orientation contribute rich intellectual resources for thinking about concepts in ways especially attuned to the politics of what concepts do, as well as how they manifest themselves and how they change.

A key feature of contemporary utopian studies is its focus on the work that the utopian performs (Anderson 2006: 694). While this has a representational dimension, the utopian is not simply a depiction of another kind of place, but a process or challenge — a mode of striving toward something else that is better — in which questions of imagination, creativity, and processes of change are deeply entwined (e.g., Dolan 2005). Certainly utopian studies is not the only field concerned with change, nor is it the only field to address the political work of concepts. However, what is distinctive and of pivotal importance for my purposes is utopia's focus on actualization, the positive example or instantiation that demonstrates what could be as well as what is. To say that utopia emphasizes manifestation may seem, in some respects, counterintuitive, for utopia in the popular imagination is deeply entangled with notions of the imagined, impossibly perfect place. However, as discussed in chapter 1, contemporary utopian studies has moved some distance away from the idea of static perfection to emphasize process, conflict, temporality, and choice. Moreover, while older conceptions of the utopian may be turned to the challenge of perfection, they still rely on the work of *enactment*, whether imagined or socially trialed. And it is in this narrated or practiced performance of other ways of living that much of the conceptual traction explored in this book can be found.

The main part of this chapter establishes the conceptual framework, developed in more detail through the course of the book. At the heart of this framework is the work of everyday utopias as "minor-stream" spaces, generating concepts not simply through what participants think and believe but also through what they collectively do. This materialist conceptual framework, with its emphasis on practice and manifestation, as well as imagining, raises some core epistemological questions: How can concepts incorporate the material dimensions of practice? Why is this important for thinking about concepts' political promise? How do concepts evolve and change? What contribution to transformative change can concepts actually make? I begin by considering some very different conceptual perspectives to those explored in the course of this book. These far more common approaches to conceptualizing treat concepts as ideas, drawn from mainstream practice, and attuned to the escalating problems of the world in which we live. My argument is not that these approaches are wrong, nor are they wholly unhelpful. However, they have limitations, particularly when it comes to thinking about concepts in new ways and to understanding the conceptual value of spaces that are innovative and unusual.

Approaching Concepts

Whether scholarship is radical, conservative, or liberal, a pervasive assumption is that concepts are ideational—elements or building blocks in the world of thought. Peter Hallward (2006: 141) remarks, "A concept renders *a* slice of chaos available for thought." Concepts help us to understand and communicate about the world, producing forms of knowledge with stabilizing or, conversely, destabilizing effects. Concepts may be influenced by social practice and material conditions (particularly when they seek to represent what is or might be), but concepts are not composed of the social world they refract or seek to alter. Nicholas Gane (2009: 87), discussing Deleuze and Guattari, describes concepts as "devices that draw on the complexities of the empirical world in order to open our theoretical imagination to things as they might be."[2]

The critical geographer Doreen Massey (2005) takes a similar approach in her thought-provoking book *For Space*. An overriding aim of the book is to provide a way of conceptualizing space that foregrounds social diversity and heterogeneity, recognizing space's generative and unpredictable capacity—that it is not all given and knowable from the outset. So Massey rejects conceptions of space that, in counterposing space and time, treat the former, but not the latter, as fixed and static. Massey's suggestions of how we might rethink space are interesting and fruitful. However, when approaching space as a *concept*, she reverts to a more conventional approach that places concepts clearly and exclusively within the realm of thought. Massey writes, "I hope . . . to liberate 'space' from some *chains of meaning* . . . in order to set it into other chains . . . where it can have a new and more productive life" (19).[3] What concepts mean, what they can signify, even their form is treated as flexible and evolving. However, their stable, permanent dwelling as ideas rather than as (or as including) material practices remains settled and uncontested.

Locating concepts within the realm of thought might seem to make a level of flexibility, creativity, and choice possible as concepts are able to develop freely in an infinite number of differently imagined directions. Conceptual scholarship, however, is usually far more bounded, developing through the historically extended interplay of intellectual engagement and debate. This can be seen in academic work on many of the concepts explored in this book, including touch, the state, equality, and property. Writers may vary in the extent to which their understanding of these terms draws *explicitly* from specific, historically situated places. Nevertheless the reliance that textual approaches place on a concept's intellectual ancestry or provenance structures and limits what particular concepts can mean. Conceptual histories become histories of elite or scholarly usage.[4] As the historian Dipesh Chakrabarty remarked, "The problem with these [European thought] universals is this: they, as thought concepts, come packaged as though they have transcended the particular histories in which they were born. But being pieces of prose and language, they carry intimations of histories of belonging, which are not everybody's history" (quoted in Dube 2002: 865).[5]

Idealist forms of academic conceptualizing have a tendency to drag the social histories and naturalized assumptions of their textual sources (or protagonists) around with them. But even conceptual thinking that does not rely on the history of ideas often draws in implicit and unremarked ways from the dominant social practices and common senses that surround it. The power of dominant social practices to structure what concepts mean, and the limits this can place on conceptual development, particularly in relation to nondominant sites and ways of doing things, can be seen in the case of legal pluralism. While legal pluralists argue that legal orders in a given social domain are multiple, there nevertheless remains a powerful tendency to draw the paradigm of law (what law actually means so one can know when it is present) from state law. Tamanaha (1993: 201) comments, "Law's conceptual connection to the state cannot be severed . . . [T]he search for the institutional aspect of norm formulation or enforcement is nothing other than a smuggled reference to the state bureaucratic legal apparatus . . . [T]he state law model inescapably provides the kernel of the concept of non-state 'law.'" Trying to conceive of law differently is clearly challenging; as I explore below, counterintuitive ways of imagining concepts, including law, face problems of resonance and impact when nobody recognizes the way they are framed. Legal pluralists, like others, are drawn to modes of juridical understanding that have salience, and if constituencies in the global North understand community norms, rules, and adjudicative processes in ways that draw on imaginings of state law (see chapter 7), it may seem foolish to ignore this. On the other hand, if scholars remain embedded within dominant state-generated notions of what law is like, they may fail to recognize other, law-like practices, particularly when these also fall outside of community members' own law-talk. But then if nobody understands such practices as law-like, what value is there in addressing them as such? The challenge of thinking about concepts in ways that diverge from both local and mainstream forms of concept-talk, and what gets opened up as a result for a transformative politics, is a recurring theme of this book.

Concepts can be understood in ways that draw *implicitly* on mainstream practice, but this conceptual relationship to the mainstream—to what is dominant, normal, or pervasive—can also acquire a more explicit cast as concepts are deliberately drawn from prevailing practice in service of a particular project. Within liberal scholarship, this has often functioned as a way of legitimating and entrenching both the concepts and the status quo—as concepts rationalize and render explicable, natural, and necessary a set of social arrangements that in turn consolidate, validate, and justify the concepts. In his work on justice, the liberal political philosopher John Rawls (1996) explicitly adopts this approach. Abstracting from prevailing contemporary depictions, or what he describes as "political traditions," Rawls articulates ideals that, in his view, can generate "overlapping consensus." He writes, "We collect such settled convictions . . . and try to organize the basic ideas and principles implicit in these convictions" (8). "Justice as fairness" is the "best approximation . . . and constitute[s] the most appropriate basis for the institutions of a democratic society" (xvii). In other words, Rawls suggests, within liberal nation-states, the normative concepts that we have derive in practical ways from the societies in which we live. By broadly reflecting and affirming the way things are, such concepts work to guide but also to maintain the status quo through time.

The limits of this approach for a transformative politics—indeed the resistance this approach places on a transformative politics—are readily apparent. Locating legitimacy in a "reasonable" consensus, other ways of understanding justice—whether they emerge from minority claims or as potential lines drawn from progressive minority practice—are disavowed (to the extent they are indeed noticed, which frequently they are not). Yet developing normative concepts in relation to mainstream or dominant practice is not the sole domain of liberal scholarship. Other scholars have also sought to develop normative or idealized concepts by reworking what seems like their common, pervasive usage. While this can take the form of extraction—abstracting concepts from contexts in ways intended to clean them of local "imperfections"—it can also work in Derridean-inspired ways through the (seemingly impossible but necessary) relationship between concepts' everyday practical and conditional usage and their infinite, unconditional, unknowable form (e.g., Patton 2010: 46–51; Dikeç 2002).[6] Recognizing concepts' capacity to extend beyond the norms governing mainstream practice makes it possible to consider normative practices, such as gifting or care, in ways attuned to these concepts' more idealized form; thus everyday utopias might be understood as instantiating what is generally understood as care or democracy, but in more desirable or "purer" ways. Alternatively, everyday utopias might be seen as working with and through the relationship between a concept's conditional and unconditional form, but doing so in a different key, where the conditional form in particular has been reframed.

Yet one challenge for approaches that seek to fashion more "perfect" versions of normative concepts is the question of emergence: namely, from where do such perfect conceptions arise? Of course they may be driven less by (the problems besetting) actual material practice than by genealogical or other epistemological strategies, but to the extent that contemporary social relations provide a ground, however shadowy, for conceptualizing, the question remains: How do mainstream relations ground what ought to be? For even if normative concepts are explicitly framed as reversals or purer forms of what exists, they remain dependent (for their existence, form, and shape) on mainstream conceptual usage and the mainstream social relations underpinning them. Trying to build progressive normative concepts out of dominant social practices remains mired in the effects such practices have on the concepts generated—a stuckness that may prove as hard to identify as it is to remove. If material life cannot be known fully or directly, its effects on (and presence within) concepts may be equally impenetrable. "Concepts' . . . generation and use are conditioned by the social world in which humans think and employ them. . . . As long as the social world which governs the generation and use of concepts is opaque, concepts do not immediately disclose their social content to the subjects that employ them" (Benzer 2011: 578–79).

The difficulty of drawing radical, normative concepts from main-stream social life, a difficulty not eliminated by simply reversing main-stream norms in the creation of such concepts, has undoubtedly con-tributed to critical scholarship's preference for analyzing instead "the contradictory, antagonistic 'real relations'" (Hall 2003: 140) alongside the cultural forms through which such relations are played out (see also Hennessy 2000), forms that are variously read as distorting, mystify-ing, generative, and necessarily interpretive (since we cannot get beyond thought). As a result, critical scholars have tended to refrain from study-ing small-scale progressive social sites. Such sites appear to be trivial, messy distractions, taking attention away from the major social relations structuring the world. Alternatively, they are seen as minor dependent places wherein the problems besetting mainstream social formations (and their concepts) are merely replicated and reproduced, despite par-ticipants' claims to the contrary. Yet, focusing exclusively on the power of mainstream life and dominant social relations to structure the con-ceptual imaginary—approaching this as the only game in town—is con-ceptually impoverishing. It neglects the possibilities posed by a utopian approach rooted in the practices, flows, desires, and projects of *nonmain-stream* places.

The failure to consider such utopian spaces comes not only from criti-cal conceptual scholarship's tendency to focus on hegemonic relations and practices. It comes also from the distinctive register in which work attuned to the future is largely oriented, with its focus on the grim ten-dencies of a worsening present.[7] Ulrich Beck remarks, in discussion with Roy Boyne (2001: 54), "Today a normative orientation to the future is ex-pressed in terms of what needs to be avoided."

Critical work on neoliberalism characteristically evidences this ap-proach. It focuses on what neoliberalism is (and is becoming), as it un-folds a vision of the world seen, unhappily, as taking shape. While not all dystopic accounts and analyses focus on the conceptual, concepts and neologisms are frequently deployed to encapsulate a broader range of anticipated and imagined processes and shifts, from Agamben's (1998: 176) work on the camp as "the new biopolitical *nomos* of the planet" to Giroux's (2008) "biopolitics of disposability," Mbembe's (2003) con-cept of necropolitics, and Bauman's (2003a) "liquid love," where humans are treated "as objects of consumption and . . . judge[d] . . . after the pattern of consumer objects by the volume of pleasure they are likely to offer" (75), subsequently being disposed of "to make room for other goods" (49).[8]

Identifying dystopia through the condensed form of the concept may be enacted neutrally, but it is often carried out in warning, its implicit or explicit imperative being that something needs to be done before it is too late.[9] For progressive and critical scholars, the portrayal of dystopia is an important part of the intellectual-political project, grounded in the academic capacity to identify trends and to foresee the force of present practice as it thrusts itself, with huge damage, into the time fast upon us (e.g., Bhavnani and Foran 2008).[10] While both utopia and dystopia are seen as mirrors of each other in the sense of deploying polarized images of what could be, as conceptual lines they function somewhat differently. Utopia conventionally depends on stimulating desire and hope in order to inspire and motivate change. Dystopias, by contrast, aim to stimulate action in order to resist or halt what is feared to be emerging. Dystopic narratives assume change, that the world is not a static or stable place but moving toward, indeed in some cases already enacting, its own ruin. Utopian discourse, by contrast, often assumes the reverse, namely that people need to be jolted out of passive acquiescence through the education of desire and the creation of belief that it is possible to destabilize and transform what *appears* an overly secure status quo. Gibson-Graham (2006a: xii) offer a similar rationale for their project of discursively challenging capitalism's perceived hegemony: "Our intervention has been to propose a language of the diverse economy as an exploratory practice of thinking economy differently in order to perform different economies. . . . Our hope is to disarm and dislocate the naturalized dominance of the capitalist economy and make a space for new economic becomings — ones that we will need to work to produce."

Toward a Utopian Conceptual Attitude

Making progressive developments visible is an important aspect of modeling and inspiring change. This book argues that such visibility should be joined to new kinds of conceptual thinking, something that remains insufficiently accomplished when concepts are approached as ideas drawn from and in relation to mainstream life and governance and oriented toward sustaining the status quo or preventing impending forms of harm. But what kinds of conceptual understandings and openings are made available by everyday utopias? And how should we approach them?

I have suggested that everyday utopias highlight the need for a different kind of conceptual framework, one that foregrounds material practice and change. In the rest of this chapter, I suggest what this might entail.

EPISTEMOLOGY FROM THE MARGINS

In recent years various frameworks have sought to counter the idealist orientation and mainstream focus of normative political philosophy and the observational axis of the elite subject. Feminist standpoint perspectives and other forms of critical reading provide relational approaches to epistemology and power that foreground the place from where analysis is done,[11] disavowing the possibility of objective or universal understandings, as they simultaneously place in question the prevailing truth-claims of the powerful (e.g., Alcoff and Potter 1993; Harding 2004; Hartsock 1997). While feminist standpoint theory has been intensively critiqued, what is important about these epistemologies from the margins, for my purposes, is their emphasis on reading social life through and from *non-dominant* experiences and forms: for instance, understanding the body through corporeal forms that are not hegemonic but female, disabled, and queer (or as viruses, transplants, or surgery); understanding property not through private ownership but through squatting, common or public lands.[12] Epistemologies of the margins are not simply intended as perspectives from which to critique mainstream, hegemonic forms; they also open up possibilities for exploring what other kinds of forms could be like. This double move recognizes the relational character of particular experiences and social locations. What it is to live as a woman or have a woman's body is structured by gender relations and the production of masculinity (as masculinity is also structured by other gendered forms), but subordinate locations or relations are not simply or only that. They also develop forms of experience, living, and knowing that go beyond mirroring or countering the status quo to traverse it at odd and complex angles. bell hooks (1991: 149–150) similarly remarks, "Marginality [is] much more than a site of deprivation. . . . It is also the site of radical possibility . . . for the production of a counter-hegemonic discourse that is not just found in words but in habits of being and the way one lives. . . . It offers . . . the possibility of radical perspective from which to see and create, to imagine alternatives, new worlds."

Utopian frameworks reveal a comparable dual aspect. On the one hand, utopian narratives, practices, and places are developed in critique

of and opposition to prevailing taken-for-granted ways of doing things —
offering a place from which to trouble assumptions of the present. But
the world-building dimension of utopia means that locally generated
concepts cannot be reduced solely to their function of opposing the
status quo. Utopian concepts do not derive simply and only from the
world they reject; they are also forged with some degree of autonomy
through their anchorage in the utopian world that is grown.

I mentioned at the start of this chapter that utopian studies, for the
most part, has not developed a thoroughgoing account of the conceptual,
even as concepts are central to its work. Utopian studies is interested in
how utopian texts (and to a lesser degree utopian practices) rethink concepts, such as gender, relationships, community, possessions, and work,
in terms of what they mean and how they are practiced. However, while
it has circled around the problem of the conceptual, utopian studies has
largely not offered an explicitly new way of thinking about concepts *as*
concepts.[13] This book aims to contribute to this project, drawing on utopian studies methods and thinking in order to consider what concepts
mean, how they work, and where they might be found in a way that is
oriented to the conceptual contribution of everyday utopias to a transformative politics.

But how are we to build a conceptual framework adequate to the task?
Starting with a commitment to another better way of living, utopian perspectives emphasize the importance of "society imagined otherwise,
rather than merely society imagined" (Levitas 2005: 14; Sargisson 2012).
While utopian scholarship, as I have said, does not belabor the *conceptual* character of normative terms, reimagining the practices and systems to which such terms gesture is a central task. Fleshing out normative terms, such as democracy and equality, by describing key features of
the utopian landscape provides a degree of political (and so conceptual)
specificity and closure; it is not change for its own sake that is desired
and sought, but particular kinds of change. At the same time, developing
concepts by means of *establishing* landscapes emphasizes the importance
of location and happening. Innovations may not be *practically* realized,
but even in storytelling or other art forms utopian perspectives depend
upon some kind of (imagined) actualization (what Jameson [1977: 11]
refers to as a "pre-conceptual thinking-in-images").[14]

In this way utopias are fundamentally different from campaigns, arguments, or slogans that declare the change they wish to see. With their

experiments and innovations in living (including in imagined experiments), utopias emphasize the importance of transformed social existence to thinking differently. As a consequence, utopian texts and methods also center ontological or human change. It is not simply about the creation of worlds or ways of living that will better meet people's interests *as they currently are*. Utopia is also centrally concerned with those changing interests, desires, identifications, and forms of embodiment that happen as people (and other forms of life) experience other ways of living (Levitas 2013). This process is a dynamic one; while older utopian currents tended to focus on timeless spaces, more recent utopias are oriented toward change and contradiction, toward human impulse and strategies, and toward action rather than system design (Moylan 1986: 49).

Out of these primary commitments to experimenting, imagining, and pursuing change come a series of epistemological elements, creative, affective, and social, which together make up what we might call, following Foucault, a utopian "attitude." Foucault (1984: 39) writes, "I mean a mode of relating to contemporary reality . . . in the end, a way of thinking and feeling; a way, too, of acting and behaving that at one and the same time marks a relation of belonging and presents itself as a task." Contemporary utopian studies emphasizes the importance of invention, improvisation, and speculative futures; it lays stress on sensation, the ineffable, and feelings such as optimism, hope, and enchantment; and it relies on bridging concepts that link present practice to a different and transformed future, from Bloch's "anticipatory illumination," *Novum*, "docta spes," and the "not yet" to more widely used notions such as prefiguration, becoming, potential, and limits.[15] Taken together, these elements provide materials for constructing a utopian approach that seeks to take concepts beyond their already established existence, to the creation and recognition of new conceptual lines. In the rest of the chapter I explore what it means to create conceptual lines, focusing on the relationship between actualization and imagining. For if the dynamic character of concepts depends on the disjuncture between how they are imagined and how they are manifested, as chapter 1 suggests, what does this disjuncture entail? In what ways can particular concepts be actualized but not imagined, imagined but not actualized, or actualized in ways that diverge from their expressed imagining?

Imagining emphasizes the dimension of fantasy, of contemplation and abstraction, of drawing from a wide range of different contexts and usages to understand (but also to visualize, sense, or form) what has been, what is, and what could be. As such, imagining constitutes a mainstay of utopian writing and practice (Jacoby 2005: 22; see also Moylan 1986). It is also a quotidian aspect of the way all of us conceptualize, moving between different contexts to imagine what a term might mean; feeling or thinking about concepts in relation to others that partner, complicate, or oppose it. As such, the conceptual imagination remains on the move. Linda Zerilli (2005: 181) writes, "Every extension of a political concept always involves an imaginative opening up of the world that allows us to see and articulate relations between things that have none (in any necessary, logical sense). . . . Political relations are always external to their terms: they involve not so much the ability to subsume particulars under concepts, but an imaginative element, the ability to see or to forge new connections." Such imagining is always partial, improvised, and unfinished; a key premise of contemporary utopian studies in its approach to imagining other worlds, provisionality applies to imagining concepts as well.

Actualization, by contrast, emphasizes the dimension of presence or manifestation, as concepts inhere within systems, structures, and other material arrangements—although the focus of this book is specifically on concepts' presence in (and as) social practices.[16] While some concepts take a tangible form and others an intangible one, in many cases presence involves a mixture of the two, especially for complexly manifested concepts, such as the state (see chapter 3). Yet particular concepts are not actualized in isolation. Just as imagining concepts depends on other linked terms—those that constitute the concept and place, differentiate, and oppose it—actualization also depends on a web of social practices. This web is important, as later chapters explore, in what concepts can do. It is also important in structuring and limiting how particular concepts can be reimagined.

Incorporating actualization into our understanding of concepts emphasizes the importance of materiality and practice; concepts are not abstract generalities floating above the "real" world; they are not elements in some kind of autonomous mental film through which a material life "below" becomes intelligible. Yet to say that concepts are actualized and mean something more than concepts, as dimensions of thought, are *shaped* and provoked by material conditions, or used by subjects in the course of their everyday life raises difficult questions. In particular, how can we get at the material life of concepts to explore the ways actualization diverges from established thought.

The relationship (and accompanying tensions) between imagining and actualization becomes clearer with an example. If we take the concept of utopia, we can think of it as embracing the different ways utopian worlds have been (narratively and socially) *actualized* and practiced— from Marge Piercy's (1976) Mattapoisett and Kim Stanley Robinson's (1993) Mars, to nineteenth-century American communities (Kanter 1972), England's garden city movement (Meacham 1999), and contemporary intentional communities in New Zealand (Sargisson and Sargent 2004).[17] At the same time, utopia is popularly *imagined* as an impossibly perfect, overly designed, atemporal place, where nothing changes. Actualization and imagining, in this instance, identify quite different things, and there appears to be a disjuncture between them. Of course, this example may seem to oversimplify the problem since the actualized instances are already identified (by their creator or by interpreters) as utopian; thus it might seem as if the distinction here is really between different visions of utopia rather than between what is actualized and what is in fact imagined. At the same time, as in most cases, we enter the relationship between imagining and actualization in the middle, where what is manifested is already identified in ways that create a conceptual link with particular kinds of imagining (even as they may seem to diverge) and where what is imagined is shaped (in mirroring or inverted ways) by some kind of practice. Thus, we move between forms of imagining and actualization already in some relationship to each other.

A driving theme of this book is the movement between imagining and actualization. However, this should not be understood as meaning that concepts form coherent entities oscillating between the actual or material world, on the one hand, and the world of ideas and fantasy, on the other. Bracketing for the moment the notion that these are separate worlds, we might see concepts as inhering rather in the movement itself. In other words, concepts are not things but processes. William Connolly's (2011: 4) words, drawn from a different context, are useful here: "It is the reverberations back and forth . . . with each folding into the other and both surging . . . that make all the difference."

Concepts keep moving, but what keeps them moving, what sustains the dynamic quality of conceptual "lines," that embedded or reiterated movement between imagining and actualization? Utopian studies suggests two distinct possibilities. The first is inherent in the concept of concepts. Since neither imagination nor material practice can ever adequately capture or respond to the other, oscillation remains inevitable and ceaseless.[18] This momentum is particularly apparent with normative concepts, which depend for their practical realization on a more idealized imagined version that is hailed, sometimes even pursued but never attained, as with Derrida's conditional and unconditional concepts (1992a, 1992b; Patton 2010). While the more perfectly imagined version of concepts such as freedom, democracy, or justice appears impossible to realize, the fantasy of what it could mean and entail, as discussed earlier, pulls on what is actualized. At the same time, the reality of social practice in a particular context exerts a conditioning and constraining force on how concepts are imagined, even as normative concepts insistently trouble the pragmatic constraints of such practice.

The second way utopian studies approaches conceptual flux relates to the longing for and process of social transformation. In taking up a utopian conceptual attitude, the pressure that both imagining and actualization can place on the conceptual lines forged is vital to thinking about change. Whether generated by new fantasies about how to live or practical experiments in living, the hopeful dimension of a utopian attitude yearns for these progressive shifts to drive change, bringing the rest of the conceptual line into line, as it were.[19] Yet, as contemporary utopian scholarship has explored, the process of change is not straightforward (Garforth 2009). Operationalizing what is imagined can come up against resistance or blockages; and of course concepts may be expressly and deliberately imagined in ways that ensure or coexist with their nonmanifestation, as explored in relation to governments' assertion of a benign state touch in chapter 3. The disparagement of wishful thinking within utopian studies speaks to those conceptualizations that seem doomed to remain at the fantastical level, thanks to a change agenda that fails to be adequately anchored in the reality of contemporary social conditions.

Yet while particular lines can be socially stymied (at least as linear processes of correspondence in which actualization and imagining are expected to resemble each other), actualization and imagining do not take shape as discrete separate worlds but simultaneously interconnect in multiple, complexly tangled ways.[20] One instance of their interconnection can be found in the case of potential. This is not just the potential for new, better practices, but also the potential of concepts, such as property, markets, and the state, to be other than they currently appear. Potential foregrounds the material conditions of the present, what is actualized and evident, yet it simultaneously depends on imagining the future and what the present could become. In this way it resonates with utopian studies' orientation toward anticipation and hope. Identifying potential, however, requires interpretation. Potential may necessarily carry with it a degree of force that shapes change over time, but potential needs to be recognized and found. In part this is because *realization* of an imagined future is contingent and uncertain; in part it is because *imagining* both the present and the future is speculative and open to contestation.

A different example of the way imagining and actualizing concepts fold into each other, one less developed within utopian studies but yet central to this book, concerns the place of imagining in the way concepts are actualized. In the case of the state, for instance, how officials think about the state constitutes part of what the state is (an "is" that also evolves). The state isn't simply a set of material apparatuses. It also incorporates reflexive fantasies held by those who contribute to its institutional processes. At one level, this may simply seem to imply that the mental images of state actors are a part of the assemblage of things that compose the state. But if the state is a more dynamic and evolving concept (in its material practices, in how it is imagined, and in the relationship between the two), what matters, primarily, about state actors' fantasies is how they are expressed, the way they shape and are brought to bear on what it is state actors do — the documents they write, the policies and laws they develop, the decisions they oppose or obstruct.[21] Participants' imaginings of the state may work to consolidate or stabilize a particular state identity, but they can also have transformative, or at least destabilizing, effects. If state actors imagine the state as, for instance, the main body capable of promoting social justice, they may seek to actualize this fantasy; such attempts then become a part of the state's ongoing story. This doesn't mean their attempts will necessarily (or even likely) succeed. They may be resisted, thwarted, excluded, or defused, or such attempts may be used to cover up the state's less seemly side. Nevertheless the presence of such attempts becomes part of the conceptual line of the state's (including particular states) evolving formation.

Reflecting on what imagining does within processes of actualization, the kinds of power available to particular actors and actions within particular contexts is important. Wishful thinking may mystify or distract from the reality of one's own powerlessness, yet imagining that things are other than they seem to be is rarely sufficient in itself to give such imaginings force. Ian Hacking (2002: 8) remarks, discussing Nietzsche, "Naming alone is never enough to create. . . . Naming occurs in sites, particular places, and at particular times. For a name to begin to do its creative work, it needs authority. One needs usage within institutions. Naming does its work only as a social history works itself out." While it would seem not to be enough, for instance, to reimagine the state as an egalitarian body for it to change to become one, the power of such a fantasy may depend (at least in part) on the authority attached and the form such expressed imagining takes.

This book explores the place of authority and usage in moving between concepts' actualization and imagining through practices of mediation. In utopian studies, the most explicit mediations are performed by creators and (fictional) visitors—in other words, by those who bridge the world of utopia and the world "outside." However, if we think of mediations as those practices through which conceptual lines are generated and worked, the kinds of practices and actors involved are considerably extended. Conceptual lines are created by utopian participants as well as by outside observers, including academics. While the latter are often treated by fellow academics as central players in forging new conceptual lines—connecting practices and imaginings in novel and imaginative ways—it is important not to reduce the participants of utopian communities (and other actors who engage with the sites) to simply following conceptual lines already laid down or waiting to be discovered. The practices of community participants are a far more creative part of the conceptual mediation process.

Writing in a different context, Bruno Latour (2005: 58) draws a useful distinction between agentic mediators and nonagentic intermediaries. In the case of intermediaries, he writes, "nothing will be present in the effect that has not been in the cause. . . . For mediators, the situation is different: causes do not allow effects to be deduced. . . . If vehicles are treated as mediators triggering other mediators, then a lot of new and unpredictable situations will ensue" (58–59). What is important about mediations is that they *do* something—whether it is to create new conceptual lines or to vary or embed further those already in existence. As explored in this book, mediating practices are extensive and wide-ranging, from document writing, speech making, and campaigns to exchanging goods, walking in the woods, managing school classrooms, giving a massage in a bathhouse, or enticing passersby in an open-air public forum.

Mediating activities and actors provide the generative ground through which concepts develop, change, thrive, get stuck, and carry power. They can, in Sarah Keenan's (2010) words, hold concepts up or impede what it is they do. Mediations can also lose or fail to exert force. Iconoclastic attempts to create new conceptual lines sometimes demonstrate this kind of failure: intentional communities unable to flourish beyond their initial impetus; utopian designs that don't take off; stories that are read as too fantastical; theoretical scholarship that short-circuits practice to reimagine concepts in ways that fail to make an impression. We might think of these as phantom conceptual lines, apparent but going nowhere, yet such disavowals should also be performed with care. A recurring theme within utopian studies is the extent to which actions written off as failed or pointless at a given moment can become subsequently revalued and appreciated as looking backward identifies "hidden" seeds and kernels that have since germinated (see Muñoz 2009).

SENSATION AND THE UNUTTERABLE

In the chapters that follow, I explore the conceptual lines generated through different kinds of mediating activities. One feature that stands out, however, about the way these lines are forged, from the perspective of a utopian framework, is the importance of the ineffable, of what cannot or simply is not said, and so is expressed, experienced, and known in other ways. Recognizing how knowledge and understanding exceed what is utterable is not limited to utopian studies. It can also be seen in other contemporary literatures, such as nonrepresentational (or more than representational) geography (e.g., Lorimer 2005; Thrift 2008). Working within this framework, Kevin Hetherington (2003: 1939) for instance writes, "We enter our homes through our slippers. . . . We sense a form of presence/present in that entry. . . . The feel of something can generate a sense of who we are and where we find ourselves—a sense of place." But does knowing our home through our slippers equate to knowing concepts, such as the home, in more than linguistic ways? Or is it, simply, that what our *particular* home means, or indeed someone else's, works best through a textile-mediated form of touch?

For writers such as Nicholas Gane (2009), feeling and the senses function as a kind of preconceptual underpinning. Ruth Levitas (2013) takes a similar approach in her rich discussion of the ineffable, utopian power of color and music. However, I want to suggest that concepts themselves, in part because they are not simply ideas but the movement between actualization and imagining, also take shape and so can be known and recognized in more than linguistic ways. We can see this with the simple example of sourness. While the term *sour* and what it means for an object to taste sour can be linguistically explained, this process is far slower, more awkward, and cruder than the initial (and ongoing) sensory recognition and recollection of sour.[22] Tasting something and knowing it is sour is not purely about effective categorization, however. What it *means* to be sour, in particular contexts, how sour is *imagined*, also extends conceptually beyond what is utterable.

Utopian studies' emphasis on experience and sensation, including in relation to storytelling texts, which work through the imaginary relocation of the reader to another world rather than through campaigning rhetoric or analytical argument, highlight the importance of these other forms of knowing. Conceptual lines may be captured linguistically,[23] but conceptual lines do not require conscious, explicit expression in order to become forged, and conceptual lines should not be reduced to what is sayable or said.

RECOGNITION

Concepts may not depend on utterances, but do they still depend on some kind of recognition, as Hetherington's (2003) example of his home and his slippers suggests? And when it comes to the question of conceptual recognition, what exactly is it that is recognized? Conventionally recognition suggests a correspondence between an imagined category and the actual thing or practice, so the thing or practice is recognized as belonging to a particular, imagined class; and where such recognition fails, either the category or the thing may need to change.

Drawing on this correspondence in order to unsettle it has been a core feature of many utopian texts. Newly imagined practices and systems, relating, for instance, to reproductive patterns and technologies, economics, or domestic life—what it means, for instance, to be a worker, give birth, or participate politically—demand new forms of identification (or changes to old ones) as existing conceptions fail to hold up to the challenge the utopian provides. Within this temporally staggered process of conceptual recognition and adjustment, nonrecognition also plays an important part. In utopian fiction, outsiders enter new worlds with bewilderment; they gaze around unable to make sense of what they observe or clearly making the wrong sense of what they observe. In William Morris's ([1890] 2003) *News from Nowhere* and Piercy's (1976) *A Woman on the Edge of Time*, visitor misrecognition is an essential element, dramatically underscoring the radical changes to have occurred, heuristically enabling the author to inform the reader about the new world they have spun. At the same time, in these novels the process of being introduced to and taken through the new world brings the visitor to a better understanding of what things mean and how they work. Thus nonrecognition is temporary and resolvable.

The power of nonrecognition also permeates everyday nonutopian political practice. When concepts are understood as mental frames that make life intelligible in particular ways, conceptual nonrecognition suggests the failure of things to correspond with or fit such mental frames (or vice versa). So practices are not recognized as being law, property, or care because they lack key accepted or institutionally determined features. Or concepts may be unrecognized as the concepts they are intended to be because their framing diverges too markedly from what is presently accepted or understood. Strategically deploying these forms of conceptual nonrecognition in the course of political activism becomes part of a process of seeking to unsettle and to reidentify practices or terms: "property is theft"; "the law is an ass." Nonrecognition here is not a goal in itself but validated by what it can accomplish—a process that often entails new forms of recognition. But can conceptual nonrecognition prove more enduring; can recognition *remain* elusive?

One concept whose contemporary deployment has deliberately sought to trouble the movement toward recognition is that of queer. While some understand the term as a synonym for *gay* and others treat the term as one of sexual deviance, queer also functions as a refusal of identification, deliberately gesturing toward that which cannot be named or rendered intelligible or normal. But even this gesture depends for its success on familiarity and notice. Queer may not seek to represent a cohort of people in the sense of rendering them transparent and knowable, but it still seeks recognition—whether of its own conceptual parameters (what counts as queer) or in the challenge it presents to other forms of thought and practice.

Approaching concepts as the oscillation between imagining and actualization, as this book does, makes a different approach to the question of conceptual recognition possible. For recognition doesn't depend on "real" things fitting linguistic terms or terms fitting, and thus elucidating, particular social practices (or indeed other imagined terms). Instead, in ways that resonate with feminist accounts of recognition as a social practice (e.g., Fraser 1997), conceptual recognition concerns a relationship to particular conceptual lines, as one of noticing, creating, following, responding to, having regard for, or being concerned about. Approaching recognition in this way does not make concepts transparent. Concepts remain elusive because actualization, imagining, and the quality of the movement between them exceeds what we can know (see note 18). Concepts also remain elusive, as I discuss, in terms of what they may become. This sense of uncertainty and improvised openness is an important dimension of contemporary utopian scholarship, with its move away from blueprint utopias to the recognized impossibility of knowing what future worlds will hold. While such an inability to know may seem a truism, its value is in what we do with it when it comes to the present imagining of concepts such as equality, markets, care, or touch. This is not simply a matter of identifying limited knowledge about the future; it is also about bringing such future openness and uncertainty into how we understand these concepts within the now (as I explore in relation to equality in chapter 4).

Destabilizing established conceptual lines can undoubtedly prove exciting, but this book doesn't advocate elusive, unrecognizable concepts either as an end or as a general means toward some other goal. While some academic work suggests that representation and doing (or reflecting and performing) are necessarily different conceptual orientations, this book treats them as far more entwined, as it explores the work performed by different conceptual imaginings and actualizations as they variously unsettle what is taken for granted, suggest new ways of think-

ing, pose strategic openings and interventions, and engage in community maintenance and development work.[24] Within utopian studies, the
shift of focus to what the concept of utopia does has focused attention
on a range of tasks, from denaturalizing the status quo to stimulating and
educating the imagination, promoting a desire for change, demonstrating the limits of what can be thought of, and performing textually and ex-
perimentally the political struggles that change invokes (Jameson 1977;
Levitas 2013). As the oscillation between what is imagined and actualized, the concept of utopia does far more than represent a particular
kind of idealized society, even as the depiction or glimpse of something
else and other is an integral part of the utopian.

Yet for concepts such as utopia to act and do things, some sort of
recognition is necessary. As I have said, approaching conceptual recognition as something other than a pure relationship of resemblance between the imagined term (or concept) and the thing or practice allows
many forms of recognition to be, in a sense, recognized. While the focus
of this book is on the conceptual lines everyday utopias can generate, it
also offers an account of recognition in some of its many different forms,
for the book treats recognition as a relationship that cannot be assumed.
Indeed it is the pervasive failure on the left, and specifically among critical academics, to recognize the conceptual life and promise of everyday utopias within the wider pursuit of a transformative politics, which
drives this book.

I begin the process of exploring the productive work of concepts
within everyday utopias with the concept of touch. My interest is in the
particular way touch was deployed by state projects to advance equality,
focusing on the case of British governance between 2009 and 2010.
While academic work has extensively explored the state's deployment of
vision as a powerful and disciplinary means of governance, far less has
been said about touch. Starting with the conventional notion of a conceptual "lens," I gaze through touch in order to consider the different
ways that contact, feeling, and relations of proximity saturate the political landscape as public bodies deploy an imaginary of touch in order to
know and to rule. At the same time, following the touch that is present
brings forth questions, both troubling and fruitful, about state engagement with progressive politics.

CHAPTER 3

CASTING EQUALITY AND THE
TOUCH OF STATE GOVERNANCE

So touch, like vision, articulates [a] . . . rich, complex world, a world of movement and exploration, of non-verbal social communication. It is a carnal world, with its pleasures of feeling and being felt. . . . And equally it is a profound world of philosophical verification, of the communication of presence and empathy with others, of the co-implication of body, flesh and world.

Paterson 2007: 2

In developing a utopian conceptual attitude, sensation and affect are important sources of knowledge. In this, the first of six case studies, I use touch to explore equality as a state-led governance project that has sought to undo structural asymmetries by targeting discrimination on specific, enumerated grounds. In doing so I ask: How does equality governance use touch to help it know? And does following the touch of equality governance, as an everyday utopia, open up more progressive and transformative ways of understanding the touching state — that is, the state that feels and that experiences, in turn, the feelings of others?

Reading state practice through (and in relation to) the senses is not new. Several writers have explored the place of odor and smell in governance relations (e.g., Corbin 1986; Curtis 2008; Śliwa and Riach 2012), and even more have considered the state's use of vision as a means of surveillance, militarism, and control (e.g., Feldman 1997; Roy 2006; Scott 1998). Far less attention, however, has been paid to touch.[1] In many ways, this is surprising given the wealth of scholarship on touch, and given also the manifold ways state governance invokes practices of contact, proximity, connection, and sensation. These practices come sharply to the fore in coercive and authoritarian state projects (from imprisonment and war to schooling and disciplinary forms of welfare, including through international aid), but they also come to the fore when states act in ostensibly more progressive ways, including in the measures introduced to advance equality.

Exploring the relationship of touch to state equality projects can take several forms. Here I want to start with touch as a lens through which the field of equality governance is surveyed. As a lens, touch frames and illuminates the object of study but is not itself reinflected in the process. In this chapter, I explore what happens when we look at equality governance *through* touch: how we find touch present in multiple ways, including idiomatically within public documents, in the discourse of good relations, and as a way of imagining state bodies touching (and being touched) differently. Yet taking touch as a lens makes it unsurprising that touch is what we find, as our imagination builds conceptual lines of resemblance into and through the practical world observed. Treating concepts as lenses has its limits; one key problem is that it explicitly envisages concepts as lying outside the domain of practice. While this book seeks to move beyond this framework of an active exterior concept making sense of a passive terrain of practice, the notion of a conceptual lens indicates something of the academic visitor's imagination as particular ideas are brought to a place or scene (see chapter 1). Here taking touch as my lens opens a series of questions about the contactful state: What does equality governance touch? What touches it back? Can equality governance generate forms of touch that challenge conventional assumptions about the coercive and disciplinary touch of the state? And what kind of state is *imagined* when we think about, and follow, equality governance's touch?

Casting Equality as an Everyday Utopia

At the heart of my account is the everyday utopia of *casting equality*. Derived from the thirteenth-century Old Norse word *kasta*, meaning "to throw," casting starts with the form something takes when it is thrown, and from there extends in rich and multiple ways to include ideas of being assigned, arranged, devised, and controlled. In this account of equality governance, I draw on three distinctive sets of meanings: the line cast, as in fishing, to extend its reach; the act of molding and shaping, as when something is cast (which includes also the act of receiving shape, a solidification that may prove impossible to undo or recast); and casting as the assignment of roles, as in a play. Casting can also suggest the creation of something not yet ready to be formed, as in a calf's premature birth. This idea of being forged too early is highly salient for utopian thinking, itself centrally concerned with the future's incipient relationship to, and presence within, the now (chapter 9).

To give this discussion of casting equality greater specificity, my focus is one particular project: the equality governance agenda that developed in Britain under the Blair-led Labour government, which reached its zenith in 2009–10, the year the Equality Bill 2009 passed through Parliament. In many respects, Britain's equality project resembled other national equality projects of its time, with its focus on removing discriminatory obstacles and enabling members of disadvantaged groups to access educational, employment, and cultural opportunities. In Britain in 2009–10 equality governance slid between its institutional and legal machinery, the "fair deal" environment it sought to achieve,[2] and the promise that all individuals would flourish by acquiring the necessary capabilities thanks to governmental action (Carpenter 2009).

Despite the range of *non*-state bodies involved, central to this equality project was the place of government, particularly central government, and of formal state instruments of governance. The central presence of the state distinguishes casting equality from other everyday utopias of this book. It also poses the question of what it means to characterize such a project as an everyday utopia. Given the pragmatic, power-laden processes that states condense and invoke, placing a state-centered project alongside the everyday utopias of civil society may seem questionable. Yet the notion of states mobilizing utopian thinking and utopian projects is not new or uncommon (e.g., Bauman 2003b; Wegner 2002). It builds on the idea of realistic utopias (see Levitas 2013) and resonates with many features of utopia explored in chapter 1. Casting equality, like other everyday utopias, is engaged in a hugely ambitious project, with its aspiration for a future better than the present, a future that it confidently seeks to procure. As Jonathan Rees, the director-general of the Government Equalities Office, declared, "Our vision is a fair and equal society for all. Equality is not just right in principle but necessary for individuals, society and the economy. In the [last] year . . . we have made good progress."[3] At the same time, as an *everyday* utopia, equality governance conveys the prosaic and orderly character of the quotidian, with its procedures, rules, concerns, and worries.

But there is also a further way in which casting equality, as something both molded and molding, constitutes an everyday utopia, a way that is central to my discussion. This relates to the project's paradoxical character as simultaneously powerful and powerless, absorbing and insignificant. On the one hand, Britain's equality agenda, during the period studied, appeared ubiquitous as it demanded that public sector reforms and programs take its mission into account. Unlike the sites discussed in later chapters, the state's promotion of equality drew on a wide array of resources and powers. Authorized through law, nation-state bodies, and European Union directives (as part of a wider transnational agenda), equality governance acquired forms of institutionalization many utopias would envy. In this sense, casting equality resembles those utopias of fiction that are able to procure the world they imagine — even if, in this case, the *nomos* (or normative world) procured was largely one of governmental discourses, networks, and institutionalized ways of doing things. Yet while the proximity of equality governance to other state processes was critical to its authority and success, it also carried dangers. As with other everyday utopias, equality governance in 2009–10 was precarious, vulnerable to marginalization and defeat by other, more powerful state agendas. Thus while casting equality as a state-led pursuit demanded attention, it was regularly evaded, pushed back, enacted superficially, deployed rhetorically, or simply ignored.

Taking touch as a lens through which to consider the everyday utopia of casting equality foregrounds several different ways of knowing. There is the observer, whose knowing and understanding come from surveying touch's paths rather than from actually touching. And there is the state. The state may know its population in particular ways as a result of who and what it touches and how. But touch, as expressed in official documents, also provides a way for the state to represent the touch it imagines. Touch, then, is not only generative in terms of knowing what is; it also provides ways of creating new forms of knowledge, from the state's urging that different communities make contact in the form of "good relations," to the potential to know the state differently through new experiences of its touch. But what does it mean to talk about the state touching or being touched through its project of casting equality? I want to start by indicating some key aspects of the touch literature relevant to this discussion and then introduce the empirical terrain. Having done so, I turn to the ways casting equality represented itself as touching, alongside those forms of touch, as a state-based project, which it ignored. From there I consider other molds that casting equality made imaginable (and in some instances partially manifested) as a state-led project that sought also to be touched and thus to "feel" differently. Finally, I turn to the problematic that following state touch—through casting equality—raises, namely the problematic for progressive politics of the "touching-feeling" state.

Touch

Work on touch is richly varied, extending from philosophy, history, and cultural studies (e.g., Classen 2005; Derrida 2005; Josipovici 1996; Massumi 2002), to nudism, museum studies, and cyberspace (e.g., Cvetkovich 2003; Grabham 2009b; Hetherington 2003; Obrador-Pons 2009). One useful text to weave together accounts and touch theorizing from different sources is Mark Paterson's book, *The Senses of Touch* (2007). Taking as his springboard the classical claim that touch is the lowest, most bestial of the senses (particularly when compared to the ostensibly refined sense of sight), Paterson explores the significance of touch to embodied existence. He writes, "The feeling of cutaneous touch when an object brushes our skin is simultaneously an awareness of the materiality of the object and an awareness of the spatial limits and sensations of our lived body" (2).

Paterson's book provides an important tracing of many of the debates surrounding touch: its development in phenomenology; the interconnections and struggles between touch and vision, from "seeing with one's hands" to touch's relationship to the "abstracted visualism" of geometry; the experience of touching (and being touched by) art; haptic technologies;[4] and the use of touch in healing. Since this chapter focuses on how public and state bodies represent and enact touch (how they touch and how they confront being touched), those debates that focus on the specific character of human or animal touch are bracketed. However, five claims about touch are pivotal to what follows.

1. Touch is inherently and meaningfully reciprocal; unlike senses such as sight, touching always involves being touched. One consequence is that those who touch chance exposing their surface — or skin — to what they touch (Manning 2007: 9). Both parties in a touch encounter thus risk being changed in the process; for example, a gallery painting may emotionally touch and transform the viewer, but the vulnerability of the painting to alteration is there in organizational signs banning touch. The two-way relationship touch invokes does not mean, however, that touch is symmetrical. It can be, as when two hands or lips touch (Irigaray 1985); however, in other contexts, bilateral touch sensations may significantly differ.[5] The sensation that comes from one's hand slapping a person's face is likely to be quite different from the touch felt by the one slapped.

2. Touching involves proximity and often intimacy. While this can be physical, it can also be emotional. This understanding of touch as affect, as a way of moving and being moved by what's around ("I was touched by what they did"), is central to my later discussion. In contrast to sight, which can manage a degree of distance (indeed states use visual techniques to govern from a distance), touch closes space.[6] Edith Wyschogrod (1981: 25) remarks, "Only touch requires contact, the proximity of feeling to what is felt." But touch, or prospective touch, can also create new spaces and distances as Josipovici (1996: 69) explores in relation to pilgrimage: "For if the goal of pilgrimage was, and is, to make distance palpable, is that not still an instinct with us today? Is not the secular visitor . . . who touches the age-old stones or the ocean . . . not so much bridging the distance between himself and these repositories of power as acknowledging their otherness and the awe he feels in their presence?"

3. Touch is a way of thinking about bodies in movement; "the act of reaching toward, of creating space-time through the worlding that occurs when bodies move" (Manning 2007: xiv). Movement includes inward- as well as outward-oriented action. So touch engages intracorporeal processes such as balance, movement, and proprioception (a felt sense of body parts' location), which work to establish the body as unified or, conversely, as fragmented. While some writing emphasizes the distinction between inward and outward touch, other work focuses on the movement or indistinct-

ness between the two (Obrador-Pons 2009; Paterson 2007; see also chapter 4).

4. While touch can thwart or upset hierarchies, it frequently works to confirm and solidify relations of power. This may take a violent form, as with war, rape, and execution, but touch can signify authority in other ways: a child's hand grabbed to cross a busy road, the employer's heavy avuncular pat on the shoulder, the healing power of the royal hand (Thomas 2005). At the same time, because of touch's power and authority, touch often works through relays and intermediaries, from the use of utensils and handkerchiefs to manage and mediate contact with bodily secretions (one's own as well as others) to the complex chains of bodies involved in state-directed governance.

5. Finally, touch suggests particular kinds of knowledge and knowing. According to Kevin Hetherington (2003: 1935), who draws on Cooper and Law (1995: 239), touch invokes "proximal knowledge"—"unfinished," "approximate," "partial," and "precarious." Hetherington writes, "Proximal knowledge . . . suggests a more fluid and uncertain composition . . . embodied, sensory and *unsightly*—it implies an out-of-the-way, out-of-sight approach to knowing the world" (1935). In other words, even as touch gets contrasted with the kinds of knowing that vision generates, touch-generated knowledge often works through its sensory and idiomatic relationship to other senses, as I explore below.

Assembling Equality

Casting equality in Britain is a project that can be narrated in many different ways. There is the story of antidiscrimination law—the development of a statutory regime attentive to "unequal" treatment in the provision of employment, goods, and services that began in the late 1960s and 1970s. Starting with sex and race discrimination, equality law expanded over four decades to take in other axes of inequality, including disability, age, religious belief, and sexuality (Dickens 2007; Fredman 2011; Hepple 2010). The year at the heart of this chapter, 2009–10, was a major moment for antidiscrimination law. It witnessed the passage through Parliament of an Equality Bill that addressed seven "protected characteristics" (otherwise referred to by the government as "grounds" or "strands"): sex, race, gender reassignment, age, disability, religion and belief, and sexual orientation.[7] While the Equality Act 2010 (as it became) addressed the standard terrain of direct and indirect discrimination, it also had, from a British perspective, several innovative features. These included the recognition of "intersectional" inequality, albeit limited to the "combination of two relevant . . . characteristics" (§14), and it placed a duty on public bodies to have regard to the desirability of reducing inequalities of outcome arising from socioeconomic disadvantage (§1).[8]

The story of equality's casting, of how the law developed to touch new forms of inequality or touch old forms in new ways—for instance, "protecting" gays rather than criminalizing them—sits alongside a second story of changing governance forms. As *promoting* equality became increasingly mainstream and institutionalized, the instruments deployed became increasingly juridical and increasingly oriented to generating and attaining external standards. To simplify a complex tale, in the 1980s with the Conservative Thatcher government in central office, the promotion of equality primarily took place in left-wing urban councils, exploiting their discretion and local political legitimacy to develop "soft" legal measures, from new employment and service-related policies to funding community initiatives, holding festivals, organizing training, and disseminating promotional publicity. By the early part of the twenty-first century, and with a new Labour government, attention shifted back to more formal instruments as a developing outcrop of legislative measures combined with an intensive array of nationally developed targets, standards, and sector agreements through which different public bodies' equality "progress" could be calculated and incentivized. Evolving modes and instruments of governance thus coincide with a story of new institutional actors, and of changing relations between those bodies—public and otherwise—involved in equality's pursuit. Progressive, Labour-controlled councils in the 1980s pursued an equality agenda in and through relations of close proximity with marginalized groups, while remaining at a well-publicized distance from the private commercial sector, from "repressive" state bodies, such as the police, and from the Thatcher central government. In the 1990s, when privatization could no longer be so easily disavowed and when Labour was looking to present itself as the party of respectability, local councils developed equality initiatives in partnership with a range of public and private bodies, including the police, local companies, and NGOs (nongovernmental organizations). After 1997, when the Labour Party took national office, local development of equality policies were in some measure overshadowed by a more visible national equality agenda, driven also by European Union directives, and the development of equality initiatives in the newly devolved nations of Scotland, Wales, and Northern Ireland (e.g., see Richardson and Monro 2012). Spearheading the new national agenda were new governance bodies. There was the Women's Unit, which subsequently became the Women and Equality Unit, and eventually the Government Equalities Office (GEO), based in the Home Office and responsible for the government's overall equality strategy and priorities (see Squires and Wickham-Jones 2002). And there was the much larger "arm's-length body" that it sponsored:[9] the Equality and Human Rights Commission, a nongovernmental public body established by the Equality Act 2006. Introduced to replace the three separate race, gender, and disability commissions, and with a new unified structure that would recognize a wide array of inequalities, the EHRC was charged with protecting, promoting, and enforcing equality across the enumerated grounds of gender, race, sexual orientation, and others; strengthening "good relations" between diverse constituencies; and promoting and monitoring human rights (see O'Cinneide 2007; Spencer 2008).

Imagining Contact

Anchored in these stories of equality's state formation, how did casting equality in 2009–10 use touch to produce particular ways of knowing? In what ways was touch imagined, and with what intended effects? The fact that governance texts deployed haptic idioms suggests notions of touch were imported from elsewhere as common, everyday conceptual lines were redeployed to support the project of casting equality. But what kinds of material processes was this use of touch's idioms intended to invoke and drive forward? And to what extent did this use of touch suggest a more utopian kind of haptic state? The discussion that follows draws on approximately thirty public documents produced mainly by (or for) the GEO and EHRC between 2009 and 2010. A growing body of academic work exists on the political and bureaucratic stakes and processes involved in generating official texts (e.g., Bedford 2009; Chilton 2004; Escobar 1995; Hunter 2008). For my purposes, what is important about these documents as textual mediations of touch is that they are *public* documents (see Geisler 2001), generated to promote, advise, and consult on new developments in equality governance. In other words, crafted with the intention to both guide and stand in for equality governance, the documents discussed functioned as mechanisms of rule as well as symbolic statements of political compromises already reached.

In considering the documents the GEO and EHRC produced, the prevalence of touch's terms is striking. Official reports refer repeatedly to *soft touch, hard to reach, embracing, unlocking, boosting, barriers, treatment, balance,* and *tackling,* as well as *arm's-length bodies* and *working-life tasters.* Such terms of course might be dismissed as commonplace figurative speech, the kind of language one would expect to find in governmental documents. However, my argument is that the use of touch idioms was far more engaged than this suggests. While comparing governmental documents between different state projects lies outside the scope of this discussion, the use of touch in casting equality had a very particular function. Touch wasn't simply a neutral way of *representing* how equality governance operated but was itself a mode (or strategy) of enactment. In representing governance in a particular way, equality documents sought to generate particular kinds of effects, producing (and producing an impression of) a state-driven network of animate, vibrant, vital bodies "think[ing] about the needs of everyone."[10] As such, casting equality as a mold that also sought to mold and stretch itself around public action invoked a political commitment to good contact, good relations, and good geometries. However, as I go on to explore, the reimagining of touch by statutory bodies during this period was not contained by (or limited to) the benign projects it foregrounded.

In casting equality, governance looked two ways: to the beneficiaries of its promise to bring forth a more equal society and to the bodies who would participate in its accomplishment. Thus documents emphasized the importance of making contact with those disadvantaged individuals and groups (women, disabled people, etc.) that constituted the key bearers of its "protected characteristics." As one EHRC document states, "Local authorities must engage with local people and communities in order to identify and tailor equality priorities to local needs."[11] Alongside those ready to be touched, equality documents of the period also signified the need to contact those deemed "hard to reach"—once lesbians and gay men, now minority ethnic women.[12] Using touch idioms, casting equality spelled out the links between contact, proximity, and visibility.[13] One GEO report from the period declares, "Inequality cannot be tackled if problems cannot be seen."[14] Another similarly remarks, "We cannot tackle discrimination if it is hidden. Shining a spotlight on the problem . . . will help employers and employees . . . take action."[15] In this way proximity and visibility become imagined as the entwined conditions that make a vigorous form of contact possible.

But such proximity, documents and interviews suggest,[16] struggles with the impossibility of a direct relationship between those national bodies pursuing equality initiatives and their far more localized subjects. Touch may involve proximity, but several relays are required as a wide array of (intermediate) bodies get cast and mobilized. Forming a kind of "touch chain," casting equality during this period imagines governance prosthetically, stretching out with increased power thanks to the bodies knitted in. These chains, formed through collaborative (and less collaborative) modes of action, are described in numerous public documents, for instance:

> To increase the number of women taking up and completing apprenticeships, the Government is working with the Equality and Human Rights Commission, the Learning Skills Council and sector bodies to improve information, broaden choice and explore more flexible . . . opportunities.[17]

> The EHRC will . . . work with CLG [the Department for Communities and Local Government] and the Government Equalities Office to make sure that public sector bodies are not just meeting their legal obligations but also adopting best practice in areas such as positive action and procurement.[18]

What these remarks reveal are the different kinds of touch at stake. At times only a "light touch" may be required; as the government declared in relation to the once planned statutory socioeconomic duty, there will be no threat of "heavy handed enforcement."[20] Such a light touch, as I

Describing their work on equality for disabled people, the EHRC reported, "Considered around 100 enforcement . . . actions . . . Pursued a formal agreement with a multinational organisation in the hotels and leisure industry to enable accessibility . . . Advised the government on how to fill [a legal] gap . . . Successfully challenged four government departments over [requested UN Convention] reservations . . . [and] cosponsor[ed] and participat[ed] at a Dignity and Justice for All of Us event with Disability Wales."[19]

discuss below, is in many ways a signature of a new form of governance. But at other moments, casting equality asserts a more formal, challenging, or coercive contact, as it imagines a touch that follows and consolidates hierarchical organizational lines, compelling subordinate agencies to bring their bodies into proprioceptive order. As Bob Hepple (2011: 322) writes, "When persuasion and dialogue fail, progressively more deterrent sanctions are required until there is compliance."

Alongside the asymmetrical touch that equality texts depict as necessary *between* public bodies, equality documents declare the need for public bodies to be touched also by the disadvantaged other. There are echoes here of the aura, the power of certain objects to touch those beholding them especially when "*enshrine[d] in the law*" (see Josipovici 1996; also Hetherington 2003: 1940).[21] Invoking registers of voice and hearing as they combine to form a political aesthetics of sound, the EHRC writes in their 2009–12 Strategic Plan, "We tell people's stories—and we learn from them. We listen and we deal with the world as it is."[22] Governance texts are clear. Those with "protected characteristics" are experts of their experience. They must be "consulted" and their words listened to (although, in some cases, even this may prove insufficient; then something more is needed, and documents speak of "involvement," a meshing of human and state bodies that exceeds the bounded communication with its set touch, which consultation entails).[23]

Disadvantaged others are not expected within casting equality, however, to touch only the state. Good touch has another dimension that takes shape through the statutory language of "good relations," a responsibility placed on the EHRC to promote by §10 of the Equality Act 2006. "Good relations is a developing concept. It started as a responsibility for local government and the Commission for Racial Equality under the 1976 Race Relations Act and has now been extended . . . to other diversity strands: age; disability; gender; religion and/or belief; sexual orientation; transgender; as well as race" (Wigfield and Turner 2010: v).

Drawing on theories of social capital, communitarianism, and human security, publicly funded reports imagine good relations in the way differently identified residents might live better together, with more cooperation, cohesion, and respect.[24] Thus good relations take shape against two opposing narratives: of no relations, where people from different communities live "separate, parallel lives with little understanding of each other";[25] and the left unsaid bad relations, where contact is

Delegates attending the EHRC event "Promoting Disabled People's Safety and Security," May 2009. © Equality and Human Rights Commission.

heated, rough, and pressured. Good relations also take shape against the unstated and to some degree uncontemplated possibility of a different kind of contact, one that fuses, merges, or undoes boundaries (see chapter 4). The injunction to interact well is anchored in the ongoing separateness of constituencies. What is sought is positive regard (or at least tolerance and civility). The Institute for Community Cohesion report for the EHRC refers to voluntary socializing, friendship, even going on vacation together, but not romantic partnerships.[26] Desire, or losing oneself in alterity, is not part of good contact.

Casting equality may promise to enact a fairer, better society; as an everyday utopia it demonstrates how a state-based regulatory touch can be expressly reimagined and redeployed. But the use of touch's idioms also reveals something of the restraints such a project, as a state-based project, is under. While casting equality has been unable to do much about the ongoing ways that the state touches poor people and migrants—coercively, on the one hand, and by the withdrawal or absence of welfare contact, on the other—I want to focus on three other haptic tendencies. What they share, along with government discourse on good relations, is a perception of contact as something that takes place between already established social forces and constituencies with a stable, defined, and separate existence.

The first concerns the lack of attention paid to an inner, constituting touch. On occasion, government bodies draw attention to their digestive system or innards, usually in relation to the uncomfortable dyspeptic effects of previous administrations. Mostly, however, the feelings that arise from internal systems remain unremarked upon. We can see this in relation to the economy. Documents, particularly from the GEO, repeatedly hail business as a key partner, stakeholder, and audience, a sector that must be supported "to grow and compete through promoting fairness" and one that should not be weighed down by "undue" or "unnecessary burdens."[27] Yet despite the clear power of the economy, it remains *external* to casting equality—at most a rocky ocean upon which this particular governmental project bobs. Its interoceptive power to shape equality governance from the inside was, in 2009 to 2010, far less explicitly remarked upon.

This silence parallels a second one: the relative absence of powerful signifiers, such as masculinity, whiteness, and heterosexuality, in official equality statements. There are some exceptions, particularly when dominant characteristics become linked to problems of underrepresentation, for instance, the declared need for more male primary school teachers, or where dominant characteristics combine with other social relations to denote alienation and underachievement, as, in the words of the EHRC's chair, Trevor Phillips, "the growing underclass of poor white boys."[28] Mostly, however, dominant social locations remain unmarked and unremarked upon. Indeed such attachments may really prove the hardest to reach characteristics within state equality projects, erased from discussion, bracketed from lines of attention, in ways that orient equality governance away from both culpability and social power.

The third troubling dimension of touch concerns the geometric models that casting equality (not always explicitly) relied upon during this period. In ways that parallel the notion of "good relations" as encounters between already existing, defined, and distinct groups, geometric representations of inequality treat the grounds or protected characteristics of gender, race, sexual orientation, and so forth as separate, contiguous shapes, able to be assembled together to form a whole.[29]

Describing the distinction between topology and a static geometry, Brian Massumi (2002: 184) explains the difference "between the process of arriving at a form through continuous deformation and the determinate form arrived at when the process stops." During the period studied, casting equality worked, at least in public documents (the views of participants were more nuanced and complex), with a largely "stopped" geometry of imagined relationships.[30] Here the experiential and sensory character of inequality in everyday life got abstracted, cleaned up, and converted into a fixed set of optical concerns. This had several effects. It stuck inequality to disadvantage (inequality's *beneficiaries*, as I have said, were largely overlooked); it separated inequalities from other aspects of social life so that inequality became something that could be removed, leaving the rest of social life intact; and, in different ways, it separated inequalities from each other. But could casting equality as a state-led project have operated with a differently imagined geometry? Could it indeed leave a settled geometry of conceptualized relationships behind?

The Feeling State

In exploring the authorized ways in which casting equality, as an everyday utopia, became fashioned, my focus so far has been on touch's idiomatic use as a way of representing and imagining relations between bodies—public, commercial, and private. Casting equality, as a governance project, imagined touch in very specific ways. These ways can be read as signaling a utopian social democratic imaginary operating within a neoliberal political environment, organized around the normative mandates of corporate power, responsible marketized subjects, and the disciplining of the irresponsible. This particular political context becomes vividly apparent when we consider the kinds of touch that remained (at least publicly) unthought. But were these limits absolute and inevitable? Were there instances where touch was imagined differently? And can we draw on the experience of casting equality within the particular historical moment of Britain in 2009–10 to imagine other kinds of governmental touch? Asking these questions highlights the importance for a utopian conceptual attitude in considering what *could be*. This is not simply a form of day-dreaming, inhabiting a social vacuum with no relationship to the conditions from and through which thinking takes place. Rather, it means working prosthetically from what exists to imagine, in Levitas's (2010: 544) words, "society otherwise."

WAY-FEELING

If being in touch suggests an attuned knowledge to what is around you, feeling your way suggests a more tentative process, less concerned with following a path that's visible and known than with moving slowly along, trying to remain sensitive and responsive, even as (and perhaps because) the journey involves unexpected directions and unanticipated obstacles. In practice governments often feel their way as the way presses upon them.[31] However, as an explicit epistemological stance, way-feeling challenges the autonomic equation of governance with certainty. As an EHRC Strategic Plan proclaims, "Our role is to create a strong vision, to transform culture and influence thought."[32]

One important dimension to way-feeling in relation to casting equality concerns how inequality is identified. This doesn't mean letting go of the line that recognizes the inequalities associated with racializing, gendering, and economic processes, among others. However, way-feeling might involve letting go of the compulsion to attach inequality to identity-based groups (even to groups at all) in order to recognize inequality's more systemic character and centrifugal effects. It might mean reading inequality as a problem of practices, spaces, and ways of living, or it might mean recognizing how historically contingent and incomplete the list of grounds actually is, as other inequalities emerge as social facts and as political claims that resemble (*or significantly may not*) those inequalities already officially recognized (see Cooper 2004: ch. 3; Ben-Galim et al. 2007; Mabbett 2008).

Something of a way-feeling approach is suggested in the EHRC's Equality Measurement Framework, with its recognition that indicators may change,[33] and with its concerns that insufficient data exist for categories such as Gypsies and Travellers, homeless people, prisoners, and others.[34] But what way-feeling also suggests is a governmental willingness to acknowledge mistakes and failures, to be ready to change, to take risks, recognizing that some will fail, and to encourage others, particularly other others, to guide. Unsurprisingly way-feeling was not especially prominent in most of the governance texts I encountered. However, more tentative, reflective stances surfaced in the handful of interviews I carried out. For instance, one senior policy officer remarked, "We don't understand enough why prejudice becomes entrenched. . . . We might be better off to pilot some projects in the voluntary sector . . . than to go immediately for a regulatory action when we don't know what we want the public or private sector to do differently yet."[35] I return to the question of way-feeling later, but first I want to explore two other ways in which touch-as-feeling gestures toward more radical forms of state-led equality governance.

BEING TOUCHED

> Emotions are suppressed because we're trying to do all this in the framework of public policy and public policy is numbers, value for money, . . . the normal measures government applies. . . . You're always encouraged to stand back from the emotional disturbance that equalities or inequalities will stir in you. . . . The prevailing wisdom is that's the only way you can do, otherwise you'd be making policies, throwing money around without the substantial evidence that it's the right thing to do. . . . There's a clear need to package [emotions] and put them to one side and have the helicopter view of the unemotional rational, analytical . . . and it's probably a good thing.
> — SENIOR EQUALITY GOVERNANCE OFFICIAL

Despite this statement, mainstream equality governance, and the bodies cast in it, do not seem to lack demonstrable feeling.[36] On the contrary, central to advancing equality as a state-led project is the production of a buoyant sense of progress. Thus a report from the Department for Communities and Local Government echoes several (including the EHRC Plan quoted above) in stating, "Over the last 60 years there have been landmark improvements in addressing the starkest aspects of inequality and discrimination."[37] But while such confidence reaches out to touch and embrace a public through a particular narrative of equality, we might think of the emotions that casting equality, as an everyday utopia, expresses through its performance of *being touched*.

A touched state might be one that feels implicated, even sorry. In other contexts, this is something several national governments have indicated, including Britain, responding to prior (and recent) histories of persecution, state excess, or colonial takeover with formalized, official expressions of shame, regret, and apology.[38] Several academics have written critically about this "sorry" work (e.g., Ahmed 2004b; Barta 2008; Goldberg-Hiller 2012). Yet, however problematic, self-serving, and boundary-setting such institutionalized expressions might prove, a striking feature of mainstream British equality governance during the period examined is the paucity of this kind of expressed feeling. Far from being touched in ways that generate shame or apology, mainstream equality asserts a kind of emotional autonomy and calculating agency. Thus casting equality is repeatedly located within a historical lineage of constant values: tolerance, equality, fairness, and human rights—values, controversially, depicted as stable themes in the continuing expression of British national identity.[39]

Glimpses of other feelings, including annoyance, frustration, and crossness, do nonetheless emerge. These feelings speak to interior cleavages and a more emotionally contactful state, where feeling isn't simply a symbolic form of outward-directed political expression but is generated through and by wider political events. One EHRC report illustrates this more responsive form of emotional touch.[40] Read in the course of reading dozens of similar documents, two things about it as a public document immediately stand out. The first is its unusual signaling and pinpointing of "mistaken" thinking and "counterproductive" policies by other state bodies, here local authorities (4). The second is its directive clarity in instructing local authorities how to act. This is not to criticize the report. On the contrary, I was struck by how different (how frank, concerned, and assertive, how in a sense "everyday") its tone appeared in comparison with the grandiosity or studied detachment common to governmental documents.

The report concerned funding of domestic violence services; it argued that funders need to recognize that targeted provision through female-only or race-based groups might prove more effective than funding only provisions defined as universal: "Having an *inflexible* approach that assumes it is better to fund mainstream services rather than single-issue groups *isn't* the right approach to begin with. . . . In the end, the effects of such *flawed* decision-making only serve to *bolster* the barriers to well-being, participation and equality experienced by disadvantaged women . . . particularly hard to reach groups, such as ethnic minority women."[41] In this example, the production of unexpectedly "un-stately" feeling demonstrates the work done by touch chains, described earlier; such chains do not simply allow state bodies to touch but cause them also to

be touched, in this case through effective NGO action. For this report followed the successful legal challenge of a decision by Ealing Council in
London to cease funding the long-established community organization
Southall Black Sisters to provide domestic violence services.[42] Thus we
might read the commission's guidance documentation as an affective expression of received touch, given shape and life by the relays of pressure,
dissent, feminist politics, and judicial decision making at several interconnected scales.

ATTENTIVE UNDERSTANDING

Reading the enactment of state-based emotion as a mediated effect of
social movement pressure takes me to a third kind of feeling: attentive
understanding (see also chapter 5). What this emphasizes, in contrast
to touch's subject-centered tendencies, is a giving over to what is felt.[43]
Absorption, immersion, and empathizing with the other have been the
subject of extensive, sometimes heated feminist debate, as writers worry
over the implications for women, in particular, losing themselves in another. However, the stakes are different when institutionalized bodies
are involved, and immersion by the state does not necessarily mean
merging. High levels of attention may be premised upon separation,
where feeling is performed in order to understand the distant and unfamiliar, even as routine, overly familiar experiences may be rendered
different and unknown by haptic forms of slow, detailed encounter.

In the context of equality governance, attentive understanding might
entail several things. It might mean feeling the texture, tensions, heat,
and shape of injustice. It might also mean, more reflexively, responding
to the ongoing, historically extensive shape institutions and institutional
actors have left on social justice politics, as the state that feels affects
what is felt. Cvetkovich (2007: 465) comments, in ways that circle back
to the question of state apology, "Affect is often managed in the public sphere through official discourses of recognition or commemoration
that don't fully address everyday affects or through legal measures . . .
that don't fully provide emotional justice. The goal is something more
than statues and monuments, something that involves ways of living,
structures of feeling."

Attentive understanding in this respect might entail being attuned to
the *different* ways different inequalities operate. In relation to the last,
during the period discussed the difficulties casting equality faced proved

Prize winners display their work at the EHRC "Young Brits at Art" competition in which young people were asked to show "what the world would look like if we lived without prejudice." © Equality and Human Rights Commission.

particularly marked as the geometry of protected characteristics, with its pie chart depiction of inequality and Venn diagram approach to intersectionality, suggested that different strands of disadvantage involved the same kind of thing (see also Grabham et al. 2009). At the same time, casting equality resisted an isomorphic approach to equality. Although official documents and interviews drew attention to connections and parallels between inequalities, emphasis was also placed on the distinctiveness not only of each inequality but of each individual as well. An EHRC report declared, "We need to think beyond strands—there is a combination of factors that affect us. . . . In practice, this means taking a person-centred approach. . . . Universal rights and values are best achieved through attention to the particular forms that discrimination takes and the specific realities of people's lives."[44]

Arguably, however, both individual and group-based approaches to inequality are of limited value if their focus on attaching inequality to subjects means they treat the ways social life is organized as a secondary effect (Cooper 2004). Yet even if the dynamic forces generating inequality are understood as socially produced and driven, a state that feels the effects of inequality on subjects raises another set of problems endemic to its fantasy of a benign state coming in close. How desirable is a touching-feeling state?[45]

Opponents here come from all sides. Critics of the so-called therapeutic state, such as James Nolan (1998), charge that feeling has replaced rationality and objectivity in state discourse and action. Others, on the left, suggest the notion of a touching-feeling state is hugely naïve, at risk of ignoring or forgetting—in its simplistic idea of a benevolent state up close—the concentrated power (and especially coercive power) states can and invariably do mobilize. Moreover even if the state could be on the side of subordinate constituencies, its advocacy of tentative thinking and nonrational feeling would do little to assist them. Thus a state feeling its way on behalf of subordinate constituencies is either not going to happen or, if it did, would involve the state in giving up the very strength it could bring to bear on behalf of the poor or dominated.

I am sympathetic to these latter claims. However, to the extent they become a confident critique of the state in general (rather than particular state formations at particular times), they risk erasing the fact that the state is not a tangible entity. It is not a physical body or thing but a concept. What it means when we talk about the state coming in close— to touch society's organization and populations, and be touched, in turn, by them, including by their imaginations of what life could be like (as in the Young Brits at Art competition)—depends (at least in part) on how the state is conceptualized, a conceptualization that also shapes and renders intelligible where the boundaries of the state, and thus what is beyond the state, are deemed to lie. In the final part of this chapter, I turn to the question of state. My argument is that following the touch of equality governance, and particularly in considering the kinds of state touch that might appear more desirable, we need to revisit the state in terms of how it is imagined and how it might be remade.

Revisiting the State

Academics have adopted a range of approaches to the question of the state's form, function, and spatial reach. However, conceptions of the state tend to assemble, in different ways and usually within a single formation, functions of territorial control and coordination, a network of apparatuses, the means by which rule is coordinated and imposed, the provision of public goods, exclusive rights to legitimate organized violence, and national modes of representation and identity production. Critical scholars drawing on Marxist, feminist, and postcolonial approaches add other dimensions as the assemblage of the state is rethought to emphasize states' central preoccupation with the reproduction of dominant social relations and their territorial reach beyond the nation-state (e.g., Jessop 1990; Rai 1996).

In considering the state's different facets — its bodies, work, purposes, powers, effects, responsibilities, and form — and in considering how they combine, connect, and become hierarchically ordered, progressive state practice (as a form of actualization) and thought paths derived from feminist scholarship (as a form of imagining) can prove useful. Progressive state practice, including the everyday utopia of casting equality discussed here, upends conceptual assumptions about what is necessary or essential to the state by demonstrating contradictory tendencies and projects.[46] Feminist theory, in turn, offers ways of understanding this more contingently assembled state through frameworks developed in relation to social subjects and personhood. Certainly feminist identity frameworks have been extensively criticized for essentialism and reductionism and for wallowing in a victim-based affect (e.g., Brown 1995; Halley 2008). But if identity is taken as linguistic shorthand for thinking about the principal social dimensions and relations (of gender, race, and class, among others) through which subjects' experiences, choices, desires, and positions are constituted and rendered meaningful, it may prove an instructive framework for thinking about those facets or relations that come together to constitute the state, dimensions that are also produced through their very assembling together as the state (see De-Landa 2006: 34).[47] Combined (or assembled), these identities gain texture and shape through a series of discursive appellations, including the welfare, security, workfare, colonial, ecological, or warfare state (e.g., Goldberg-Hiller and Silva 2011).

As with the social composition of subjecthood, imagining the state's identities raises certain core questions. These include the relationship between doing and being, appearing and performing, and between those identities readily recognized—whether by the subject or others—and those uncovered (or unmasked) through critical (some might say "paranoid") readings and encounters (see Sedgwick 2003). Yet if casting equality steers us toward (by inciting the need for) a more contingent, socially embedded conception of the state (as well as particular states),[48] how does thinking about the state's multiple "identities"[49]—and I include as identities those refused or declined identifications that nevertheless constitute the state relationally in different fields of violence, legitimacy, rule, bodies, and so on—help us think about the touching and touched state that casting equality both materializes and imagines? I want to approach this question in two parts. First, what effect has casting equality had on the identities of the British state? Second, what strategic possibilities does it suggest for how such identities might be assembled differently?

Casting equality may have affected social life in various ways; nevertheless its effects on the assembled British state seem limited. Certainly it provided a platform through which a differently imagined state could be expressed, illustrated by the somewhat remarkable statement from the Department of Community and Local Government in their public consultation on equality planning: "Government is committed to making sure, in every community, in every corner of this country, people know we are on their side. No favours. No privileges. No special interest groups. Just fairness."[50] But this may be an instance of the phantom conceptual lines discussed in chapter 2, imagined and narrated but unable (perhaps indeed not intended) to drive a resembling form of practice. A more realized revision in the British state's identity, achieved by casting equality, might be instead the development of horizontal and facilitative forms of governing.

Equality governance, without question, made use of vertical techniques of monitoring, requirement, and judgment, but it was weighted toward other modes of contact, involving encouragement, partnership, contract, training, and modeling. The public documents I studied were replete with references to such things as "pilot outreach programmes," Exemplar Employers "sharing their best practice," "trailblazer" public bodies as "champions, ambassadors and mentors," even the statement, "Through an online tool, being developed with Ernst & Young, we will work with those involved in recruitment to help them learn to recognize and address any biases and prejudices they may have."[51] Partnerships with commercial bodies and grandiose claims may generate skepticism. However, the forms of horizontal governance depicted are not unique to casting equality. In many respects, they can be seen to echo wider shifts in the interorganizational relations of the neoliberal state (e.g., see

Clarke and Newman 1997; Newman 2001, 2007) variously explored and conceptualized as policy networks, the "hollowed out" state, and governing at a distance (Rhodes 1994; Rose 1996).

At the national level, then, it appears wildly optimistic to suggest that casting equality generated a newly manifest state, with different state identities assembled together in different ways. But can we make a more modest claim? Is it possible to see the conceptual lines of the state generated from following casting equality's touch as suggesting certain new imagined strategies — strategies that, in turn, reframe the problematic of the touching-feeling state?

Imagining state power in a country such as Britain suggests a force that comes from and is augmented by the tight intersections and formative interconnections between different state identities. To put it at its strongest, state coercion and violence emanate from specific state apparatuses, linked by hierarchical techniques of state governance, with authority over a defined realm. But what happens if these interconnections are looser or partially dismantled so that the state is not a tightly interlocked composite entity but a concept whose imagining and actualization reveal bits sticking out in all directions? In his discussion of British state sovereignty in relation to the EU, the legal scholar Neil MacCormick (1993: 17) poses a related question: "Can we think of a world in which our normative existence and our practical life are anchored in, or related to, a variety of institutional systems, each of which has validity or operation in relation to some range of concerns, none of which is absolute over all the others?"

A contemporary British instantiation of such trends toward polycentrism or state fragmentation is privatization, particularly in its global, corporate form. Here "state" functions are performed by nonpublic bodies whose primary goals and interests are commercial, who can be domiciled beyond the state's territory, and who may be inadequately controlled through modes of state rule. A similar trend is evident in Guiraudon and Lahav's (2000) discussion of European nation-states' externalization (and delegation) of migration control as responsibilities were moved upward to transnational bodies, downward to local government, and outward to private partners (see also Gill 2009). Privatization and the delegation of migration control suggest a thinned and stretched out state, clearly *antithetical* to advancing equality, but might thinning and stretching have other, more progressive effects?

British municipal socialism offers one such instance. In councils across the country, the Labour Left of the 1980s refused to comply with a host of central government edicts, denouncing hierarchical modes of rule and disavowing conventional relations between state bodies, to advance a series of agendas antithetical to central government that included gay equality, local democracy, environmentalism, and workers' rights (Cooper 1996; Lansley et al. 1989). Whether mainstream equality governance, even at its 2009–10 height, constitutes a similar instance of "thinning out" is debatable. Certainly some scholars have worried over this, concerned its imposition (rather than its bottom-up deployment) reduces the vital linkages that critical proximity requires between equality as a project and governmental modes of power (Squires and Wickham-Jones 2002). But does the thinned-out state have unrealized political mileage when thinking through the touching-feeling potential of casting equality?

Located within the thick state of liberal modernity, feeling as a state ethos brings, as I have suggested, a raft of problems. Fundamentally it appears too close and too dominating. Whether state power is mobilized to feel people, objects, inequality, emotions, or its own way, the state seems too heavy and powerful not to destroy, radically transform, or upset those things felt in its wake. Advocacy of a weaker state is well-trodden ground within libertarian and anarchist writing (even as others condemn weak and failing states), but such advocacy is not my aim here. The material elimination or weakening of particular state identities might not diminish state power or authority overall. It could lead to multiple (quasi-)states, with different identities (or differently configured identities), coexisting across the same territory; ditching certain state identities might protect or augment powerful others; and the decoupling or withering of specific identities might simply reflect emergent, newly dominating interests and projects (see Hansen and Stepputat 2001: 30). Even privatization, with its mobilization of profitability and commercial involvement, does not unequivocally support a declining state thesis.

But if we focus instead on the articulations and linkages between state identities, it becomes possible to imagine (and perhaps even to actualize) certain state identities free of their "normal" baggage. Earlier in this chapter, I explored the recasting of equality governance in terms of feeling—of a state feeling its way, expressing feeling, and feeling what is there. Associated with the thick British state, feeling seems troubling.

But what about feeling in the context of a thinned-out state where specific state identities have been pulled away (stretched out) from their established articulations? If the ties between welfare and coercion were loosened or very differently articulated, we might imagine the state's welfare identity (the reciprocating touch between citizens and government) extending toward sensual pleasures, creativity, and human fulfillment (rather than work, security, discipline, and risk), without necessarily bringing the penal state along too. Or if the state's pedagogical ethos were less tied to the state's role as regulator, welfare provider, or referee, greater reflexivity and tentative thinking (a state feeling its way) might not necessarily have the same repercussions for other aspects of its operation. Likewise if reassembling the state's network of bodies (public organizations, commercial providers, NGOs, partnerships) to get experientially closer to injustice had a far more mediated relationship to the state's coercive and penal work, less might be risked for communities in getting closer to the state.

Stretching state identities in ways that cause some identities to overhang or to hinge differently to others suggests ways a more radical politics might be folded in, or brought into contact with certain state parts or elements, with less risk of hazardous forms of incorporation. But while we can imagine this, actualization is far more difficult. Decoupling, recoupling, or reforming state identities is a hugely complex task as a deliberate, progressive project. Indeed in some cases it might prove impossible as particular combinations, at particular temporal-spatial junctures, are unable to be reformed, let alone pulled apart. Nevertheless what a strategy of stretching and rearticulating reveals is a way of engaging with the state that centers the imaginative and improvised pursuit of its re-creation, and in imagining what this could be like, the actualization that state-based everyday utopias offer are important educators of desire and inspiration—if not guides.

Concluding Remarks

While states in the global North tend to be viewed as far from sensory formations, this has not discouraged academics from exploring them in this vein, focusing on the senses as both targets and techniques of rule. Work addressing the state's use of vision, for instance, has explored how states can govern (or attempt to govern) at a distance by rendering people, things, and processes visible from far away. Sight also allows for other forms of contact, including through weaponry, while the reality or threat from another's scrutiny and surveillance habitually steers people into governing themselves (explored further in chapter 7). Governing through vision appears efficient, clean, asymmetrical, and fast. But what about governing through touch? How does touch structure relations between institutions, subjects, governmental technologies, and politics? In many respects, touch as a mode (or register) of governance seems to offer something of a counterpoint to vision. Where vision speeds up governance, touch slows it down; vision can see panoptically, touch works serially; while vision may not be reciprocal (rendering the one who sees as vulnerable), touch always touches back; where sight takes, touch reflects; where sight is certain and finished in what it knows, touch is uncertain, open, hesitant, and reflexive.

In this chapter I have adopted a less romantic approach to touch. However, rather than focus on the materially unequal ways in which states touch, how they consolidate social relations of inequality through the very practice of touching, my focus has been on the ways touch is imagined within a progressive state project. Casting equality did not imagine touch in a vacuum. Mediated by the politics of producing official documents, the conceptual touch-lines created were intended to have specific effects—legitimizing, informing, declaring, warning—in the course of expressing a vision of an animate, sensitive, responsive state. Thus official texts used the language of touch to touch in particular ways. But as active elements within the social democratic project of casting equality, these texts also did other things. As such, they reveal how notions of touch can be deployed to make certain things unknowable and unthinkable; they also offer glimpses and evidence of other kinds of touch. In this way, the public texts of casting equality open up other, more speculative, ways of imagining the touching state as one that is also touched—concerned, sensitive, and attentive to the harm and damage of systemic social inequality.

Yet while casting equality allows us to envision a transformative kind of state touch, imagining such touch poses troubling political questions, specifically, how touching-feeling should the state be? Studies of the state's deployment of vision foreground critical and analytical questions about how states work; focusing on touch in the context of casting equality as an everyday utopia opens up a series of normative questions regarding our relationship to the state and what it could be. These questions require us to think again about how we conceptualize the state, a process that invokes the constant move, as I discussed in chapter 2, between actualization and imagining—between the specificity of particular state formations and fantasies of what a state is and of what it could be (in the light too of imagining different, other states also). This process opens up various places where intervention might occur, including through the strategic pursuit of a thin or extended state, in which state identities are both reconstituted and reassembled.

In chapter 4 I continue to explore the development of an equality project in ways attuned to questions of touch. However, rather than focusing on equality as something that can be abstractly formulated and then delivered by top-down state practice, I examine equality as something that is protean and always in formation. In particular, I explore equality as a normative concept expressed in everyday noninstitutional practices. My focus is the social terrain of nudism, particularly nudist appearances in public.

CHAPTER 4

PUBLIC NUDISM AND THE PURSUIT OF EQUALITY

The vanishing of clothes has done more for human equality than all the philanthropists' efforts, or the anarchists' steel blade.

Dickberry [1904] 2006: 240

June 2011 in London witnessed two public naked events in a city that usually lives its life clothed. At the start of the month *Un Peu de Tendresse Bordel de Merde!* by the choreographer Dave St-Pierre opened at the premier dance venue, Sadler's Wells.[1] In this work not only did dancers spend time on stage naked, but they also brought their nakedness quite literally into the hands and across the faces of theater audiences, as they clambered over people sitting in the stalls. One journalist commented, "As a group of blonde-wigged, naked men scamper through the auditorium . . . we find ourselves being kissed, hugged, and sat on, up close and personal with the arses and genitals of complete strangers."[2] A week later, on June 11, the London part of the world naked bike ride passed through the city center. I watched it go with my partner and friends, quite unexpectedly, as we were making our way around Westminster and stopped at a crosswalk while it passed. Several hundred people cycled through, stopping traffic, in a highly embodied form of advocacy for cycling and against the environmental damage caused by reliance on cars and oil. Strongly resonant of the dramaturgical aspects of carnival culture (see chapter 8), bodies went by in all shades of paint and attached accessories, as well as in the buff, women being noticeably less naked than men.[3]

Public nudism, of course, has no special attachment to London. Media stories circulate globally about people appearing naked on streets, cliff walks, rugby pitches, and in public buildings, as well as at festivals and on beaches. While a limited range of naked performances are deemed acceptable, most are not. In Ontario, Brian Coldin, a naturist resort operator, was charged and prosecuted in 2011 for using restaurant drive-thrus without clothes.[4] In response, Coldin challenged the constitutionality of the law, claiming that the criminal offense of being nude in a public place or exposed to the public in a private one hindered his freedom of expression.[5] Coldin's challenge failed. Yet his prosecution was no isolated instance. The discriminatory treatment of nudists, nudist organizations, and people who choose to live part of their lives naked raises serious questions for equality politics. Indeed nudists have long pointed to what they perceive as the unfair, preferential treatment of the "textile" world, those parts of society that take being clothed for granted.

In chapter 3 I considered equality as a governmental project, a mode of public address that indicates particular ways of thinking about reform, about the problems requiring solutions, and about the fantasies of what it is that is to be done will do. With the development of equality and antidiscrimination measures within large numbers of liberal states, the everyday utopia of state action striking at unfair disadvantage has extended and multiplied, even as it takes shape in close proximity to state action directed at quite other ends.

Conceptualizing equality as a project of ameliorative and regulatory action, undertaken by state and other powerful bodies in pursuit of an imagined better world, provides the ground for much academic writing on equality. Indeed the extent to which contemporary equality scholarship is organized around the problematic of state action, whether in the form of philosophical thought experiments and modeled solutions or by engaging with law and policy, is striking. At the heart of much of this work lies the question: Which equalities matter, and for whom, when, and where (e.g., Dworkin 2000; Phillips 1999)? Responding to this question, writers have explored the composition of equality's subjects, whether it be individuals, groups, living beings, or humankind; they have debated what it is that should be equalized, whether opportunities, resources, outcomes, or dignity; and they have explored equality's role, remit, and animating conditions, from providing a vital dimension of democratic representational politics to shaping workplace relations, the use of public and commercial services, and the life course (e.g., Baker et al. 2004; Harding 2010; May 2010). In the process, writers have addressed the strategies, laws, and policies that equality's pursuit requires, from treating like alike (which of course depends on knowing what is alike) to undoing systemic relations of power (Cooper 2004; Fraser 1997; Young 1990), and they have addressed the question of equality's "why" (or inequality's "why not"), finding in nature, humanity, or principles of social justice the rationale for reform.

One helpful contemporary framework to combine these different elements in a way that places systemic power relations at its heart is Sandra Fredman's (2011). Anchored in the legal and policy operationalization of equality, Fredman argues for a "multi-dimensional concept that can incorporate four overlapping aims." She calls these the redistributive dimension "to break the cycle of disadvantage"; the recognition dimension "to promote respect for dignity and worth"; the transformative dimension, which "accommodate[s] difference and aims[s] to achieve structural change"; and the participative dimension to enable people to participate fully, "socially and politically" (25).

Certainly there is a lot of very good work on equality, including Fredman's (2011). However, with a few exceptions, recent discussion on equality has largely stuck to established paths, with little more novel work. In this chapter I want to move away from that more familiar terrain of equality scholarship, which, by focusing on the who, what, where, and when of equality, treats equality either as a model for allocating resources (or something else) or as a discursive frame for social movement or policy ambitions. Instead I consider equality as a set of normative organizing principles that wrap together actuality and imagining in the course of conditioning present practice and future (as well as past) fantasies. Approaching equality when it takes shape as something that is not quite a project, discourse, or explicit set of political aspirations means we can identify equality's presence in contexts where these other elements are not especially evident. This broadens the range of contexts in which equality can be identified and opens up possibilities for developing new conceptual lines.

To extend this process fully, this chapter deliberately focuses on a social practice—public nudism—that diverges from many of the conditions that animate conventional equality theorizing. Understood here as the deliberate decision to be unclothed in shared (or publicly visible) spaces,[6] public nudism is something that is done rather than sought; it is often unorganized, and, in contrast to much left-wing theorizing on equality, it concerns ways of living and appearing (rather than structures of domination). This is in no way to disavow equality analysis's more usual focus on gender, class, race, sexuality, and disability. However, choosing to focus on public nudism offers a hopefully fresh perspective on what equality (or undoing inequality) might entail—one that may be helpful for thinking about better known forms of inequality as well.

Yet approaching equality through public nudism immediately confronts a problem. For equality frameworks have been far from paramount in nudist activism, which has tended to prefer discourses of health, nature, rights, freedom, and expression. This begs the question: Why use nudism to think about equality? Wouldn't nudism have more to say about those political discourses *actually* deployed?

Moving beyond a reliance on the effable may be particularly salient in relation to nudism, an experience that is often felt to elude or exceed verbal description (Obrador-Pons 2007; see also chapter 5), and in chapter 2 I explored how concepts can be present and expressed even when they remain unuttered. In developing a utopian conceptual attitude, decentering the conventional reliance on speech and texts, and being attentive to other ways of knowing—for both participants and observers—is important, opening up conceptual lines beyond those already verbally established. These conceptual lines can be driven by new forms of imagining or by practice. This chapter's focus is the latter. Yet, exploring equality's *presence* as a normative set of principles within public nudism does not mean equality exists in any simple sense. Finding it rather depends on the movement between imagining and actualization as equality takes shape in three different temporally configured ways: as a presupposition, as something expressed, and as potential.

Presupposition concerns the norms required to be in place for a particular practice to be intelligible, appropriate, or possible. Such norms may become apparent only as new practices take shape; they may also be invented or asserted by those claiming legitimacy, as past conditions get *imagined* as already there in order to drive their future reality. As a presupposition, equality is particularly evident in the conditions animating nudist activism. The contemporary focus of nudist politics may largely revolve around rights and freedom, but these are authorized and gain meaning through notions of a moral equality between nudists and others. As Todd May (2010: 58) writes, discussing Jacques Rancière's work, "The presupposition of equality does not have to be consciously recognized in order for it to be effective, in order for a democratic politics to occur."

Nudists can speak because—at least from their perspective—their equality as speaking subjects is presumed. Moreover claims for nudists' rights frequently deploy analogy in ways that, implicitly or otherwise, are premised upon equivalence. In other words, as many movements have done before them, contemporary nudist politics link nudists to the struggles of those now perceived as having acquired legitimacy and official recognition. In doing so, nudists use these latter struggles to validate their own in ways that largely disregard the political limits others have identified in such analogy drawing (e.g., Lamble 2012). So, Andrew Welch, a British Naturist representative, commented, after losing access to a beach, "If we were an ethnic or religious group this sort of thing would never happen."[7] In a similar vein, an American nudist activist, Terri Sue Webb, remarked, "To be offended by another person on the basis of visual appearance is prejudice akin to racism."[8]

Equality, then, appears as a presupposition, shaping and influencing nudist political claims despite being rarely invoked explicitly. Equality also appears as a presupposition in relation to the less instrumental forms of public nudist practice. Being naked in public asserts the foundational claim that bodies have an equal entitlement to express themselves; and that it is legitimate for bodies to appear in authentic ways, namely as undressed. But equality isn't manifested only as an imagined animating condition; it also takes shape as a form of expression constituted and conveyed by action. Within the context of postindustrial societies within the global North,[9] there are limited authorized public places in which naked bodies can appear or gather. As a result, out-of-place nakedness, along with those places where public nakedness is allowed, become conveyors of meaning and force. Rancière (1995: 47) describes how strikes similarly can function as a translation and practical demonstration of equality. In the case of public nudism, what is expressed is not so much an equality already materialized as a set of organizing principles that govern what is, but rather a set of normative claims about what could (and should) be.

The third way equality appears is as potential. This is not potential in the sense of what materially should be (as just described), but the conceptual potential of equality itself to be differently imagined and opera-tionalized. As I discussed in chapter 2, potential combines temporalities in complex ways. It exists as a presence within the now that is predicated on an imagined future concertinaed back to uncover or re-recognize what presently exists. Potential exists only to the extent it is found, and its finding is subject to what it could become if the conditions — knowable and unknowable — proved to be right. Identifying equality's conceptual potential to become other than it currently is, to disavow for instance the splits and divisions (between groups or subjects) that conventional equality thinking relies upon, depends on creating new conceptual lines. These may be mediated by nudist practitioners; however, when equality operates as a form of expression and potential, the conceptual lines that move from what is to imagining what could be importantly rely also on other interpretations, finding equality's lines where others may not. This does not mean equality is completely free-floating, able to be shaped into any pattern one desires. In all three cases — of presupposition, expres-sion, and potential — the particular effects of context are vital to bear in mind. Equality as a set of normative principles is not hermetically sealed. It takes its shape from the norms, anxieties, systems, and *ethoi* it encoun-ters and within whose terrain it resides.[10] Recognizing the adulteration (or contamination) of normative concepts such as equality is important to avoid overidealizing what it is and what it could become. I do not want to produce a perfect conception of equality out of its imperfect practice (see chapters 2 and 5).

I begin with the everyday utopian character of public nudism, and the discrimination, even criminalization, that nudists and nudism routinely face. The rest of the chapter explores enactments of nudism through dif-ferent registers of publicness; in doing so, I address the different concep-tions of equality that various forms of public nakedness can bear. My ac-count draws on diverse documentary sources, including contemporary nudist publications and media stories.[11]

Public Nudism: An Everyday Utopia

Over the past century, modern nudism — as the deliberate choice to be naked beyond transitional moments of dressing, undressing, and bath-ing — has taken various forms. These include "associational," "in shared space," and "personal" nudism. Associational (or club) nudism developed as the public face of nudism in the early twentieth century, its presence

Naturists feeding meerkats at Newquay Zoo in England during a visit by nearly one hundred naturists in June 2011. This event was one of many during a weeklong naturism festival attended by 350 people in Cornwall. Reprinted by permission of British Naturism. Image courtesy of Steve Betts.

being particularly marked in central Europe, although it quickly developed in Britain, the United States, and Canada, among other places. Associational nudism proved distinctive for its highly organized and regulated form, and, particularly in the United States (and to a lesser degree elsewhere), it strove to establish nudism as a family activity completely divorced from sex. In many countries, camps and other outdoor spaces owned by societies or pro-nudist individuals provided private venues for weekend and holiday gatherings (e.g., Hartman et al. 1970). By the turn of the twentieth-first century, associational nudism had branched out to infiltrate the usually clothed spaces of the textile world. Nudist societies organized group trips to tourist attractions, rented public pools for naked swimming sessions, chartered planes, and held clothes-free shopping nights.[12]

"Shared space" nudism, by contrast, refers to the diverse range of places in which collective nakedness occurs. These include nudist and clothing-optional beaches, as well as commercial holiday venues, such as hotels, guesthouses, resorts, and even the occasional cruise ship. The expansion of commercial nonassociational nudism has been characterized as a growing feature of the contemporary nudist scene, particularly in the form of up-market leisure facilities and venues (Woodall 2002), used by individuals, couples, and families who want to enjoy the occasional clothes-free environment. Participants may enjoy the presence of other nudists, but they don't necessarily share a commitment to nudism as a social project in the way club members tend to, nor do they share a commitment to the norms, rules, and ethos apparent and enforced in nudist associations.

The third form of nudism, "personal" nudism, takes place in private and public spaces, including the home, beach, or woodland. While other nudists may be present (including partners or family), their presence — and particularly the presence of naked nonintimates — isn't necessarily desired or deemed an enhancing dimension of the experience (see Schrank 2012). Availability of legitimate spaces for personal nudism varies considerably between different jurisdictions, with continental Europe, for instance, being far more permissive than the United States. When it takes the form of solitary nudism, personal nudism is more likely than the other forms of nudism outlined to transgress normative, and often legal, boundaries, by venturing illegitimately into clothing-required spaces, as I discuss below.

Associational, shared space, and personal nudism identify the main forms nudist activity takes. However, since this chapter focuses on nakedness in public arenas, it also draws in other, more sporadic forms of festive, aesthetic, or protest-based nakedness. These don't necessarily involve people who regularly appear naked in public but includes those willing to undress to demonstrate their strength of feeling in relation to state or corporate action (and inaction) (Alaimo 2010; Misri 2011; Sutton 2007), for carnival (Gotham 2005; Shrum and Kilburn 1996), or because they are taking part in a television show or art event. Other kinds of organized but infrequent forms of public nudism include cycling events, such as the world naked bike ride, festivals such as Michigan Womyn's Music Festival (Browne 2009), nude lounging on town streets, and the dramaturgical deployment of nudity in the form of "guerrilla pranksterism."[13]

Nudist beach carnival, Queensland, Australia, 1998. Photo by Ruth Barcan.

Different forms of public nudity, advocated and practiced by often very different kinds of groups and individuals, may seem to have little in common. However, bringing them within the frame of everyday utopia causes diverse gestures of public nudism to become instances of a loosely common form, a form that brackets those social nudists who equate legitimate nudism *exclusively* with private or commercially owned space. Public nudism's utopian character lies in several features. It signals the fantasy of a better way of living, one that stretches dress informality to the utmost in the nudist dream of a people living unclothed (less true for those who undress as one-off moments of protest than for others). Introducing Frances Merrill and Mason Merrill's book *Among the Nudists*, John Langdon-Davies (1931: ix) remarks, "In the future all reasonable governments would insist, on grounds of public morality and health, on the removal of all clothes."

In posing another way of being, nudism seeks to educate desire (see chapter 5), stimulating people, through the experience of nudism, to become far more attuned to their sensory, and especially tactile, relationship to the world around them. Public nudism also highlights the multidimensional character of everyday utopias' relationship to time. On the one hand, it refuses to postpone the better, undressed society until some future, undefined moment. Yet to the extent that public nudism is part of a *political* project (as I discuss below), it is oriented to bringing about a different future. In that sense, it might be read as a prefigurative practice—a utopia in formation, where undertaking what appears to be novel (carrying out everyday activities naked) provides a way of experiencing, demonstrating, and bringing into being its more developed (even institutionalized) future reality.

Nudism also speaks to utopia's signaling of the impossible, absent place. Like other utopias, nudism seems to function as a (multidimensional) domain only when viewed from within. From outside, it may appear incredible or unbelievable. Too unusual or "freakish" to be taken seriously, public nudism is largely ignored in wider discussions of dress or appearance. Yet despite its utopian aspirations and regular disregard, in common with the other sites discussed, as a way of living (at least from the perspective of nudist regulars) nudism is firmly rooted in the textured concerns of the routinized everyday. Organized associational nudism, in particular, is replete with rules, conventions, and etiquette in an attempt to preempt external prejudices and to confront and resolve the micro-problems of "normal" life deliberately lived unclothed. How to cook, deal with menstrual blood, manage sweat and other personal secretions, and make eye contact in nonsexual ways (discussed further below) are all the subject of nudist rules and customs. Yet, more than this book's other sites, in some ways nudism centers that which is most quotidian: namely, how bodies *appear*, making banal that which gets fetishized elsewhere. As an article in *Time* magazine on American nudists commented, "They . . . have learned to see the naked body as mundane."[14]

Whether nudism is a good idea—whether it provides a means of emancipation from the restrictions imposed by clothes—remains largely, for reasons explored in chapter 1, outside the scope of this discussion. At the same time, in considering the transformative potential of public nudism's conceptual life, it is important to recognize the difficult relationship associational nudism in particular has historically had to other equality projects. While early twentieth-century European nudism embraced a spectrum of political affiliations from anarchist to far right,[15] a dominating concern was the good, healthy body, which for many nudists meant also the good healthy race. European nudists (and naturists) argued that sun contact (heliotherapy) and physical exercise would improve bodies; some also suggested it would generate "better" spousal

Relaxing in a naturist spa. Reprinted by permission of British Naturism. Image courtesy of Steve Betts.

matches, as love, kindled by a more fully displayed beauty and by the development of bodily strength, would drive sexual selection (Kenway 1998: 109; see also Jeffries 2006: 83; Peeters 2006; Ross 2005). Nudism's early, highly problematic associations with eugenics and racism are well established.[16] However, later twentieth-century developments continued to demonstrate associational nudism's racialized imbrication within the global North, from the racism of nude aesthetics and naked parties in postwar East Germany (McLellan 2007, 2009) to the white bias of photographic imagery within mainstream nudist publications (Woodall 2002: 271–72).

Nudism also has had a complex relationship to progressive gender and class politics. One promotional claim often made about associational nudism is its practical commitment to minimizing economic status asymmetries. Commenting on a Socialist Party nudist club near Hamburg, Frances and Mason Merrill (1931: 130) remark, "The lack of clothing contributed, if anything, to the ease of everybody. One barrier, at least, was eliminated: there was no class distinction of dress" (see also Dickberry [1904] 2006). Maurice Parmelee (1929: 231) similarly states, "Dress is one of the principal means of making [class and caste] distinctions." Historically nudism has also been presented as promoting gender equality, challenging the hypocrisies of female "modesty" and supporting women and girls' ability to move about freely without restrictive garments (e.g., Parmelee 1929).[17]

However, in recent years the equality-extending claims of early nudist advocates in relation to class and gender have been countered by writers attentive to the historical and ongoing ways such inequalities structure nudist activities (Bell and Holliday 2000; Ross 2005; Woodall 2002).[18] In relation to gender, in particular, early twenty-first-century feminists, including those sympathetic to nudism, have challenged nudism's claims to enhance women's liberation, exploring how women's bodies are sexualized on nudist beaches and in naturist publications (see Barcan 2004; Holmes 2006). Less discussed but still strikingly apparent from nudist and naturist magazines and websites is the ongoing social and cultural orientation of associational nudism toward an able-bodied heterosexuality,[19] whose contemporary racial and geographic politics (particularly as up-market naturist tourism brings naked white bodies to the global South) largely remains unexamined. Equally unexamined is the grooming that mainstream nudist bodies seem to receive, especially in the images used in nudist magazines (many of which rely on sales to a nonnudist market). The Western aesthetic of hairless, smooth, shiny, taut, fair bodies suggests that, rather than simply seeing nudism as rendering the utopian everyday, we might see the everyday in a sense as having been made utopian—in some sanitized, racially gendered form.

The equivocal relationship between nudism and other progressive politics begs the question: Would we do better to read nudism (or at least organized nudism) as an everyday utopia of the right? While this argument can certainly be made about some historical (and contemporary) forms of associational nudism (including conservative Christian nudist communities active today in the United States), exploring equality through *public* rather than associational or club nudism, that is, through practices that legitimate naked bodies in publicly owned or publicly visible spaces (and not just private ones), may orient nudism leftward. As a mode of *public* appearance, nudism encompasses a heterogeneous array of naked activities, including those one-timers or annual participants who strip to cycle naked through London, take off their clothes at a women's music festival, or participate in one of Spencer Tunick's art events. Yet while these cultural contexts indicate public nudism's lawful face, much public nudism, particularly when it is ad hoc and individual, remains illegal.

Contemporary states in the global North seem able to disregard nakedness when it is an integral aspect of some established or recognized creative project; however, the regulation of "inappropriately" naked bodies is extensive and intense. Nudity is forbidden in a range of locations, including streets, courtrooms, universities, and mountain paths, and those who breach place-based prohibitions by walking, cycling, or otherwise appearing undressed face official, as well as unofficial,[20] sanctions (Arneil 2000; Valverde and Cirak 2003). While the legal regulation of nudism varies by jurisdiction, most postindustrial societies have some form of control over public nakedness. Indeed what stands out in accounts of nudist regulation is the severity of some states' responses, notably toward people who repeatedly appear naked in public spaces, and particularly in elite public spaces, such as courtrooms. Britain's "naked rambler," Stephen Gough, according to the *Guardian*, has spent "nearly all of the last six years in Scottish jails, including long periods in solitary confinement at Perth prison, after repeatedly being arrested for failing to wear clothes in public or in court. He was nude again at Kirkcaldy sheriff court on [August 23] to face another charge of breach of the peace."[21] Indeed the mass media is replete with narratives of individuals arrested, charged, tried, and in some instances jailed.[22] And these narratives don't just invoke a dispassionate law telling people to put their clothes back on. One striking and disturbing feature of several media reports, most notably in the United States, is the use of taser guns to make docile those naked bodies deemed, because they remain determinedly naked, out of control.[23]

Regulating nudism is a fast-moving international domain, one not restricted to the immediacy of confronting naked bodies with the criminal law. Other forms of regulation target associational nudism, such as the seizure and prosecution of nudist organization magazines (and other literature) on grounds of obscenity. Media and community websites also tell stories of nudist organizations facing hostile local residents over the establishment of proposed nudist communities, of discrimination from financial service providers, and of activities closed down or intensively scrutinized on the grounds of possible child sexual abuse.[24] Even when nudism is lawful, opponents — whether community groups or public authorities—use legal, governmental, or grassroots means to undermine its development and enjoyment. And the stigma attached to lifestyle nudity in many jurisdictions, although not all, means it frequently remains a covert choice.

The treatment of nudists and of nudism sharply and clearly belies any notion that nudism is an accepted way of living within the postindustrial societies of the global North. Certainly there are nondomestic spaces where nudism is permitted, but internationally they are largely restricted to commercial or privately owned places. One tension, then, unsurprisingly, to arise between different nudist organizations, with important implications for equality principles, concerns the status of property rights, a theme explored further in the rather different, educational context of chapter 7. Mainstream organizations have frequently sought to protect and legitimate nudism through ownership claims, arguing that as property-holders and corporate bodies they should be treated like any other when it comes to contracts, licenses, and renting and when it comes to determining what people can do in privately owned land and buildings.[25] Mainstream organizations have campaigned for access to public lands, such as clothing-optional beaches and parkland (if to a lesser degree, certainly, in the United States than other groups might like). However, the politics and style of mainstream nudist politics distinguishes such organizations from more radical groups, such as the U.S.-based Body Freedom Collaborative, which seeks not only to extend public nudist spaces and to affirm nudism's social value but to use nakedness in the process as a political tool. As they state on their website, "Why not fight for body freedom by doing good in public while naked? We call this type of activity civil nudification."[26]

Beach sunning, nude bike rides, swimming sessions in municipal pools, or stripping naked at meetings, on city streets, or in the theater can happen for many reasons. In the discussion that follows, I want to follow the path of being publicly naked in order to explore how equality gets manifested through practices that implicitly or explicitly challenge nudism's marginality, subordination, and erasure. If public nudism constitutes a utopia, or at least one in formation, it provides a place from which to critique what is and to instantiate a move toward what could be. Equality, in this sense, exists as an enacting presupposition that brings certain forms of nudist practice into being; it is expressed practically (if not verbally) by them; and it inheres as a more open, if nevertheless interpretively found potential. But what content do these forms of equality when attached to nudism invoke? Drawing on parallel debates within feminist and queer politics, we might imagine nudist equality according to a range of possibilities that could include "equality of place," where the nudist/textile divide concerns the fair distribution of dressed and undressed spaces; "equality of entitlement," making it possible for people, however they align themselves, to exercise their preference to be clothed or unclothed anywhere; and an "equality of who," reducing the dressed/undressed distinction to one of insignificance. But linking equality to plurality can also exceed this model of equivalence. As queer has done for sexuality, so nudism might invoke multiple forms of dressed and undressed practice, exploding the clothed/unclothed distinction. It might also, like queer politics and lesbian feminism, open up and destabilize what is possible, sought, and desired, so that how people appear cannot be reduced to fixed, preexisting preferences.

Nudist equality can suggest many different things. And once we move away from a governmental account that treats equality as a program or project that is deliberately arrived at, enunciated, and then installed, the relationship between equality—whether as a presupposition, expressed norm, or potential—and the social context that gives it shape becomes far more muddy and entangled. This complexity is often omitted in work on equality and public life. Despite the different ways public is understood—from geographical work on public spaces to social theoretical perspectives on the deliberative public sphere—the relationship between public and equality tends to be addressed in terms of the conditions for inclusion; how people are treated in public once included; whether publics can encompass diversity; and the value of counter-publics explicitly molded around minority interests and expression (Fraser 1990). In other words, equality is incorporated into discussion about public spaces and public spheres as a clear (often calculable) political project that will transform or revitalize public practice. However, what gets lost here is equality's ability to be far more inchoately present in part because of the complex ways in which conceptions of equality (as the movement between imagining and actualization) absorb, adapt, and respond to the norms, pressures, desires, fears, and constraints of their conditioning social environments. Focusing on the environment within which public nudity takes place rather than the environment conditioning its interpretation, the absorptive character of equality is foregrounded in the discussion that follows.

Bringing Nudism into Mainstream Publics
CIRCULATORY PUBLICS

I start with the notion of circulatory publics, a term I draw loosely from Michael Warner (2002). Warner uses the idea of circulatory publics to characterize the creation of an open-ended formation of strangers organized around and through particular circulating texts and discourses, a newspaper-reading public being one obvious example. I draw on the idea of a circulatory public in order to explore the equality norms that inhere within the interactions of an open-ended body of people, constituted as a public through the movement of a shared text or practice, which somehow involves nudism. However, as the instances described below reveal, nudism can circulate in very different ways—with very different implications for equality norms.

In the first instance, a naked person privately engages with a circulating text. To the extent the text remains unmarked by nudism, the so-called difference of the naked reader is contained, bound off from the rest of the public sphere. This kind of circulatory public captures the idea of an equality of inattention—familiar to feminist and sexual politics activists who have struggled both for and against an inclusion contingent on the private management of one's difference. In the second instance, the circulating text bears a discursive imprint of nudist brief-carrying—a letter to the editor, for example, from a naturist organization. Here we see the equality of liberal public sphere politics. Differences constitute legitimate discursive positions or objects for debate so long as they comply with the conventions of proper form, being coherent, intelligible, and restrained, and so long as they operate according to the conditions that signal an authority or legitimate right to speak and make contact.[27]

However, it is a third way of inserting nakedness into a circulatory public that most interests me, a way that combines speech and body, as when a naked writer's picture is printed beside her or his article,[28] or when naked participants take part in a predominantly clothed face-to-face debate. Here the equality articulated is not only about what is said or written and by whom; it is also an equality given texture, sensation, and weight by bare, claims-making bodies.[29] Attaching naked bodies to nudist speech in the context of nonnudist publics troubles forms of nudist subordination (or minimal equality) that rely on the physical and sensory bracketing of that about which they speak reminiscent here of the embodied protest kiss-ins of lesbian and gay politics in the 1990s. Bringing bodies right in troubles a vision of equality as allotted space that depends upon clothed and unclothed practices remaining apart.

Instead, as nudism circulates through nonnudist spaces, it speaks to a conception of equality that takes shape in and through desire. Like an earlier generation of revolutionary gay politics which identified gay sexuality as a potential available to all that would gain equal value as more people chose it, desire here also passes, intensifies, and becomes transformed as nudism stops being a minority preference and becomes something that engages many (see McLellan 2007: 64). As the young man who introduced the Americans Frances and Mason Merrill to 1920s German nudism remarked, "If all the opponents of *Nacktkultur* could be got into a *Freilicht park*, undressed, just for a day, by evening there wouldn't be any opponents" (Merrill and Merrill 1931: 11). Evert Peeters (2006: 455) similarly emphasizes the experiential aspect of being won over in his discussion of nudism in Belgium in the early twentieth century. Echoing Obrador-Pons's (2007) account of beach nudism at the start of the twenty-first century, Belgian nudists (almost a century earlier) believed the truth accessed by nudity couldn't be lectured or taught; it had to be *felt*. The power of public nakedness as a sensation and experience is evident also in the comments of participants in the contemporary mass naked art events staged and photographed by Spencer Tunick; more than one described the freedom that came from temporarily laying aside the burden of being more than "flesh."[30]

A circulating nudism, then, gestures toward an equality that goes beyond the fair distribution of textile and naked spaces, challenging the notion of predefined subjects stably attached to one mode of appearance rather than another. At the same time, for those to whom nudism constitutes a dangerously seductive harm, the force emanating from nudism's desirability and enticement underscores its threat; in David Scott's (2003: 129) words, nudism can "infect us, like a plague." Alongside the alarm posed from "catching" nakedness reside other contamination fears of catching something else from the circulation of sweating, leaking, unclothed bodies. In nudist clubs and venues, the profusion of hygiene anxieties mean barriers, such as towels, come down to stop anything spreading. But beyond the *nomos* of associational nudism, the main fear of contagion concerns children. What will children catch from nakedness circulating? And is it (representations of) naked children that are circulating as well (see also chapter 7)?[31]

The anxieties and panics mobilized in relation to contemporary nudism structure and, in the short term, seem to limit equality's potential as measures are introduced to curtail what circulates and to whom. (Some public authorities, for instance, have prohibited children from being present during certain nudist activities, such as municipal swimming sessions.) While the force and power of such anxieties obviously are shaped by time and space, what they reveal is the power of particular contexts to redirect equality's potential. Rather than being carried by the spread of desire — as the infectious quality of nudism touches more subjects — nudist equality gets cornered and domesticated. In turn, the potential of nudism to bring forth new interests and desires among transformed subjects becomes reduced to a restricted equality in which nudism circulates freely only among a micro-public of nudist participants.

ORIENTATIONAL PUBLICS

A second form of publicness is constituted not by what circulates but by the relationships forged between a provider and a group of strangers. Orientational publics vary widely, from witnessed arts performances to welfare use. However, what they share is a reciprocating, projective relationship; as publics are turned toward a particular object (a play or public service, for instance), that object is also turned toward them.[32] In orientational publics, welfare providers, fundraisers, performers, and arts producers attend to the social composition of their public, both imagined and actualized. To the extent that nudist constituencies come to function as a recognized category of interest (or need) — for instance, in seeking a mass bike ride permit, permission to use a public swimming pool or establish a nudist beach;[33] less favorably, as objects of court or police scrutiny — this attention may extend to them too. At the same time, in contrast to circulatory forms of public engagement (where participants transact with each other through and in relation to the circulating thing, which might of course be their own or someone else's nudity), orientational publics interact minimally — if at all — among themselves. Demonstrating the kind of civil inattention that Goffman (1963) discusses, such publics rarely get to know one another and show little reflexivity or interest in themselves either as an entirety or part.[34]

What happens, then, when naked bodies appear within nonnaked orientational publics? While nudists may be recognized as legitimate public subjects, including by theatrical producers, unexpected audience undressing seems to trouble rather than support the undoing of nudist subordination. Anecdotal media stories suggest attendees who distract proceedings by undressing become *spectacularized*, the most frequent instance being the sports field streaker. Undressing or undressed, they become the temporary object of interest, amusement, annoyance, or anger as they reorient what counts as the show.[35] Indeed one might speculate about the outcome at Sadler's Wells if, during the naked clambering of dancers performing *Un Peu de Tendresse Bordel de Merde!* among the audience, members of the audience had started taking off their clothes as well.

Incidents of theater audiences undressing appear quite rare, however. But what kind of equality might be present as a presupposition, expressed norm, or potential if it did happen, particularly if the undressing extended beyond individual acts? Certainly, in the context of current gender practices, the equality fantasy that imagines this as anything other than a rather risky event is hard to come by. Yet in those contemporary contexts where the sexualization of gendered inequalities do not predominate, such as a women's music festival event (e.g., Browne 2009), we can imagine such side-by-side nakedness as expressing an equality framed by sensation—of the body that's adjacent or proximate as limbs (moving and at rest) touch. Yet outside such liminal, other-worldly (other-normative) spaces, naked bodies' presence in contemporary, predominantly clothed spaces—as a way of undoing nudist subordination (and the boundary between *separate* naked and clothed spaces)—seems likely to confront several obstacles or mediators. For the *circulatory* publics (constituted around communication, expression, and influence), exclusions (such as of those children) may operate to limit the infectiousness of naked bodies that appear too appealing, risky, or leaky. But what mediators exist in the case of *orientational* publics?

Certainly we can imagine other means being brought to bear to manage and temper nudity's interjection into the relations between publics and their object, or between public members themselves.[36] While skin could become, in a sense, a different kind of skin,[37] signaling contact's necessary boundaries rather than any merger or blending (also chapter 3), distance — both physical and functional — might also be drawn on to thwart and limit the challenge of proximate naked bodies. So a local authority considering a nudist group's request for regularly scheduled swimming sessions might have in place a series of formalized expectations of how such a group should behave in making and following up their request, to maintain the council's distance and separateness from the nudity in question.

Undoing nudist subordination through nakedness performed in non-naked orientational publics thus confronts a series of tensions to do with contact and connection, distance and alienation. These tensions structure equality's normative principles as nudists oscillate between demanding recognition from providers as a constituency of equal value to denying that the nudist/textile distinction is itself meaningful and worth retaining. In the first, equality is fashioned as a relationship of parity and equivalence between differently marked (client or audience) groups. This is the kind of equality presupposed in nudist claims for public swimming sessions, justified in part because other "minority" groups have them also. But equality can also signal forms of relating in which individuals' different (transient) markings — as dressed or undressed — become bracketed as insignificant. Extended further in its normative scope, it also becomes possible to observe, in the side-by-side relations of touching bodies in public, the potential for an equality oriented toward connection rather than comparison, indistinction rather than separation.

What nudism as a case study begins to identify beyond notions of parity between different groups and beyond the transformation of desire that opens up nudism as a more widely desired as well as available choice is equality's *sensory* potential. As Obrador-Pons (2007: 128) remarks, "Nudism is first and foremost an expressive and affectual practice, a way of accessing the world through the body and a sensual disposition." An equality of indistinctness is not simply equality between people *judged* to be the same; it is an equality attuned to connection, blending, and physical contact — to transformed sensory and tactile relations between people. Conventionally equality has had little to say about touch; this is no doubt unsurprising, given equality's traditional deployment within debates on political representation and the distribution of social resources, respect, dignity, and recognition (see chapter 3). Indeed as a set of conceptual lines, equality's discursive history and continued juridical orientation toward comparison has caused it to assume (even perhaps to produce) divisions between the units of its gaze. Public nudism can certainly be read according to a politics of calculation and comparison given the preferential treatment clearly afforded to the textile world. However, taking seriously the *materiality* of naked bodies touching pushes us to consider what a more haptic version of equality might entail. This is a version of equality that doesn't simply seek to make touch more equal but that approaches touch — as contact, feeling, and a reinflected interior space — as a core dimension of equality also.

Yet the notion of nudism as the harbinger of some more tactile, connective version of equality should not be overstated. Processes of undoing subordination, like inequality itself, get forged compositionally, and the equality that animates and is created may also be one that seeks or depends upon other forms of distance or separation. Nudist clubs, especially in the United States, have historically used compensatory devices extensively as a substitute for clothes, from norms and rules about looking and touching to bans on alcohol use, sex talk, nude dancing, photography, body accentuation (such as with makeup or jewelry), and single or unmarried male membership (see Smith 1980; Weinberg 1965).[38] These devices work to make the side-by-side contact of fellow members safe, respectful, and possible. But in doing so they limit the possibilities for new conceptual lines predicated upon the proximity of physical exposure to others and what this could mean.

APPEARING IN PUBLIC

Clothing is a language of publicity, folding the body in what is felt as the body's own privacy.

—M. WARNER 2002: 23

Underpinning the two public modes discussed so far is a concern with those norms governing public appearance. Certainly being constituted as (or in) public is not restricted to human subjects. Yet whether public appearance concerns spaces, things, or people,[39] it treats the accomplished subject as something (or someone) that cannot be assumed. As a stylized, normative way of being, appearing in public is regularly over- or underperformed. Nevertheless when people enter public space unexpectedly naked (whether in an auditorium, meeting, or some other arena), their accomplishment of being properly public is perceived to have broken down.[40] Unorganized, ad hoc, public nudity is deemed a grave bodily mistake—that the body has become so forgotten or neglected it has failed to be hidden (or tucked away) or, conversely, that an individual's overvaluation has placed it deliberately on show.[41]

Out-of-place nakedness not only breaches social norms; it also foregrounds the power of proprioception (the internal sense of bodily movement and location). The stigma and anxiety attached to unbounded, nonorganized forms of public nudity, that is, to nakedness outside of reality television or well-publicized mass events, such as the world naked bike ride, reveals something of the significance of individual proprioception (sensing where your bits are) to modes of public appearance.[42] But out-of-place nakedness invokes not only the anxiety of misplaced body parts; it also invokes the power of a *social* proprioception, collectively attuned to the movement and location of parts of the body social. This goes beyond *knowing* the right place for particular forms of (clothed and unclothed) activity, to the social capacity to *feel* (and to regulate through feeling).

Proprioception, then, can be understood as the process by which norms relating to proximity, distance, contact, and place are experienced, collectively and individually, as feelings and sensations rather than as obligations or right thought. While the positive sensation from experiencing nudism might encourage its growth, set against it is the power of social proprioception to inhibit a spatially random nakedness. Social proprioception doesn't make nudist equality impossible. Nevertheless it inclines toward an equality of settled allocations, in which naked activity—wherever it occurs—occupies its own *already proper* space.

Linked to the social processes that recognize through feeling where things are and should be is a related process in which individuals and the social body sense or feel "right" and conversely "wrong" time (see also chapter 6). While the force of right time underscores the deviance associated with temporally improper nakedness (e.g., outside church on a weekday morning or in a closed government building at night),[43] it also gives such nakedness power, including the power to denote more than formal equality. In her discussion of whiteness, Sara Ahmed (2006: 131) draws on Merleau-Ponty to suggest that bodies bear their whiteness as a kind of train that extends their motility and reach. To the extent that contemporary nakedness gets associated, positively or negatively, with infancy, sex, or transitional daily self-management (getting out of the bath, undressing, etc.), untimely nakedness bears a train of other (often liminal) times. Inserted into the flow and circulation of the proper, these wrong times inject a phantom replay of other time-spaces.

Proprioception, then, whether it relates to individual bodies, social spaces, or scheduled (or generational) time, identifies social strains, secures existing (as well as new) norms, and gives a troubling weight to improper nakedness. Clearly where nudism feels right can change, including through sustained acts of impropriety. Nevertheless proprioception's orderliness harnesses (and is fortified by) similar tendencies within equality's own normative principles. As a promise or set of claims, equality is usually mobilized when the worth of a constituency, place, or practice has already been identified. Equality claims may be rhetorically and instrumentally deployed against a marginality or subjugation that becomes knowable through the very terms in which it is protested, but equality tends to remain a distant or weak murmur until constituencies, identities, or lifestyles cross a certain threshold of socially recognized (or constituted) value. Nudists and nudism can, and in some places have, crossed this threshold. However, to the extent that undoing nudist subordination depends upon *extending* where and when nakedness appears, it comes up against equality's governmental disdain for the improper (even when a nongovernmental equality is at stake). In this sense, public nakedness precipitates exposure — not only of the body overly undressed and overly present but of equality also — as public nakedness makes all too readily visible the limits in equality's contemporary imagining and scope.

ENVIRONMENTAL TOUCH

I realized that mankind is most in harmony with nature when nude.
— PARMELEE 1929: 18

Although views differ about suitable public nudist spaces, beaches and woodland have tended to be so coded (Daley 2005; Parmelee 1929; Saldanha 2005), as advocates forge nudism's ideological and symbolic associations with nature and celebrate the feeling of sun, wind, and sand on the body. Conceived as a desire for the prelapsarian—a re-tuning to wilderness, purity, and what's natural—nudism is unsurprisingly associated with and located within imaginings of unspoiled or authentic rural idylls (Bell and Holliday 2000; Daley 2005; Peeters 2006). Thus in this context we might imagine nudist equality extending resonances and associations that already exist, perhaps by claiming (or legitimizing) new parts of the countryside for naked bodies. But what is at stake in thinking about equality as an allocation of spaces and options that goes beyond nudism's association with the rural?

When it comes to urban spaces, the presence of naked bodies is, for the most part, intensely regulated and proscribed, including in countries with a more relaxed approach, in general, to social nakedness.[44] Indeed nudism has often had an antagonistic relationship to the modern city. Discussing Australian nudism, Caroline Daley (2005: 155) explains how removing clothes symbolized the removal of the constraints and taint of modern urban living. While nudism's relationship to the urban is a complex and certainly racialized one, I want to suggest that expressed in this sense of incongruity is the unsettling touch deemed to move between body and built space. In contrast to the benign relationship of *resemblance* struck between the rural landscape and the naked body, in urban contexts it is the ostensibly nonresembling contact between body and place that unsettles, evidenced in the often harsh treatment of randomly naked adult bodies in public urban spaces. But beyond the fear of what touch carries is an anxiety simply about touch itself. Despite naturism's claim to build hardier, less physically sensitive bodies (Peeters 2006), naked bodies are seen as vulnerable (see chapter 5). This is not simply fear that, in a densely thronged urban space, without clothing's protective barrier, incidental physical intimacy might occur. It is also a reading of the urban as itself touching (and debilitating through touching).

What kind of equality might naked bodies in urban space suggest? Certainly we might *imagine* naked bodies legalized on present-day city streets, but given the character of urban design and street furniture — of uncomfortable, dirty benches and tarmac roads, of wind tunnels, narrow pavements, and looming high-rises — this is an undoing of the textile/nudist divide arguably at the level of formality alone, since dressed choices would seem to remain far more comfortable and practical. Can urban nudism go any further? Can it express a version of equality that exceeds the "formal status" equality, which permission to go naked might enact?

Thinking *with* public nudity speaks to the presupposition, but also to the claim, that cities are for people in all their diversity, and this means *accommodating* naked living as a *public* practice too. Establishing cities that fit naked bodies begs all sorts of questions about the urban environment, including its textures, materials, and temperature. Enacting nakedness within public urban environments is obviously not enough on its own to cause cities to be rebuilt (though see Dickberry [1904] 2006: 244). However, regular events, such as the annual naked bike ride, offer forms of practice from which new conceptual lines might be drawn. These approach equality not as the fair allocation of nudist/textile spaces but as the basis for *reimagining* what is sought and desired in our urban environments, whether it is greater sensation or greater comfort.[45] Thus public urban nudism has the potential to contribute to wider forms of social dreaming and to visions of better cities (Pinder 2002), for what might suit those who choose to experience urban space naked may also benefit others, such as the young, elderly, and homeless.

Concluding Remarks

While writing on equality politics focuses on explicit, calculated forms of action (and activism), this chapter has focused on the ways equality as a normative concept is actualized within a particular field of practice. Equality isn't something to simply exist or not. Instead it takes shape in the ways past and future are narrated into and folded through the present. Public nudism, particularly unorganized public nudism, can be interpreted in different ways — as signaling mental distress, antisocial behavior, exhibitionism, disruption, and deviance. And read as such, the moments accounted for in this chapter are unlikely to herald the start of anything politically new, simply taking their place within a flow of incidents that might be read as alienated, dysfunctional, ad hoc, random, or simply insignificant. What follows from this is the importance of the interpretive frame brought to moments of public nudism. This is crucial to understanding the meaning such moments can bear and what they can open up.

As a presupposition, as that which animates public nudism, equality of rights and entitlement come to the fore. For public nudism depends on participants, in particular, perceiving themselves as subjects entitled to act, including by removing their clothes (even as who counts as a nudist subject can be restricted through status-based prohibitions such as those imposed on child participants). A sense of entitlement does not only foreground the equality presuppositions public nudism depends upon. It also can be seen as something that public nudism *expresses*, including as a claim of what should be. But notions of the kind of equality that public nudism should be granted vary. As explored in this chapter, public nudism may express a moral right to inclusion within the public sphere, to a share of public resources, to the value of experiencing life undressed, and to the need for spaces, such as cities, to make different ways of living possible — equality rights grounded in the presuppositions of democratic politics, of individual freedom, and of the "natural" body.[46] At the same time, the equality that public nudity expresses cannot be separated from the other norms that saturate and circulate through its practice. These norms include propriety, orderliness, legitimacy, and harm — particularly the harm associated with contamination, and they very clearly structure what nudist equality can mean and entail.

Recognizing the presence and power of other norms is important to understanding what equality as a set of normative principles can express in a given context. However, equality is not limited to the normative principles that it currently bears (or expresses). Reflecting on equality's *potential* within public nudism highlights how a practice can signal other, future possibilities. This does not simply mean that public nudism in the present can create (or gesture to) a form of future social organizing, in which nudism's legitimate material place is other than it currently is, for that would simply be to repeat the promise of equality (or at least its normative claims) that public nudism expresses. Rather approaching equality as *potential* indicates new future forms of imagining as well as actualization. What these will be is, of course, unknown. However, if we approach public nudism as a practice that gives rise to new imaginings, albeit imaginings that require mediation, interpretation, and enabling since they cannot be assumed to take shape, these lines might take up the challenge public nudism proffers of an equality oriented to touch, plurality, and indistinction, disavowing the separation, order, and equivalence that conventional conceptions of equality rely upon.

Exploring potential ways of imagining equality that particular practices can generate is clearly speculative, as Ruth Levitas (2010) helpfully discusses (also Levitas 2013). Its value, however, lies not in its capacity to represent what is or will be, but in extending our imagination of the present, identifying generative aspects of a practice, such as public nudism, routinely discounted by many on the left. But is it right to claim public nudism because of its rich potential as a source of new conceptual lines? Is this a form of appropriation, drawing on nudism to service some other political project? Or does it simply reveal the contingent and un-determined character of change and transformation—that what things may come to be and mean do not belong to any particular constituency?

In chapter 5 I explore the politics of boundary drawing and belong-ing in a different context. My discussion centers on the everyday utopia of a sexual bathhouse for women and transgendered people in Toronto. Building on the themes of touch, equality, pleasure, and sensation, I con-sider what happens when a casual sex space for women meets feminist care ethics.

CHAPTER 5

UNSETTLING FEMINIST CARE ETHICS
THROUGH A WOMEN'S AND TRANS BATHHOUSE

One of the things we talked about, if women are traumatized, should we have a room with a counselor and herbal teas. . . . It's interesting we had the conversation, but we said no—women have to take care of themselves . . . . One of the principles the organizing group articulated was we won't police women [who are] already very policed.

Bathhouse committee member

Feminist care ethics (FCE) has had a remarkable life since Carol Gilligan's (1982) work on "a different voice." Refusing "to relegate care to a realm 'outside morality'" (Held 2006: 10), FCE promised an alternative normative framework to the androcentric approach that dominated moral reasoning, epistemology, and psychology, with its valorization of rationality, autonomy, abstraction, impartiality, and the public realm. Feminist perceptions that these values were not uncontestable or neutral and that they privileged masculine life experiences generated a series of care-based counternorms that, it was claimed, emerged from and, importantly, would validate women's lives. These counternorms converged around ideas of context, feeling, intimacy, and, importantly, (inter)dependency.

Since the late 1980s FCE has developed in diverse ways, as scholars brought care ethics into an ever-expanding set of fields. By 2010 these included international relations (e.g., Robinson 1999), feminist jurisprudence (Drakopoulou 2000), the environment (e.g., King 1991), child caregivers (e.g., Cockburn 2005), and animals (e.g., Donovan and Adams 2007), alongside more established domains of parenting or mothering (e.g., Held 2006; Ruddick 1989), nursing (e.g., Barnes and Brannelly 2008; Cloyes 2002), public welfare provision (e.g., Sevenhuijsen 2003), dependency work (e.g., Kittay 1999), and support for people with disabilities (e.g., Hughes et al. 2005). Feminist care ethics has not been without its critics (e.g., Beasley and Bacchi 2005; Cockburn 2005); however, the cluster of feminist texts that trouble FCE's claims and assumptions are largely drowned out by the torrent of work deploying its terms.

This chapter contributes to debates on feminist care ethics by reflecting on its terms and premises from an unlikely caring site: a casual sex space for women and transgendered people. By exploring the assemblage of elements that come together as ethical care from the standpoint of the bathhouse as well as from feminist care ethics, I want to take forward the utopian approach to concepts developed so far. Specifically this chapter builds on three themes: the importance of actualization within the minor stream spaces of everyday utopias to imagining concepts differently; the limits of idealist conceptualizing, in the sense of creating perfect normative concepts as well as developing concepts purely through thought; and the way conceptual lines can be forged through sensation and feeling rather than just through what is said.

Imagining care in relation to mainstream caring practices, feminist care ethics articulates a set of normative principles that include attentiveness, responsibility, competence, and responsiveness (Tronto 1993: 127–36). Developing these principles in ways that put pressure on professional care policy and practice is valuable; so too are the explorations of what care ethics might entail in fields, such as international relations, largely governed by other norms. However, the rapid growth in feminist care ethics has caused it to solidify into a framework of judgment that parses everyday social caring according to its terms. In the light of this hardening, what contribution can the everyday utopia of a casual sex space make to thinking about the relationship between ethics and care, questioning and resettling the way ethics and care are articulated? To the extent a casual sex venue manifests both care and ethics, does it open up other conceptual lines and other forms of imagining? Approaching the Toronto bathhouse in this way emphasizes its value as a space of conceptual creativity. As such, it is more than a passive terrain spread open for analysis; instead it is an active participant in a two-way deliberative encounter. Mieke Bal (2002: 24) makes a similar point: "Concepts can only do [their methodological] work . . . on one condition: that they are kept under scrutiny through a confrontation with, not application to, the cultural objects being examined."

Adopting a contextual approach to care and ethics, I explore feminist and sexuality politics as they extend beyond the terrain of inequality, resituating both sexuality and gender in relation to pleasure rather than (or at least as well as) pain. While feminist concerns with oppression and discrimination circulate through my discussion of the politics of this particular bathhouse, focusing on care and ethics also places vertical social relations (that is, relations of asymmetry) in a different light. Both care and ethics are engagements whose value lies in the differentiated and in a sense *unequal* character of the encounter. The difference is that here, compared to other kinds of unequal encounter, inequality functions as a way of advancing equality (by empowering the subordinated party) rather than sabotaging it. Feminist care ethics also unsettles equality's presuppositions of separation and division. While FCE has generated considerable debate over the question of immersion and loss of oneself in the other, and while equality has the *potential* to center touch and connection (as chapter 4 explores), care ethics' orientation toward bonding and binding contrasts with equality's inclination to locate equivalence in separation. (Things can be equal because of or through their difference.) The relationship between an ethics of care and a politics of equality (sometimes read as justice) has received considerable attention within feminist care ethics (e.g., see Clement 1996; Cockburn 2005: Sevenhuijsen 1998), and I will not retread these debates here. Rather, centering a space oriented to pleasure in dialogue with an academic framework oriented to caring, I want to explore what's at stake in how we think about and *recognize* care and ethics, both as these terms come together in the fused framework FCE advocates and when they are otherwise articulated.

A Women's and Trans Bathhouse

Much has been written about men's bathhouses, particularly by sociologists studying their practices, norms, and geographies in order to understand how sexual forms of conduct in a site oriented to brief and anonymous voluntary encounters can become familiar and even routine (e.g., Berubé 1996; Binson and Woods 2003; Tattelman 1999, 2000; Tewksbury 2002). Far less, however, has been said about women's casual sex venues. In a sense this is hardly surprising since few such spaces for women exist. But as a consequence it is equally unsurprising that a thriving women-initiated bathhouse, active for more than twelve years, would precipitate academic interest and a clutch of scholarship. Work has examined the site's promotion of women's sexual agency and erotic culture (Hammers 2008a, 2008b, 2009a, 2009b; Nash and Bain 2007), its governance ethos and distinctiveness (Cooper 2009), trans participation (Nash 2011), the methodological challenges involved in conducting field research (Bain and Nash 2006), and the police raid in 2000 and subsequent court hearing (Bain and Nash 2007; Gallant and Gillis 2001; Lamble 2009). This chapter benefits significantly from such earlier work. However, since my aim is to consider the bathhouse in relationship to ethical care, my primary material instead comes from interviews with approximately thirty organizers, volunteers, and other bathhouse attendees over a period of about five years.[1]

The Toronto Women's and Trans Bathhouse (TWTB), initially known as Pussy Palace, opened in the fall of 1998 as an occasional event to be held at a local men's bathhouse in Toronto, a city with a long history of bathhouse activity and a gay community with considerable experience in defending men's bathhouses from the state.[2] Initiated by women who were active in the city's polyamorous adult sex education and sexual health networks, TWTB aimed to promote a healthy, positive attitude to sex among queer women and, subsequently, among those who identified as transgendered. Organizers sought to celebrate the range and diversity of sexualities; invest nonstraight female culture with a more overtly raunchy, "in your face" eroticism; and signal women's sexual agency to wider society.

The Toronto bathhouse intrigued me from my first encounter, walking along a neighborhood street in North London with one of its founders in the late 1990s and hearing her ambitious, fully committed description of what the space was intended to be and to do. I was struck by her pedagogical ambition and by the idea that women (the focus of early bathhouses) would learn new sexual skills from volunteers offering lap dances and G-spot orgasms. The Toronto bathhouse didn't just *dream* about developing women's sexual desires. In ways that echo the utopian writer Abensour's (1973) account of extending desire—to desire more and desire better—TWTB sought to create a place where participants would acquire new sexual wants, learn new techniques, and develop new ways of being sexual subjects.

The Toronto bathhouse was also an everyday utopia in another respect (see chapter 1). As a queer feminist space, it committed to modes of governance that were democratic, participative, and open. At the same time, aspirational norms of governance confronted the legal and social realities of running an innovative sexual space, one that encountered state attention and monitoring in several guises, including most sharply in the form of a police raid two years in. Out of the mix of concerns and pressures, organizers introduced a series of measures to ensure bathhouse nights ran smoothly, safely, and securely—from rules about where sex could happen to rules about alcohol, BDSM (bondage, domination and sadomasochism), and "oppressive behavior" (Cooper 2009). But perhaps the governance provisions that best exemplified the quotidian character of the bathhouse as an everyday utopia were the techniques deployed to get participants to be sexually proactive, to understand the etiquette of how to behave in a bathhouse, and the challenges volunteer sex providers faced in managing time, demand, and their own pleasures. As one volunteer told me, "When you're volunteering, you need to make dates for *after* your shift ends, because you've a line up outside your door, and you're there to serve a population."

In exploring the bathhouse as an everyday utopia, as with the other sites, it is also important to recognize how the space evolved. The Toronto bathhouse changed in many respects between 1998 and 2011. As one organizer commented, "The first bathhouse, we had no clue how many people would come—we thought there might be twenty and there were four hundred. . . . There was such euphoria, women sitting out in the rain for hours [waiting to get in]. . . . From 1998 until 2000, it calmed a bit. We put more systems in place, how we organized volunteers, we put a lot down on paper, bathhouse etiquette, anti-oppression stuff. . . . After the raid [in 2000] people attending got scared and cautious." Many things changed after the 2000 raid. Alcohol was withdrawn to avoid the surveillance and regulatory vulnerability that came with holding a liquor license (the ostensible cause of the police raid), and rules prohibiting sex in publicly visible or "risky" areas were described by some interviewees as more firmly enforced (although others disagreed). Other changes were prompted by non-raid factors. One was the challenge of dealing with institutionalized inequalities within the context of a casual sex bathhouse. Developing policies, procedures, and rules to counter overt bias seems to have been in large part driven by incidents and frustrations that put pressure on the organizing committee to respond as discussed below. Other developments were less reactive as organizers sought to *stimulate* sexual encounters for those attending and as new volunteers tried out new ideas, using the range of structured opportunities which the design of a male bathhouse made possible. Alongside a changing menu of "special interest" rooms, other kinds of bathhouses also started to be organized after the initial flurry. These included service-free bathhouse "lites" and the Sugar Shack for women and trans people of color.[3]

Bathhouse Care

While the ethical care of FCE is relatively narrow in scope, when I asked bathhouse interviewees whether care happened, examples were plentiful. Participants drew on conceptual lines imported from other contexts in order to recognize, and in some cases re-recognize, a wide sweep of actions and encounters, especially between people unknown to one another. One participant said, "Well, I think it was definitely very caring. . . . Organizers definitely put a lot of thought to making us comfortable with each other and enjoying ourselves . . . providing supplies for us to use, lubes, you know, condoms for our dildos and things like that. . . . There was a lot of thought put into that. . . . There were numbers so we could leave messages for women . . . and even workshops [in advance of the event] on how to meet people in the bathhouse." Alongside references to the care organizers showed, participants described individual acts of kindness and consideration among those attending. They commented on the range of services provided by volunteers and on the importance of taking care of oneself.

In the light of my earlier work on the Toronto bathhouse (Cooper 2007, 2009), I want to focus here on three particular care constellations: vertical care providing, horizontal stranger care, and the problem of too much and too little care. The first I take from the perspective of volunteer service providers, the second from the perspective of sex between attendees unknown to each other, and the third in relation to the organizing committee's response to charges of racism.

Between 2005 and 2010 I spoke to a range of volunteers performing roles from security duty and cleanup to organizing and working the butt room, G-spot room, and breast play space. In talking about care, these unpaid erotic service providers emphasized the importance of their role and the responsibilities that flowed from it, specifically that they were engaging in erotic play in order to provide a service, not to satisfy their own desires. One volunteer explained, "While I really enjoy doing it, it's definitely a bit of a role. So, it's not being aroused with somebody. The intimacy at the end where [the client] wants to hug and kiss me; it's not me, it's a persona. . . . It feels a little inappropriate. . . . You haven't really had sex with *me*."

As service providers, volunteers were required to be impartial, servicing all who presented themselves, unless there was a good reason to say no. Bathhouse attendees, in general, could not demand that others attending should desire or have sex with them, but they could expect "public" service providers to treat them equally. This distinction became particularly explicit in relation to nonsurgical trans women participants. Organizers worried that despite the institutionalized injunction that discrimination and intolerance were unacceptable, trans women (with penises) might find it hard to attract a sexual partner. Volunteers, however, could not turn them down. An organizer explained, "We spent a lot of time talking about [volunteers'] comfort levels . . . and at the same time, making sure they really understood their role. . . . This wasn't at all a place where they could offer different services depending on their attraction levels. While at the same time being very clear about the importance of them trusting their guts and being able to say no to certain things . . . to help women and men doing the volunteering to think about what their boundaries might be ahead of time. . . . So if a trans man came up and you wouldn't lap-dance for him, don't do lap-dances." In other contexts, however, volunteers were allowed considerable discretion to set their own parameters in managing sometimes awkward scenarios. For example, a volunteer told me, "I had one customer . . . and [she] came in, got up on the bed, bent over, and she was quite dirty. And that was one moment in which I was, like, what do I do? Do I tell her to go clean up and come back, but fortunately, at that time I'd been supplied with these wipes . . . and so I just put on some gloves, and just said something like, "hmmm, you know I'm going to have to give you a wipe." . . . And it was not pleasant . . . but in the moment that was my choice: do I just take care of it . . . or send them off?"

While volunteers stressed a caring that was vertical and client-oriented, participants described a more horizontal, reciprocating kind of stranger care, even as the idea of strangers in a casual sex space used mainly by women was an equivocal one. One woman described it as like "dozens and dozens of circles of friends." Another remarked, "Our community is so small, so there's no such thing as real strangers, but . . . it's definitely like, you know, somebody that's not in your immediate circle. . . . It could be . . . somebody you've seen passing around the community a few times and haven't got a chance to talk to because you don't run in the same circles."

While some came to have sex with lovers or friends, having sex with people not already known was highly vaunted. Elsewhere I have discussed the stress participants placed on self-care on these occasions (Cooper 2007). Many I spoke with said that their sexual parameters would vary depending on how well they knew someone or whether someone else could vouch for the person. Thus they might choose not to venture into a private room, avoid transmission of body fluids, and ensure they were not in a position of vulnerability or restraint, such as being tied up. A participant described the situation this way: "You are in a room full of strangers so I think you have to have your wits about you. . . . You've got to play safe and not get yourself in a situation with people you don't know and give them trust when they really haven't done anything to earn it. . . . It's an environment where there are a lot of people having sex and there are body fluids going around and you don't know everybody. . . . So, it's just being smart and putting down a towel before you sit . . . and [if] you are having anonymous sex . . . you know, use gloves, use things."[4] However, the care mobilized in relation to strangers was not just a self-care enacted by participants determined to protect themselves from harm. Participants also, importantly, described the ways sex with unknown others *created feelings* of caring, in part through shared experiences of intimacy.

A wall gets dissolved when engaging with someone in that way. . . . [You] are no longer a stranger—when I see them again, even if we don't talk—it never feels like a stranger. (Participant interview)

If someone comes because of what you're doing to them, it's very intimate . . . how to get me off, know the sounds I make . . . things not normally disclosed so casually. (Participant interview)

In ways that resonate with the other main stranger space of this book, Speakers' Corner, several participants commented that sex with an unknown person was exciting because you didn't know where such an erotic encounter might lead. Foucault (1988: 328) characterizes such excitement or attentiveness as care—a curiosity about what might exist. One participant told me, "It's still exciting but still more exciting for those who've never been before; who knows what will happen if you get an erotic massage or pick someone up."

Yet openness to the unknown, and its risks, lay somewhat in tension with a key bathhouse norm: that sexual encounters should follow the lines of what had already been verbally agreed upon. Interviewees described the importance of taking care and of ensuring that all participants—in what one interviewee described as a "contractual negotiation"—got what they sought, even as they recognized not everything could (or should) be pinned down: "Everything needs to be consensual; we flirt, talk about what we want, say limitations and then figure things out. Sex might follow what's agreed, but you still don't know the other woman so it's exciting."

Participants also spoke at some length about the less contractually negotiated issue of postsex care between sexual partners unknown to each other. Such care ranged from how to end a sexual encounter on the night and whether to exchange names and contact details (something attendees said became easier to negotiate and avoid through growing familiarity and ease with bathhouse sex)[5] to how to behave in subsequent chance encounters or sightings of a sex buddy: "I know that sometimes I've got the name of someone and it's not their real name, it's their play name. . . . But to me I prefer that because, well, now I know where you stand. I know you're probably not out. I know you obviously have a persona when you're in here so if you saw me in the street you probably wouldn't want me running up to you in front of everyone going, 'Hey, remember the other night? That was fun.' You know, things like that. It really lets you set the stage and lets you know what the boundaries are basically."

In building a bathhouse community, sexual exchange was not the only thing at stake. Also vital, since the community in question was feminist and queer, was a demonstrated commitment to an anti-oppression politics. The Toronto bathhouse expressed this commitment verbally, in its texts, in ventures attempted, and in various other ways. A foremost commitment here was the evolving emphasis on trans inclusivity. Anti-trans behavior was explicitly prohibited in the bathhouse's rules, and trans participation was flagged in the bathhouse's changing name and identity as the organizers sought to provide a relevant welcoming place for people with diverse gender identities. The Toronto bathhouse also recognized the challenge many disabled people faced in participating. Organizers commented that the lack of available venues for hosting the bathhouse, since many men's bathhouses seemed unwilling to accommodate an occasional female event, meant the primary space they could use—a multistory, old house—was not good for people with mobility difficulties. Bathhouse organizers tried to compensate with volunteer helpers, portable toilets, and ramps; they also tried to reduce the costs facing people with other disabilities, offering free entry for attendants and signers for deaf participants. Many I spoke with praised TWTB for its open, plural "beautiful *bodies*" norms (a point addressed also by Hammers 2008a). One participant commented, "At the bathhouse, there was like, 'look at my chub, who cares'? And it was lovely. . . . There was a real celebration of the female body and shape and size—sort of anything goes." However, while bodies may have varied, interviews suggest that participation by people with disabilities remained limited.

The ability of organizational care to secure a diverse, egalitarian, democratic bathhouse was also challenged from a different direction. Early in TWTB's life, concerns were expressed that women and trans people of color were not fully welcomed and involved. While many interviews, particularly with white participants, conveyed the emotional charge of racism's allegation rather more than the details of specific events, a series of incidents appears to have sparked a conflagration that burned at different levels of heat, particularly among organizing committee members, for some years. Incidents described to me included a carding episode, where some women of color were turned away for lack of identification, while white women without identification were simultaneously let in; incidents of rudeness or abruptness by white participants to people of color at bathhouse events; and early publicity with images of white women only.

As I talked with bathhouse volunteers and organizers about racism, accounts and perspectives varied; however, the question of what constituted racism seemed a central area of contestation. One woman commented that while no one would deny that racism was a structural element of the bathhouse, there was more disagreement about what could be attributed to racism and what could not. Sarita Srivastava (2005) identifies similar tensions over naming racism in her research in other Toronto feminist and women's organizations. She argues that in many organizations, white women saw the charge of racism as challenging their identity as feminists, and as participants engaged in alternative politics: "The effort to maintain an ethical, innocent, and nonracist face often produces an emotional resistance to antiracism" (40–41). At TWTB the social, cultural, and psychological difficulties involved in recognizing incidents as racist was something on which several interviewees commented.

While interviewees disagreed on how to characterize incidents and on what to do—could a feminist bathhouse, for instance, ever tackle racism adequately?—they converged in their accounts of the remedial measures taken. These included increasing representation of women of color on the organizing committee and in publicity; bringing in a facilitator to try to resolve some of the organizational tensions racism's charge had generated; ensuring those attending were clear that racism and other forms of discrimination would not be tolerated by giving brief talks and disseminating rule sheets to participants as they arrived; and holding bathhouse events specifically for women and transgendered people of color.

Writing about the struggles over racism within the Toronto bathhouse is complicated by many factors, including the not surprising reluctance of many of those most deeply involved to discuss events with a white, academic outsider. Yet in thinking about care, what stands out in relation to the charges of oppression, and the many measures introduced in response, is the question of what care can (and cannot) do. In her discussion of feminist care ethics, Kristin Cloyes (2002: 10) argues, "Care is seen as an antidote to . . . [domination and oppression], and the conclusion is drawn that if only the world were more caring . . . then there would be less power used in the world, or it would be used more justly, more equitably." Cloyes's discussion of remedial care is salient here. The Toronto bathhouse stands out from the other sites I discuss for the intensity of its expressed concern to do something about racism and in the measures taken. And caring—as a practice, orientation, affect, and hailing of the self—was clearly evident. Certainly racism wasn't the only process to generate care. There was care shown in relation to the inclusion of trans men and women and the inclusion of people with disabilities; bathhouse attendees were careful about other people's feelings and, to varying degrees, about their own and other participants' sexual health. But while emotional and physical safety *may* indicate care's more straightforward application, the risk in seeing care as *the* way of dealing with inequality, which racism's charge exposed, lies in the negative cycle that failure can generate. Some care may be helpful: being attentive to who gets noticed and who gets ignored, to who is welcomed and assisted to have a good time. But the risk, as interviewees in different ways identified, is that expecting solicitous behavior, feelings of investment, and attentiveness to others to undo inequalities such as racism may eventually turn care—when it fails to do what it is supposed to do—inward. So caring as a practice or relationship with another can segue into a surfeit of care*fulness* oriented to protecting the self, now understood—at least by the self—as vulnerable, from (further) perceived attacks.

"Caring for equality" raises profound questions for feminist care ethics. While some critics of the turn to ethical care focus on the problem of FCE's asymmetry, with its risk of diminishing the one cared for, particularly when this gets mapped onto wider systemic inequalities, other challenging questions also arise. These include the temporal direction care takes—backward to meet existing needs or forward to what might be created; the question of what need is when it comes to inequality; the power of interpersonal interactions to enact, exacerbate, or undo systemic processes; and the power of particular sites to make good the injuries generated by wider webs or formations. More generally, using care to tackle oppression foregrounds the troubling relationship between the caring dyad (or network) and the social environment in which it is enmeshed. This relationship sits at the center of the discussion that follows.

Recognizing an Ethic of Care

Caring by service providers, between fellow participants, and in relation to structural inequalities are some key ways bathhouse participants identified the care taking place. But to what extent do such practices constitute care from the perspective of feminist care ethics? Do the lines FCE draws between imagining and actualization converge with those of bathhouse participants? And if they do not, does this matter? Or can we find in this divergence some fruitful challenges for how we imagine ethical care?

CARE RELATIONS AND CONDITIONS OF VULNERABILITY

For Berenice Fisher and Joan Tronto (1990: 40), caring, at its broadest, is everything "that we do to maintain, continue and repair our 'world' so that we can live in it as well as possible." However, for the most part, FCE has been interpreted more narrowly, including in subsequent work by Tronto. Accounts of care tend to be organized around two axes: care's registers, which include caring about, caring for, taking care of, caring, and care; and the elements that combine to produce these registers, namely attentiveness, responsiveness, responsibility, competence, respect, and needs (Engster 2007; Sevenhuijsen 1998; Tronto 1993). Variation in how care is conceptualized interconnects variation in FCE's mission. In a sense, the aim of early work, such as Gilligan's, was to revalue context-specific, relationship-based moral reasoning. However, for the most part, FCE has moved away from simply revaluing "different voices" or ways of living to designating and advocating *particular* values and principles. Virginia Held (2006: 10), for instance, writes, "The ethics of care stresses the moral force of the responsibility to respond to the needs of the dependent."

Care is fundamentally grounded in the premise that we all have needs and thus need care, to varying degrees at different times, to survive but also to flourish (Sevenhuijsen 2003: 183; Tronto 1993). According to Daniel Engster (2007), the general moral principle to care derives from our desire to be cared for. Since we believe others should care for us (when we need it) and since we know we may rely on their care, we must see care as a good (40–51). He writes, "We all have made use of the general moral principle that capable individuals ought to care for individuals in need" (49). Grounding an obligation to care in our own valued or accepted dependency means certain groups can't be morally excluded from care simply because they lack the power to reciprocate.

At the same time, Engster, like other feminist care ethicists, supports a differentiated approach to care responsibilities. Drawing on Robert Goodin's (1985) model of "assigned responsibility," Engster (2007: 55–58) advocates a framework of care obligations based on concentric rings. Here individuals' primary responsibilities are for themselves, then for those intimately known, after that for those with whom there are looser relationships, or circumstantial dependency, and finally for "distant strangers." Engster writes, "Caring is best practiced in particular relationships where caregivers can be attentive, responsive, and respectful to those needing care" (55). A concentric rings model of care obligations, however, has not received unequivocal support among feminist writers on care or among those drawing on feminist care ethics. Unsurprisingly several writers have been disturbed by the notion of care obligations decreasing as social, emotional, and geographical distance grows, and there is a growing body of critical work on care across uneven geographies (Raghuram et al. 2009; Silk 2004). However, as Engster's approach represents the mainstream within FCE, I want to stay with this tranche of work to think about the ways the Toronto bathhouse refracts—in the sense of splitting and illuminating—different aspects of these care obligations.

Feminist care ethics draws on different relational paradigms of caring, including friendship and sisterhood. However, for many, underlying a relational approach to care is an idealized, deliberately utopian model of motherhood or parenting. According to Virginia Held (2006: 26), "The ethics of care . . . takes the experience of women in caring activities such as mothering as central." If we associate care with relationships, particularly those organized around warmth, affection, and intimacy, bathhouses might appear to be a kind of anticare, deliberately established so sex can happen outside of (and unrestrained by) the other-centered focus of long-term, dutiful, obligation-generating coupledom. Weinberg and Williams (1979: 165), for instance, discuss the men's bathhouse as a pure case of impersonal sex, in which partners are fungible and interaction moves easily from one person to the next as participants pursue purely sexual objectives. But not all work on casual men's sexual spaces characterizes them so exclusively as self-oriented market exchanges (see also chapter 8). Tattelman (1999: 90) comments on the presence of *re-*

lationship: "The surprise is the willingness one finds, a willingness to be touched, to be connected, to be put into a position one would not normally be in."

Connections like these surfaced in many of my interviews. Particularly for those most involved in developing TWTB, the care shown appeared deeply tied to commitments to both sexual freedom and community. Indeed there are interesting resonances here with professional care scenarios where the primary, enduring commitment and loyalty is to an occupational community or set of intangible norms and values rather than to the specific one cared for. A similar resonance was apparent also in the shared reliance between professional caregivers and bathhouse service providers (as well as some bathhouse participants) on time-demarcated commitments. The temporal boundaries placed on bathhouse encounters were described, with perhaps brutal honesty, by one participant, who remarked. "For me, I'd say that . . . [empathy] would extend only so far as, you know, we're doing something together and when that ends, that's it—don't expect anything from me after that. I wouldn't treat it as [if] we're friends after or anything like that."

The Toronto bathhouse also converges with FCE more generally in its shared concern with vulnerability. Feminist care ethics has taken forward Robert Goodin's (1985) claims that we have a moral duty to protect individuals who are vulnerable to our actions and, importantly, to our omissions to step in and act—duties that extend beyond the particular time and place of professional responsibility. At the bathhouse vulnerability may not have had the same standing as a *moral* justification, but it proved a commonly deployed discursive rationalization for acts of kindness and compassion. As one participant said, "People are a lot more conscious [at the bathhouse] that everybody is feeling pretty vulnerable and I think they tend to be a lot more conscious of that and . . . more kind, I think, than they would in a club environment. . . . Once you get everybody stripped off and in a towel, you know, everyone is a lot more caring to each other." Participants recognized their own (and others') vulnerability in the risk of rejection, of being undesired, and in the possibility that interactions would prove unsatisfying, awkward, and even harmful. Yet while bathhouse vulnerability, as manifested and imagined by participants, resonates with FCE's concern for those whose ability to manage is fragile, in significant ways the two also diverged.

First, in contrast to FCE's emphasis on the asymmetrical character of vulnerability, at the bathhouse vulnerability was seen as widespread and shared, even as "newbies" (bathhouse first-timers) were deemed particularly susceptible. Second, vulnerability was seen as *acquired*. At the bathhouse people *became* vulnerable to infection, embarrassment, or outing by *deciding* to participate. While organizers especially went out of their way to help people feel safe and secure, by, among other things, providing safe-sex kits and guidance such as that what happened at the bathhouse should stay there, vulnerability was nevertheless seen as arising from choices consciously made.

Organizers' encouragement to participants to seek out a kind of vertigo — as vulnerability was largely understood (also chapter 8) — suggests a major distinction between the bathhouse and FCE. In care ethics, vulnerability comes largely from *existing* relationships. Feminist care ethics is positive about the relationships even as it sees the vulnerability that relationships produce as a problem; it isn't good to feel exposed, disoriented, or fragile. A sexual environment, however, inverts these norms, and in doing so suggests a more ambivalent, or multivalent, conception of vulnerability or exposure. Interviewees described the disorientation, unsettlement, and nervousness that comes from "playing on the edge" as integral to the site's success as an exciting educative space (Newmahr 2011; also chapter 8). One organizer commented, "The bathhouse is boring if you don't take a risk, if the situation isn't new. . . . You could just be in a social area, which feels a lot like a dyke bar."

Revaluing risk may be one reason why care theorists have sought to keep sex outside of care ethics. If domination, pain, control, lack of control, and uncertainty are sexy (albeit if only for some), then bathhouse care may validate interactions (if not relationships) that FCE would strongly eschew. Cloyes (2002: 210) makes a related point; she argues that care ethics seeks to "fix" and domesticate power, "what is thought of as the harsh masculinism of sheer politics and the starkness of power, where power is always conceived in negative terms: power is bad, and care is good. This approach fails to illuminate the ways in which care tacitly enacts power on multiple levels." At the bathhouse interpersonal power is managed, as in other edgy sexual events, through a care that is focused on consensuality. Willingness to experiment with one's own limits is encouraged, safeguarded only by the requirement for agreement-reaching conversation and the inalienable right to say no. Thus sexual vulnerability is treated very differently from other forms of bathhouse vulnerability, such as discrimination or prejudice, where the bathhouse's retrospective approach, oriented to remedying or protecting existing vulnerability, resembles care ethics far more closely.

COUNTING AS NEEDS

Just as the bathhouse sought to create and sustain a space of erotic vulnerability, it also sought to sustain and to some extent *create* needs; indeed vulnerability can be read as such a need, in the sense of an imperative required for bathhouse encounters to be successful. In thinking about needs and the obligations placed on others to meet them, I want to briefly consider two questions that arise from the way the bathhouse coincides with but also challenges feminist care ethics. First, whose needs count? In particular, do self-needs count? Second, what counts as a need? Specifically should sex count? These questions are central to thinking about TWTB as an ethical space.

For the most part, feminist care ethics has developed in ways that center the largely naturalized needs of the cared for. Held (2006: 10) writes, "The central focus of the ethics of care is on the compelling moral salience of attending to and meeting the needs of the particular others for whom we take responsibility." Within FCE caregivers' needs are recognized, particularly those needs that arise out of or need to be met in order to sustain caregiving. However, with its focus on relational understandings of what makes human life viable and livable, care ethics pays little attention to one's own needs-meeting. This doesn't mean that action to meet such needs is morally wrong. For many care ethicists, self-care is primary, and an entitlement to receive care from others comes only when one's own needs exceed one's ability to meet them. However, in contrast to FCE's rich elaboration of what caring for another entails, the limited attention paid to self-care, and the equivocation on whether and when such care is ethical, is striking.

What does this mean for the bathhouse? Does its orientation toward self-care on the part of participants place it outside the scope of how FCE imagines ethical care? At TWTB self-care took several forms. In some instances, such as organizers' support for volunteer bathhouse sex workers, the care that was shown resembled FCE's focus on nourishing and aiding caregivers so they could provide good, sustainable care. In other cases, as when participants halted sexual encounters for reasons of their own health or safety, the interests of self and other appeared, at least superficially, to diverge, making it harder for a care ethics formally oriented to the vulnerable *other* to provide an adequate moral structure. Yet whether care ethics should include self-care, and how it might go about doing so, begs a prior question: What purpose does care ethics serve? Is its aim to influence public policy, promote relational understandings of people's interconnected lives, legitimate an already existing "different voice," or figure out how people (and other bodies, including states) should behave? Arguably feminist care ethics encompasses all of these strands, causing self-care to be in turn ignored, downgraded, presumed, and partially included. But in thinking about whose needs count, we also need to consider a related issue: *What* needs count?[6] Specifically, can and should care ethics embrace sex, whether this means providing nonsexual care to support sex-based "needs,"[7] providing sexual care to meet other needs (such as for self-esteem), or meeting nonsexual needs nonsexually in a venue dedicated to sexual adventure?

With its orientation to the sighs of suffering rather than of pleasure, for the most part FCE ignores sex. Tronto (1993: 104), however, writes explicitly that the pursuit of pleasure, play, and desire does not generally constitute care. For Engster (2007: 26) too, sexual activity "falls outside the scope of caring on the grounds that it is not essential to survival and functioning." Given Engster's focus on core, universal, obligation-generating wants — wants that are serious and impose enforceable duties upon others, including governments — it is hardly surprising that sex is excluded. But is there a good reason to read the need underpinning care ethics so narrowly? A narrow reading might be advisable if particular nonconditional obligations on others, and especially governmental others, are intended to follow, but if definitions of need carry less policy weight, or if what follows from being designated a need is not already determined, are there still good reasons to exclude the erotic?

When I started talking to bathhouse participants, I expected to hear many women describe sex as a need. However, for the most part this didn't happen. Indeed I was struck by the ambivalence women demonstrated in talking about their need for a bathhouse. For example, one participant said, "As a one-off event, it plants the seed for the idea that women's sex does extend further than what our perceptions of it have been to date, but because it's a one-off event it doesn't carry through, . . . whereas with the men's bathhouse, you know, it's open twenty-four hours seven days a week, where men can go if they want to have sex. . . .

It's there and expected, right? *It's that idea that men have that need and it's an immediate thing that needs to be filled, whereas you don't get that with women.*"[8] Here I encountered something of a paradox. On the one hand, participants described a variety of vulnerabilities and bathhouse needs and the caring work carried out to meet them. On the other hand, sex — the bathhouse's primary focus — was largely not described as a need. Does this suggest we should read care, and its relationship to needs, differently? Rather than identifying care as a way of meeting needs that are already in existence — needs with a tendency in the context of sex to be stabilized around (and in turn to stabilize) categories of sexual orientation and gender — does the bathhouse suggest a value in attaching care to *potential* needs (see chapter 4)? Can we think of care as forging or responding to what *might* emerge, to needs being built, including by being met? One organizer suggested something of this formative process when she commented, "We've a *need* to celebrate our community."

At the bathhouse games, rules, services, and individual acts of kindness were performed to help women and trans people develop more sexually confident subjectivities and more sexually expansive, proactive repertoires. Certainly some feminists would question the direction of such empowerment, with its celebration of fucking, erotic display, power games, and phallic simulations. It is too simple to celebrate new capacities, wants, and needs simply because they become asserted. But for reasons explored in chapter 1, I don't want to go down the path of politically and critically evaluating the sex project that the Toronto bathhouse advanced. Instead I want to use FCE as a provocation to think differently about bathhouse ethics, focusing on ethics (like needs) as something created. Yet while creating needs suggests the establishment of something imperative and urgent, of something that must be met, ethics by contrast focuses on the creation of dilemmatic responsibilities — ways of reflecting, feeling, and deciding that emerge and are shaped by the social practices within which they arise.

From Care Ethics to Bathhouse Ethics

Feminist care ethics and care at the Toronto bathhouse both foreground key elements associated with ethical care: connection, vulnerability, need, and self. Yet while bathhouse participants positively identified normative forms of care as present in many aspects of bathhouse life, many of these forms of care exceeded FCE's ethical care framework. As a normative framework, oriented to how individuals, communities, policy actors, and governments *should* behave in responding to those with less power and greater need—those detrimentally affected by others' actions—FCE has little time for a venue organized around sex, stranger interactions, voluntarily assumed vulnerability, self-pleasure, and the creation of new needs. Of course, it is possible to extend how we imagine care ethics so that more bathhouse activities and norms come within its scope, but this is not my goal. Rather I want to use the situated instance of the bathhouse to suggest another way that care and ethics can combine, a way that offers more promise for thinking about the ethical lines generated through everyday utopias.

One of the main limitations of feminist care ethics, despite repeated claims by advocates to the contrary, is its inadequate situatedness.[9] This contextual inadequacy is evident in two main ways. First, it can be seen in care ethics' sanitization of body work. Feminist care ethics repeatedly refers to the situated body and to situated embodied care, but there is a notable absence of *real* descriptions of embodied encounters—with their odors, textures, and discharges—and the dilemmas that uncontained bodies can pose for ethical care in the contemporary era, as illustrated in my example of a bathhouse volunteer confronting a dirty bottom. This was not the only such instance to emerge during interviews. Although sensory distaste didn't dominate people's accounts, several participants commented on the ethical and practical dilemmas of bad breath, genital infection, loud noises, semen odor, chlorine smells, dirt in the whirlpool, and unappealing surfaces on which to sit. Emissions, dirt, and smells are central to much care provision and a key factor in caregivers' low status. Yet despite the strong and persistent claim within feminist care ethics that care work should be revalued, scholars implicitly confirm care work's stigmatization in their own apparent unwillingness to "lower" their scholarship to the bodily functions care both responds to and produces.

This lack of odor and grit reveals a second problem, which surfaces as a result of FCE's inadequate material anchorage. This problem is certainly far less evident in more applied care ethics accounts. However, for moral and normative philosophers in the field, despite their repeated emphasis on the importance of context, the ethical principles that are to guide or define ethical care are treated as if they can be generated from without (e.g., Engster 2007; Noddings 2002).[10] This does not mean contexts are altogether absent. As discussed in chapter 2, mainstream contexts are often drawn on explicitly or implicitly as academics contemplate concepts such as care. But if feminist care ethics works with idealized conceptions of care abstracted from mainstream care practices, what value can it have for approaching care in other contexts, particularly contexts that are unconventionally normative, such as the everyday utopias discussed in this book? In such circumstances, what legitimacy and worth can externally wrought and imposed principles—the "moral guidance" Held (2006: 12) refers to—have?

This question echoes a host of similar ones generated in recent decades, as feminists and others, with varying degree of heat, have debated the legitimacy and value of an "external" normalizing judgment (e.g., Deckha 2011). Notions of domination-free communication are rightly rejected by feminisms attentive to social power and its impact on what can be known, thought, and said. But if an ethics of care is not simply to be imposed from the outside, what other options exist? Certainly we might think of care ethics circulating hermetically within its own authoring communities or as emerging and taking shape within individual decisions or in those decisions made more collaboratively within care relationships. But can we think of ethical practice as being open to multiple possible decisions, while being simultaneously less bounded by *decision*?

The Toronto bathhouse is clearly an ethically porous space, involving participants with a vast array of normative dispositions, including those emanating from feminist and new age politics, as well as those brought in from other queer sex-play spaces. The bathhouse is also a space in which ethical practice is closely tied to sensory experience and affect. Consequently thinking about ethics through its actualization at the bathhouse supports a move not only away from ethics as external guidelines and asserted moral principles but also from the assumption that ethics is only about *decision*. Selma Sevenhuijsen (1998) claims that judgment and responsibility in relation to ethics can involve deliberation rather than applying rules; she writes, "Ethical issues arise in concrete situations, in the form of questions such as 'how to act?', or 'how to lead a good life?'" (37). However, I also want to trouble the notion of deliberation itself. One perhaps surprisingly useful resource for thinking about ethics in this way is the work of Michael Oakeshott (1962, 1990), which resists a rationalist approach to morality in which the good or right thing is predetermined and laid down. For Oakeshott (1990: 63,

64, 79), morality is practical, "a vernacular language of colloquial inter-course . . . a continuously extemporized dance whose participants are alive to one another's movements and to the ground upon which they tread. . . . It is learned only in being used. . . . It is only in books . . . that moral conduct appears as an incessant lurching from perplexity to per-plexity. . . . Moral conduct is not solving problems . . . but a practice in terms of which to think, to choose, to act, and to utter."

Oakeshott's practical morality is firmly tied to a conservative politics intent on protecting "tradition" and accepting, at most, slow, gradual, *organic* change. Ardently opposed to radical transformation or deliber-ate, programmatic political action, Oakeshott's work offers little help for thinking critically about mainstream moralities within the global North. Yet in relation to *new* emergent spaces (or communities) based on *new* moral principles, Oakeshott's approach is useful. Leaving to one side what Oakeshott might think of a casual sex bathhouse, his empha-sis on moral practice allows us to think about ethical development as something that is not entirely reliant upon, indeed *exceeds*, speech and rational thought, as it also exceeds what can be known and laid down.

Oakeshott's (1962, 1990) focus, however, is morality. Still, I want to draw on his practical approach in order to locate ethics as one part of a broader mosaic of value-based practice. Thus my aim isn't to be *for* ethics (and against everything else) but to locate ethics within a wider assemblage of normative practices, entwined with morality, politics, and values but having its own particular cast. Specifically I want to use ethics to foreground agentic responsibility, reflexively forged in contexts of un-certainty, dilemma, and indecision. In this sense ethics diverges from Oakeshott's emphasis on moral *habits*; it also diverges from the growing top-down use of ethics to identify organizational codes intended to pro-cure employee compliance with broader institutionalized projects. "By getting organizational members to commit themselves to the corporate ethical standards and values of the company, the responsibility for ethi-cal behavior becomes a collective effort shared by all members of the organization" (Rossouw and van Vuuren 2003: 398).

Certainly there are many occasions and many issues wherein the value of doing what is expected or agreed seems more important than the burden of being ethical (as this takes shape through the cultivation of open-ended, uncertain choice or feeling). At TWTB community prin-ciples, from avoiding racist and trans phobic conduct to not bringing in alcohol, coercing someone to have sex or having sex in unauthorized spaces, were treated with considerable seriousness. Bathhouse rules stated, "If you do not respect the rules of the Pussy Palace, you will be asked to leave and your money will not be refunded."[11] The distinction between rule-based obligations and (ethical) choice as it took shape in a space governed by queer feminist norms was made explicit by one volunteer, who commented, "We say this is the kind of space it is, and this is what we won't accept. You can fuck your brains out but no oppressive behavior."

Thinking about ethics as a dilemmatic practice indicates the centrality of care. For FCE, ethics certainly seems all about care, but this is care as a way of behaving ethically—care as a filling in of ethics' substance. Care as a register for behaving morally and well was much in evidence at the bathhouse, as I have explored. But if ethics centers on uncertainty and the weight of being pulled in competing directions, then the place of care shifts. It is no longer how to be ethical but instead provides the preconditions for its practice.

Elsewhere I have suggested understanding care as "weighted attentive action" (Cooper 2007, 2009),[12] a reformulation based on "taking care" or "exercising care" that draws more explicitly on care's Old English roots as *cearu*, with its invocation of sorrow, anxiety, or serious mental attention. Exercising care or attentiveness can be directed to the needs of others, as FCE suggests (Tronto 1993: 127–31).[13] But it can also be directed to oneself, including as the awareness of one's own prejudices, biases, and limits (Bowden 1997), as well as in less moral forms of self-interested attention (Cooper 2007). What care centers is a close, observant engagement with what's around, with meaning-making (that draws on what is occluded and to come, as well as what is currently witnessed). As one participant remarked, in ways that highlight the challenge of rendering the bathhouse a disability-positive space, "You get a sense with a lot of them, when you talk to them and look them in the eye. That's one thing you don't get with Internet dating—looking them in the eye; that can say so much."

Care, then, involves sensitivity, including, in the bathhouse context, to both one's own and others' eroticism (see Hammers 2008a, 2008b). But it also suggests responsiveness. While one might be an attentive voyeur, attentiveness is arguably incompatible with passivity (see Koehn 1998: 103). Attentiveness means bringing oneself into events, a close-knit, dynamic, and interactive form of engagement with what is happening and changing (see chapter 9). The care that attentiveness can generate thus emerges fully in relation to challenging forms of novelty that also matter, as participants navigate and seek productively (and properly) to inhabit unfamiliar activities and places. Care arises when things break down, when things that should work don't. Attention in overdrive was something several bathhouse interviewees alluded to, even as the focus of their attention—other people's behavior, their own feelings, the "messages" they and others were "giving off," their sensory experiences, anxieties, and the venue—varied and as the stakes (or things that mattered) varied also.

If TWTB, as a playful space of disorientation, surprise, challenge, and stimulation, constitutes a space in which considerable care was shown, we can see how care, as weighted attentive action, *supports* ethical engagements. Choosing, deliberating, agonizing, and second-guessing, feeling regret, pleasure, anger, annoyance, or self-worth—these features of ethical encounters are *enabled* by the attention that navigating and doing well, in a new kind of highly sociable and contactful space, engender, where things are not as they normally are. One instance of care's occurrence, mentioned earlier, concerned how to end encounters. The desire to avoid rejection, brusqueness, objectification, and disposal in the light of different people's interests in prolonging the connection or in treating it as an overture to something else (and more) battled with a desire to do casual sex expertly and efficiently. As one volunteer commented, "There's a little bit of a risk being a volunteer in the service rooms, where you might end up with people who don't know how to navigate the bathhouse, and on the one hand that's fine, but you don't want to end up being their date for the evening."[14]

At the bathhouse participants found it hard to shake the anxiety or tension invoked in doing casual sex well. At the same time, because dilemmas were, in some larger sense, chosen and open-ended, they became important to participants' evolving, projected sense of self. During interviews I was struck by the number of people who used examples of their own caring practice to demonstrate the kind of person they happened to be. In the desire to be ethical that their words expressed, we can hear echoes of Foucault (1997: 267) on "the kind of techniques you use in order to . . . constitute yourself as a subject of ethics." At the same time, I would be reluctant to read the moral agency given voice as a narcissistic forging or gratifying of the self, where participants' ethical actions principally operated as a way of displaying, proving, and improving on their goodness—something Srivastava (2005) identifies in her work on antiracism in Toronto's feminist organizations. Moreover ethical practice isn't only something that individuals do. To the extent that agency is expressed through an assemblage of players or through action built up from multiple interconnecting encounters, the ethical "subject" may be equally composite. Thus I take on board Rosi Braidotti's (2010: 44) claim that the "ethical instance" may be located "in a set of interrelations with both human and inhuman forces." The bathhouse's development of its antidiscriminatory rules, then, is an example of how rule-*making* can be an ethical practice for complex organizations even if individual *compliance* may lack the necessary elements of tension or undecidability.[15]

Ethics, then, includes conscious, deliberate choosing in dilemmatic situations. But an important dimension of a utopian understanding of concepts is the principle that concepts are not restricted to the effable (or what is uttered). I want to draw on the discussion of more-than-linguistic concepts in chapter 2 and Oakeshott's claim that moral practice can be retrospective, interactive, and nondeliberative to move ethics away from the exclusive domain of things that get talked about and decided. Ethical practice, of course, often takes this latter form. But as the bathhouse clearly demonstrates, dilemmas can arise and be expressed in other ways, including as feelings or emotions that, whether arising simultaneously or after the fact, do some of the work of deliberative reasoning on which ethics theorists tend to rely. This was something several participants described, from one volunteer's uncertainty about whether she had pressured two women to have sex with each other (or just made a positive opportunity available: "I wanted to encourage it and move it forward") to another volunteer's annoyance at being let down by others who failed to show for the post-bathhouse cleanup (but who decided out of feelings of responsibility [trumping fairness] to just do it herself) to an organizer's expressed regret that the bathhouse may have allied itself, in the aftermath of the police raid, with affluent gay men rather than marginalized and poorer lesbians (see Cooper 2009).

Feelings are not simply the expression or consequence of ethical decisions already taken. Rather, just as choice may become apparent only in retrospect—embedded in interactions in ways that only make sense after the fact — so ethical dilemmas within ongoing and complex social practices may also only become known, indeed in some cases may only get *constituted* as ethical dilemmas, through feelings that subsequently become generated or felt. This was graphically described by one participant who commented that she would never again have oral sex with unknown women at the bathhouse after the experience of smelling, in her words, like "another woman's pussy when my lover arrived — it was embarrassing and disrespectful."

It is tempting to describe the bathhouse as a highly ethical space, and in many ways the extent of the ethical dilemmas, as well as the movement between the undecidability of ethics and the solidification of moral guidelines and rulings, is striking. But what is also striking and important about the bathhouse is the extent to which, as a space of casual sex, it moderated the injunction to be at one's best by bringing other values and goals into play. Within the business ethics literature, moving up the ethical ladder has been a central goal (e.g., Rossouw and van Vuuren 2003). At the Toronto bathhouse ethics' presence and practice were uneven and deliberately tempered.[16] Organizers wanted and encouraged people to do well, yet "doing well" was about accomplishment as well as morality, and often the first trumped the second. So it didn't mean having sex with people undesired out of a sense of fairness or kindness, nor did it mean staying with the same person all night or disclosing to a sex partner your real name and contact details if asked for. To the extent that bathhouse ethics involved a working on the self, that here included the collective and organized self, the ethical call was both encouraged and held in check (as the quotation opening this chapter illustrates). Having fun and taking risks constituted a bathhouse form of excelling that could take precedence over caring about others. Moreover while the bathhouse as an organization continued to develop and regulate its own distinctive ethical temperature, individual practice both exceeded and undershot it, contributing in the process to the evolving ethics and morality of the bathhouse itself.

Concluding Remarks

The Toronto Women's and Trans Bathhouse provides a rich site for thinking about ethics. As an event provocatively geared to casual, no-ties sex, it is saturated with ethical practices, feelings, and dilemmas in ways that beach feminist care ethics as an overly idealist set of obligations imposed on life (as it is lived) from a sanitized distance. At the same time, the contribution that ethics, as discussed here, can make to a transformative politics is uncertain. While feminist care ethics has developed into a framework of principled conduct—what should happen and be done—a more dilemmatic approach to ethics emphasizes uncertainty. As such, ethics cannot be deployed, as business organizations attempt to do, to engineer programmatic change. But that does not mean a more dilemmatic ethics disavows politics. Rather what it contributes is an emphasis on situational responsibility as actors try to respond in ways that they perceive as right, drawing on varying principles from other domains, principles that (temporarily at least) become imported into the bathhouse site. What a dilemmatic ethics also contributes is an emphasis on complexity, concern, attentiveness, feeling, and uncertainty (principles associated also with the feeling state, see chapter 3).

Feminist care ethics has proven to be an immensely influential feminist framework, extensively deployed by feminist writers and regularly alluded to by nonfeminists as an intuitively correct set of norms. Consequently it has come to monopolize the terrain of ethical care. The example of TWTB, however, shows that care and ethics can combine in other ways, that care can be the basis for ethical practice rather than its substance. Yet in centering ethics rather than care, there is a risk that ethics becomes the terrain of normative idealization, with care just the means of its arrival, so everything good then gets piled onto ethics. But do we want ethics to hold so much of value? Do we want care to? What's at stake in the tendency of normative theorizing, as instantiated by care ethics, to build up particular concepts as the repository of all that is good?

Inflating concepts in this way is not limited to conventional normative theorizing. Similar tendencies can be found in critical writing that works, not always consciously, to build terms such as *queer, feminism, even touch* in idealized ways—that is, in ways drawn from the world of thought (rather than from other kinds of social practice). As those involved commit themselves to particular concepts, such as care ethics, these concepts grow in nuance and complexity. Advocates fortify their concept's boundaries, determining the exact relationship between care and justice or care and love, as they determine whether self-care, voluntarily assumed vulnerability, pleasure, and sex can fit within their ethical perimeter. In the process, a host of questions get closed down as academic debate fixes on the flaws, contradictions, and subsequent repair of the concept in question. Energy flows into justification—why care is the best way of conceptualizing and carving out good relationships—and successful concepts move into, and indeed sometimes colonize, new discursive terrains.

In thinking about the contribution of concepts to transformative change, would it be better, then, to work with "thinner" concepts, ones that are less idealized, lighter in their attachments and investments, and more equivocally constructed? Care and ethics are easily valorized as inherently and only good things. Yet caring practices can be excessive, providing aid, intimacy, support, or attention that is undesired (see Dahl 2000). Ethical responsibility may also be unhelpful, regressive, or insufficient, where the responsibility assumed works to disempower others or is unfair to the self (which might also be the collective self), where lack of institutional authority renders the ethical subject too weak, or where agonizing about what to do and second-guessing what has been done paralyze or deplete all the pleasure and vitality an everyday utopia can and should manifest. In developing a utopian conceptual attitude, I have argued against the drive to build idealized normative concepts. While this might seem a paradoxical claim given the popular association between the utopian and perfection, in earlier chapters I explored how utopian studies and utopian texts have moved away from notions of flawless, static ideals to a concern with process, change, and conflict. Earlier discussion also emphasized the importance of material practice to concept building—that concepts should not be understood as cognitive ideas alone. In chapter 2 I described concepts as the formative oscillation between imagining and actualization. The problem academic scholarship confronts, as a social practice, is when it ignores this interrelationship. For the risk of its disregard, and particularly the disregard of actualization (or how concepts are practically manifested) when it comes to the development of everyday normative concepts, such as care or ethics, is that concepts can grow without restraint within the social imaginary. This is not simply an argument that concepts need to be *applied* or properly anchored within their (separate and nonconceptual) material settings. The importance of actualization is that it shapes what concepts come to mean as I discussed in relation to equality in the previous chapter.

Recognizing that normative concepts are *necessarily* imperfect—that they are part of a multitude of imperfect concepts — does not lead, however, to a *diluting* of political, ethical, or value-based commitments; on the contrary. Overinvestment in any particular concept, whether it be equality, touch, or care, can be problematic when it reduces the ability and willingness to recognize a concept's limitations and, perhaps more important, when overly elaborate terms and dimensions impede activist and academic ability to work through and across different, overlapping terms. In their work on men's bathhouses, Styles (1979) and Tattelman (1999: 73) identify casual sex spaces as gestational sites for multiple communicative repertoires — repertoires that include looks and posture as well as sometimes speech. Participants at TWTB may have proven, in the main, less experienced and less ready to rely on nonverbal modes of casual, erotic communication, depending more on conversation to build connection and desire. Nevertheless what talking with organizers, volunteers, and participants revealed was a multilingual openness, motivated by the desire to forge an inclusive and diverse community event and by the desire to communicate erotically with (often unknown) others. The readiness of bathhouse participants to communicate across and in different registers raises interesting questions about what it might take for others, including theorists on the left, to incline similarly — treating normative (or good object) concepts in a similarly provisional, multilingual manner.

In the three chapters that follow, I continue to develop a situated approach to normative concepts, but I do so across different terrain. While the first three case studies, with their focus on touch, equality, and ethical care, have centered concepts that progressive forces and scholarship tend to avow, the next three chapters, on trading, property, and markets, tackle concepts about which the left has traditionally been more suspicious. But if drawing materially embedded conceptual lines through everyday utopias unsettles typically progressive concepts, can it also open up more positive ways in which to reconfigure typically conservative ones? My discussion starts with the challenge of creating new local monies and trading networks in order to rebuild community economies. My focus is Local Exchange and Trading Schemes, an ambitious and inspirational local currency network project that captured international attention in the 1990s.

CHAPTER 6

NORMATIVE TIME AND THE CHALLENGE OF COMMUNITY LABOR IN LOCAL EXCHANGE TRADING SCHEMES

I joined to meet people in the community, and because a friend who does things for me, it made me feel less indebted paying in . . . the local currency. And her partner also did stuff for me, drilled holes in my wall, and he wasn't a friend so it was easier. We have one trading day a month. People bring food and sell goods; about eight people go to trading days. Not much trading of services happens. I wanted help with gardening and offered lifts to the airport. There was a question about whether I'd be insured using my car as it wasn't in the course of domestic use. I was once asked for a lift and couldn't do it. I never asked for gardening. I felt diffident asking someone to do something who I didn't know, unless they'd asked me already. At trading days, we'd lament no one was trading services but nothing much was done about it.

LETS member, North Midlands

Local Exchange Trading Schemes (LETS) were the big local currency story in Britain in the 1990s, an ambitious venture in which people would exchange goods and services with those living nearby using community currency checks. One person might walk the neighbor's dogs and use the credit gained to purchase local handicrafts, a massage, or fresh bread. A brilliant instance within a far longer and broader story of alternative economic networks and community currencies (North 2007), LETS promised to relocalize money as a medium of exchange so people could obtain the commonplace things they needed, along with goods and services that were harder to access, all the while developing friendships and social networks on their doorstep.

In many respects, LETS exemplify the notion of an everyday utopia, of quotidian practices performed in an organized, ambitiously counterhegemonic manner. In a context such as Britain, where national currency reigns supreme and where money remains intricately tied to modes of capitalist accumulation, the creation of currencies intended to operate *only* as a means of facilitating exchange is a bold and striking move. But LETS were also utopian in another key respect. At the heart of their vision of good community life was the dream of revitalizing neighborhoods through the development and strengthening of sociable, mutually supportive, *economic* ties.

Given the tremendous amount written about LETS, and local currencies more generally (e.g., Aldridge and Patterson 2002; North 2006; Seyfang 2001a, 2001b; Williams 1996a, 1996b), the ambition to develop grassroots, locally controlled money has inspired and intrigued many. Yet despite the sometimes esoteric scholarship to which community money has given rise, LETS proved in many ways a homely structure addressing everyday needs — house repairs, cleaning, laundry, gardening, car lifts — even as the goods offered, and largely wanted, presupposed a certain kind of propertied life.[1]

In the light of LETS' ambition and optimism, this chapter centers on the challenge British LETS faced, and ultimately seem to have lost, in turning an imagined ideal, "community labor" (with its promise of sociable trading that would build community), into actuality. Focusing on failure may seem contrary to a utopian ethos. However, utopian thinking is not dreamy-eyed. To go beyond wishful thinking it is necessary to understand the relationship between existing social conditions and change possibilities. And the failure of particular conceptual lines to take shape is an important part of this process. In interviews, LETS documentation, and secondary texts, the virtuous cycle imagined for community labor was repeatedly expressed. As Jill Jordan remarked in a foundational LETS speech in 1991, "It's a tool which rebuilds our communities again. It re-unites people; it's relationship trading."[2] Organizers and activists argued that success was assured as economic exchanges and services provided by neighbors for local money would build ties of friendship and acquaintanceship that would, in turn, develop community feeling and further willingness to trade. This didn't happen; the conversion of community labor from promise to actual practice proved far harder to accomplish than advocates imagined.

Exploring reasons for this failure to convert, I want to build on my discussion of earlier chapters, which has considered from different angles the relationship between concepts' imagining and their actualization. Here I ask, What happens when there is no actualization (or very little)? Of course, actualization can simply involve the expression of imagined ideals or the presence of potential, as discussed in chapter 4. However, in the case of a virtuous cycle, where mutually interacting *practices* are intended to reinforce and build upon each other, the work imagining does is very different from the work actually materialized practices perform. Indeed for LETS, the difference between the concept of community labor expressed as a vision (and promise) and actually operationalized proved to be the difference between failure and success. Without community generating trades and trades generating community, LETS could not grow and flourish. Why did this virtuous cycle prove impossible? Why were LETS unable to manifest or actualize community labor in anything like the form advocates imagined? This chapter focuses on one particular set of factors: the normative temporalities LETS mobilized, crafted, and ultimately depended upon. Focusing on the two temporalities to most prominently surface — community time and labor market time — I explore their centrifugal force in pulling community and trading apart.

The Promise of LETS

The origin of LETS as a particular kind of local currency system can be traced back to the work of Michael Linton and others who founded the Comox Valley LETSystem in British Columbia, Canada, in the 1980s. The aim of the system was to enable local people to exchange goods and skills, despite the depressed, cash-starved character of their economy at that time. From there the momentum to establish LETS networks internationally quickly grew. Colin Williams and his coauthors (2001: 121), conducting an extensive survey of British LETS in 1999, found 303 networks with an estimated 21,800 members and estimated turnover of £1.4 million.

While British LETS varied in some respects, as I discuss below, the basic premise was that all members within a scheme (which might be anywhere between seventy-five and five hundred people) would identify things they both wanted and could offer: such as plumbing, dog walking, language lessons, fresh vegetables, and computer use. All wants and offers would be regularly publicized to members, usually through the production of a monthly newsletter, with lists indicating who wanted and could provide what. Trades performed would be immediately paid for ("acknowledged") with a check (or credit note) given to the seller, who would send it off to the LETS administrator to enter on a spreadsheet that made everybody's balances visible. As a "no interest" scheme, people could go into debit ("commitment") without cost. Thus the network could, and was intended to, be kick-started by demand-driven activity. While most British LETS were member-led and organized, a smaller number were initiated or significantly resourced by public bodies as part of their local economic development or antipoverty work. These latter schemes tended to focus on particular constituencies — public housing tenants or mental health service users, for instance — and were often heavily dependent on funded workers to run the networks and facilitate trading. Public bodies were also involved in limited ways as members within other schemes. Alongside a handful of associational and commercial members (such as health food co-ops), local councils offered services, such as printing and room rentals, that could be paid for with LETS currency. The involvement of firms and public bodies as network members was seen by some activists as an essential aspect of LETS growth, extending the items that could be brought into the LETS economy. Yet the involvement of the for-profit sector, in particular, divided LETS members, forming part of a wider schism within the British LETS community as two (mutually antagonistic) models emerged: LETS schemes and LETSystems (Lee et al. 2004; North 2006).

Disagreement between the two models fundamentally revolved around whether LETS were exclusively currency-based structures or sociality structures as well. System advocates, including the founder Michael Linton, argued strongly for a pure self-regulating monetary system, on the grounds that the social benefits of community building depended upon and would follow getting the currency right. Linton is quoted as saying, "A money system that needs grants or volunteers to operate is a boat that don't float."[3] Scheme advocates, by contrast, felt local money was only one part of a wider, *integrated* project. Currency systems alone could not develop people's skills and economic confidence, nor could new money by itself craft an alternative economy (see generally Lee et al. 2004: 606–11). While trading networks were central to community building, scheme advocates also believed that successful trading networks depended on establishing social connections between members, a process that involved some level of organizational activity, coordination, and stimulation.

As everyday utopias, schemes — to a greater extent than system networks — cohered around an explicitly countercultural vision of the "good society," in which pro-ecological practice was linked to egalitarian, trust-based, and communal forms of work and trade. Thus schemes encouraged people to offer work they enjoyed; aimed for greater parity in terms of rates for the "job"; and organized a wide array of complementary social, cultural, and educational activities as a means of encouraging trade and as part of their community enhancement function. Yet while disagreement between scheme and system advocates proved a major force field running through the world of British LETS in the 1990s, in practical terms distinctions were often less sharply rendered. Many LETS networks combined or moved between the two approaches over time, and individual members did not necessarily sign up to (or always know) the orientation of their particular network. In the discussion that follows, I draw on a paradigm of LETS situated somewhere between the two extremes — that is, neither highly interventionist and proactive nor completely dependent on currency systems alone to get things right.

Beyond LETS Potential

I began researching British LETS in 2001, as it became increasingly clear that early heady expectations had proven overly optimistic. By the turn of the twenty-first century, LETS in Britain appeared in free fall, with many networks having folded, been abandoned, or struggling to survive as membership levels plummeted and trading collapsed.[4] My aim was to interview a cross-section of members from different networks around the country to understand better what had gone wrong. Between 2001 and 2010 just over fifty interviews were conducted with coordinators and LETS participants.[5] While many remained optimistic about the future of LETS, others saw survival as an ongoing struggle. A former organizer and participant of a North Midlands LETS commented, "It's been a great journey for me; I'm not bitter, I'm just sad that it hasn't swept the country. . . . [to himself] Get *real* . . . it hasn't swept its own back yard! We all got carried away about the excitement and potential of LETS; I've read hundreds of chapters on the Internet about the potential of LETS. But no one has written about why people *don't* join and why people *don't* trade."

Academic and policy writers have certainly not been idle. Work on LETS has addressed its contribution to new monetary systems (e.g., Robertson 2005); its value as a means of combating local poverty, unemployment, and social exclusion (Aldridge and Patterson 2002; Williams 1996a, 1996b; Seyfang 2001b); its contribution to alternative economic development strategies (Purdue et al. 1997); its relationship to environmental sustainability (Dauncey 1988; Seyfang 2001a); and the demographic background, values, beliefs, and commitments of LETS members (Barry and Proops 1999; North 1999). However, as the North Midlands ex-organizer quoted above said, with some notable exceptions, such as Aldridge and Patterson (2002) and Evans (2009), British LETS scholarship has been far better at explaining LETS economic and environmental *potential* and participants' hopes and optimism than addressing in any detail the fundamental challenges organizers and members faced.

Among organizers, however, accounts of the difficulties in sustaining LETS proved plentiful. One former organizer from southwest England whose scheme had folded remarked, "People get the impression that nearly anything they might want to have done or obtained can be obtained through LETS. We didn't have many people providing services, and a lot of people were looking for somebody to fix their car or do some plumbing or wiring and other DIY. I mean most of the time, people that have those skills are actually fairly fully employed and getting a living from that. So a lot of the services being offered were all very similar — and some complimentary therapy-type things." Another coordinator from west England said, "We've had new members, but we haven't been able to give them jobs they want to do or provide for their needs, so that's been a bit of a failure. We had an artist who offered to do classes but we don't have enough people . . . who have the free time to take that offer. So it's really difficult; you really need a lot of people to make it successful."

Writing about LETS, Aldridge and Patterson (2002) identify several factors that retarded success: the limited range of (largely nonessential) goods and services available; the risk for welfare claimants that LETS income might generate benefit deductions; psychological barriers, particularly of indebtedness by purchasing services in advance of earning (something LETS encouraged); the costs of participation, which, while relatively low, remained excessive for some; insufficient administrative support, causing directories of wants and offers to be out of date; and lack of trust and community feeling between members in many LETS networks. These factors are important. However, in my own research, exploring with interviewees why membership and trading levels flagged, one theme that repeatedly emerged was that of time. Interviewees commented on the difficulty in finding people with time to participate (and even more to help run the network); on the time involved setting up a trade; on problems of no-shows and tardiness by both clients and providers; and on excessive time spent traveling to the one traded with. These interviewees weren't particularly negative about LETS overall; indeed many were strikingly positive. However, alongside complaints about the lack of diversity in LETS goods and services, time was a constant source of complaint.

At first glance, these problems appear mainly to concern inadequate resource time—a familiar problem for many community projects. However, what became increasingly apparent was the fact that time difficulties weren't simply those of scarcity. What people's complaints and dissatisfactions also indicated was the presence, indeed the competing presence, of two normative temporalities: community and labor market time. In relation to local currency networks, community time signaled a relaxed, generous approach to time's rhythms and duration, often with a nostalgic relationship to the past. By contrast, labor market time emphasized the importance of efficiency, economy, and reliability, including the need to overcome the hindrances of the past in order to procure a thriving, expanded, work-based future. The force of these different temporalities has been explored in other contexts, as writers address how community time and work (or capitalist) time get enacted, organized, managed, and experienced as both contemporary and historical processes (e.g., Crow and Allan 1995; Gross 1985; Rau 2002; Rifkin 1987). For the purposes of this discussion, two particular dimensions of these temporalities are important: normativity and plurality.

The concept of normative time, as both imagined and actualized, combines material and ideational dimensions. On the one hand, it is oriented to notions of good, legitimate, authorized, or right time, how time *should* be organized, managed, and experienced—including, importantly, also the possibility of time being nonnormative, of being resisted and organized in other ways. Yet normative time isn't just about values or temporal preferences, however significant and visible these may be in the things people say. Normative time is also centrally concerned with the standard ways time's rhythms, tempo, signaling, duration, phasing, interconnections, and distributions materialize, and the impact of this materialization on the shape, legitimacy, and force of what is considered to be "right" or "proper" conduct.

While time frequently acquires a normative, often institutionally enforced cast, in a country such as Britain, normative temporalities do not take shape as unitary assemblages monopolizing the entire social field. Multiple temporalities coexist — combining and colliding in complex, constantly shifting ways — as time's accrual, signaling, passage, rhythms, and other features get stitched and restitched together. To consider this process in more detail, as I do below, I draw on the parallel schema of legal pluralism, an area of legal anthropology and sociolegal studies that focuses on the coexistence of multiple *legal* orders (e.g., Merry 1988; Kleinhans and Macdonald 1997). While there has been considerable debate within legal pluralism over what counts as a legal *order* and whether legal and normative orders can be usefully treated as equivalents (e.g., Tamanaha 1993), what is particularly useful for my purposes is the way legal pluralism centers the interactions *between* orders, as, for instance, in the ways state and customary (or religious) law combine and interact within particular contexts, or, as I discuss in chapter 7, how a school's organization of property relates to the property order of state law.

According to Sally Merry (1988: 873), "plural normative orders are found virtually in all societies. . . . At the center of investigation [is] the relationship between the official legal system and other forms of ordering that connect with but are in some ways separate from . . . it." She continues, "Research . . . emphasizes the way state law penetrates and restructures other normative orders . . . and, at the same time, the way nonstate normative orders resist and circumvent penetration or even capture and use the symbolic capital of state law" (881). These kinds of reciprocal interactions between diverse normative orders are central to my discussion of time. At the same time, recognition of temporal reciprocation needs to also incorporate recognition of unequal power. Legal pluralism (usually) acknowledges that some forms of ordering have more power than others, even as it is committed to exploring the effects of their interconnections (without assuming in advance what these will necessarily be). Normative temporalities, likewise, coexist unequally. Liberal postindustrial capitalist society may generate diverse temporalities, but these temporalities are far from evenly matched in their social force. This unevenness penetrates microsocial spaces, such as LETS, too as they become compelled to manage the flux and flow between the temporalities they create and those wider temporalities they confront.

Imagining Community Labor

Sociability is important, but it needs to be based on a trading. It's not just a friendship; it's people doing things for each other, and I think you need one for the other to take off.

— LETS COORDINATOR, WEST ENGLAND

The promise of community labor lay at the heart of LETS' autofantasy in which its value and ability to build both an economy and a community through mutual interaction was assured.[6] While the co-constitution (or reciprocal embedding) of sociality and trading are well-recognized features of any economy, LETS gave this relationship particular prominence as something to reimagine and foreground.[7] This reimagining had four primary dimensions: friendly trading, friendship through trading, social contact as a prerequisite of trading, and forging community through labor.

The first, friendliness as a *trading norm*, directed exchanges to be conducted in ways attentive to the voluntary character and pleasant camaraderie expected of LETS encounters. In conditions of equality, unlike conventional capitalist relations, friendliness meant neither patronage by the purchaser nor an obligatory supplement by the provider but a mode of relating expected of both. Because LETS trading was not essential to members' economic survival, interviewees suggested people could (and would) skew their trading toward those who made the experience pleasurable (see North 2006). Friendly trading, then, can be seen as an integral part of building and being attentive to the cultural and symbolic meaningfulness of exchange-as-contact, in contrast to narratives of routinized, disengaged trading cultures in the global North.

Second, sociality, in the form of hospital visits or befriending, could be the service explicitly offered or sought. Yet as a community-*building* network, LETS more commonly encouraged people to trade other goods *in order to* make friends or social contacts. One participant and coordinator from an East Midlands LETS commented, "By being involved with someone else you start to build a relationship." Interviewees from my own and others' research described how establishing social ties and overcoming isolation were major motivations for joining LETS schemes, especially in the case of newcomers to an area. One ex-organizer from Wales described how she and neighbors decided to establish a LETS because they were conscious of an influx of people to their district without local ties: "It allows people coming into the area to join up and make out a few people and get friendly with them and so they don't get isolated; that was the reason for setting up in the beginning. . . . There was a lot of people coming into this area . . . and they seemed to be a bit left out . . . and some of us, we were thinking about [it] and we got a bunch of people who're always thinking about these things; and we thought about what we could do and thought if we had a LETS scheme it would help them to resettle."

While trading was seen as a way to build social contacts and friendship networks, prior contact was also characterized as a prerequisite for LETS trading (an interesting contrast to the case of the bathhouse in chapter 4, where erotic desire and sex were stimulated by a *lack* of prior interpersonal contact):

> Trading tends to go on more when people know each other, or can put a face to a name . . . than between two strangers. (Participant and coordinator, East Midlands)

> I do like people to come to a meeting and get to know each other because I think really the whole point of LETS is that you need to know people before you ask them to your house to do anything. (Coordinator, west England)

Recognizing many people's unwillingness to trade in LETS currency with unknown others, schemes organized trading days, ice-breaking socials, cultural events, and fairs to help people make social contact.[8] Some schemes also introduced volunteer brokers, a strategy institutionalized further in Time Banking.

Finally, community labor designated work that was socially conscientious, community-based, and nonalienated, where labor and exchange formed the cornerstones to deliberate, realizable community building

A Tea and Tarts Party in 2008, Cambridge. Members were invited to bring a tart and give 2 lets (a local currency) to the host, who provided the tea and the venue. Image courtesy of Cambridge CitiVillage.

through the performance of trust and the experience of mutual benefit (Dobson 1993: 125). In a useful article on informal transactions within both poor and more affluent neighborhoods, Williams and Windebank (2001a) explore how both bonding and bridging social capital — involving ties of friendship as well as weaker forms of acquaintanceship — could be generated through alternative trading networks. These collective benefits were keenly promoted within the LETS literature and later on LETS websites.[9] "This is a great way to get the help you need, support local people to use their skills and make new friends as our trading events are good fun too!" one LETS coordinator wrote.[10] Schemes portrayed local trading and work (in conditions of nonalienation) as a vital community-building device. At the same time, many schemes struggled with the tension between a community orientation toward affinity and an economic need for diversity.

LETS Time

In talking about the failure of community labor, it is important to distinguish between community labor as a thin account of the mutually constitutive, inherent interconnections between economic and social life—that economic relations are *always* social relations—and the thicker, deliberately normative form promised by LETS in which community labor constituted a self-perpetuating upward cycle where trade would enhance community relations and feeling, and community would strengthen and energize local trading. Certainly as an expressed idea, the upward cycle of community labor appeared both logical and viable. However, as a material practice, more was required. To explore this further, I want to start with the temporal orders constituting LETS, and then consider how they knit—or, more precisely, how they *didn't* knit—together.

COMMUNITY TIME

LETS community time took shape against a particular version of capitalist time. While academics have explored capitalism's own internal discrepancies and conflicts (e.g., Gibson-Graham 2006a; Hope 2009), LETS worked with a particular vision of capitalist money-time as simultaneously compressed, calculating, roller-coaster erratic, alienating, and controlling, dominating other (particularly nonwork) temporal registers (Pacione 1997).[11] Against this vision, and surrounded by other movements also oriented to more attentive, sustainable, slower ways of living, LETS sought to develop a radically different temporal model from that of global capitalist trading, interpreted by some as a "gift relation" (Dobson 1993; compare Raddon 2003; see also chapter 8).

Central to understanding LETS as a gifting structure was the bestowal of labor time in a context where currency constituted a means of enabling and representing the flow of favors rather than a mechanism for capital's accumulation and labor exploitation. For this to work, however, members' labor time needed to be valued with some degree of parity. Consequently schemes variously introduced thresholds, ceilings, and norms to limit earning disparities between different people's work. LETS also adopted an approach to resource time that inclined toward plenitude. Certainly schemes and members expressed awareness of the competing demands on people's time. Nevertheless norms of not complaining, socializing with others while they worked for you, and being relaxed about delays in setting up trades or no-shows pointed to an expectation of resource time ease (also North 2006).

Against the speed, compression, and exhaustion associated with capitalist time,[12] LETS trades manifested a slower rhythm. Unlike mainstream capitalist norms, which value money for its capacity to accelerate the gratification of desire, in LETS gratification was often delayed in the face of other commitments and the need to build a relationship. At the same time, LETS exchanges inclined toward *mutual* satisfaction or enjoyment. LETS foregrounded the pleasure involved in spending time with others, whether through trading, working on joint projects, or participating in LETS events.[13] In this sense, labor time was less substitutable since expectations that purchasers would interact socially with providers meant that paying someone for a service didn't necessarily release the purchaser's own time. Nor was providing a service for others intended as a means of accumulating leisure time later on. Opposed to future-oriented modes of living in which the present is simply to be churned through or treated as an envelope for resource accumulation before one's "real," better life started, LETS schemes (more than systems) emphasized the importance of doing what one enjoyed now, whether this was repairing bicycles, providing driving lessons, baking cakes, growing plants, dog walking, giving massages, or home decorating.

This emphasis on the present didn't block off other times, however; LETS folded in very particular narratives of both the future and past (see also chapter 9). In one sense, LETS can be read as an ambitious forward-facing initiative, intent on establishing closer, stronger, more self-sufficient communities—even as the incessant emphasis on localism sometimes obscured the political stakes involved in disparaging more global forms of trade. At the same time, LETS' community was explicitly anchored in a multilayered past. This emerged as a practical effect as well as a culturally imagined one. Mending, for instance, represented a salvaging that refused to waste previously satisfactory items in pursuit of an unsustainable faddish consumerism in which things lived truncated lives among temporally truncated communities (see generally Appadurai 1986). LETS' emphasis on patched and recycled goods also spoke to a sedimentary vision of multiple generations reworking and leaving their trace upon things as, through this reworking, the extended life of things became visible. Also rendered visible were local geographical his-

Plants sale, 2008. Image courtesy of Cambridge CitiVillage.

tories. LETS sought to embed their economies within situated stories of the past, albeit stories oriented to certain narratives rather than to others. This was most publicly visible in the naming of currencies (tales in Canterbury, bobbins [for spinning] in Manchester) and in the naming of schemes, such as Avalon LETS in Somerset. Through their deployment of imagery and symbols, LETS told particular, often nostalgic stories of pasts worth recuperating within instantiations of the local present.

It is easy to read LETS as a community experiment intent on countering the out-of-control, strained, precarious, and alienated character of social and personal time under capitalism. However, this is not the whole story. I now turn to a different instantiation of normative LETS time. According to this second account, far from presenting an antidote to capitalist temporality, LETS demonstrated, in its centering of trade,

accounting, skills enhancement, calculation, and instrumental rationality, the authority, legitimacy, and breadth of labor's commodification
and capitalism's empire.

Central to LETS practice was the valuing of time as *labor* time. While particular modes of valuation, as I have suggested, may have distinguished
LETS from conventional capitalist labor markets, and while the value of
LETS currency was not that of state money, LETS depended on the utility
of time as a resource that could be bought or sold. Indeed a key claim of
LETS advocates was that items and services, impossible to buy in other,
more formal trading contexts, could be purchased through LETS. Idiosyncratic offerings such as help buying a van, personalized services and
hobbies such as tarot card reading and ear candles, and amateur skills in
home repair were all brought within LETS economies, as members were
encouraged to think outside the box in terms of what they could offer
and in terms of what they might need. With its nonscarce currency, rejection of deferred purchasing, and organizational injunction to participate *economically*, LETS encouraged members to see their network as an
effective alternative to the mainstream economy. In LETS a wide array of
items could be easily and competently purchased; likewise a wide array
of skills could be sold.

LETS' complementary value as a supplement to mainstream labor
markets did, however, raise substitutional concerns for some commentators and observers, who feared that underemployed adults might
spend their work time in informal, peripheral economies, such as LETS
(which could not undo their impoverishment), rather than in more
mainstream (economically sustaining) employment. Yet little evidence
exists of LETS schemes actually functioning in this way. What LETS advocates emphasized instead was LETS' contribution to contemporary labor
self-management—a role that not only emphasized LETS' proximity to
mainstream economic markets but also sought to insert LETS within the
patchwork formation of working life. Aldridge et al. (2001), for instance,
describe LETS as part of a wider diversification strategy, while Williams
and his coauthors (2003) consider LETS within a context of full *engagement* rather than full employment.

The blurring of work/home boundaries, described by a number of au-
thors, including Brannen (2005), Maher (2009), and Tietze and Musson

(2002), underpins both descriptions and certainly shaped LETS normative culture. While people could say no to trading requests, and while many organizers recognized LETS as a "spare time" activity (particularly in those more middle-class LETS schemes revisited in 2010), LETS' logic frazzled the perimeter around personal time as something lying outside of the market's reach. Given the organizational impetus to increase trading levels, the "good" LETS member was generally available. While LETS were certainly not a major force in wider moves to "full engagement" or "stitched together" labor time, their successful functioning was tied to this growing entrepreneurial momentum with its "responsible worker" norms.

Yet while members and activists may have been attracted to new, less bounded models of work, LETS' early appeal to state-based economic development agendas was somewhat different. Here LETS were valued less as a permanent supplement to mainstream labor markets and more as a temporary support during times of economic crisis—a support that, importantly, established pathways for the unemployed and underemployed *into* work. Those I spoke with described a progression in which members might initially offer a service in local currency, with the aim of subsequently offering it within the mainstream economy. However, when networks pursued municipal funding and commercial interest, they emphasized employability rather than self-employment, which tended to also mean employment within the *private* rather than public or NGO sectors (see Peacock 2000: 74). With its (implicit) promise of creating reliable, workable workers refamiliarized with the expectations of formal market employment—which depended upon efficient and punctual work— LETS presented itself as a regeneration practice oriented to and rationalized by a particular vision of a reinvested, hopeful future, involving skilled, employable people and stable communities (see generally Bourdieu 2000).

However, while the enhancement of mainstream employability posed a particular normative blending of present and future, LETS' economic strategies were also underpinned by narratives of *enduring* harm, as certain individual and collective histories—of poverty, mental ill health, and female oppression—left a residue of poor confidence, inadequate skills, and limited work adjustment that would impede present-day employability. As a consequence, several targeted (and publicly funded) networks were introduced for poor communities (e.g., Pacione 1997), while a few others targeted women (including one specifically aimed at Asian women) and mental health system users (see Manley and Aldridge 2000). Here, in contrast to LETS' deliberate attachment to particular, valorized historical narratives of place (discussed earlier), capacity-building strategies sought to detach particular constituencies from what was seen as their injury-bearing past. In ways that resemble the equality governance discussed in chapter 3, funded LETS sought to break the hold of histories that were deemed to keep repeating.

Incompatible Temporalities

We can read LETS' time, then, according to two different normative tendencies. In the first, LETS functioned as a community-building, gift-based alternative to the alienated rationalities and social recklessness of capitalist time. In the second, LETS' proximity to, indeed its imbrication within, the mainstream economy necessitated and, in turn, consolidated mainstream temporal norms, as efficiency and reliability were presented as helping to free workers (and potential workers) from the stranglehold of their nonliberal past. In the rest of this chapter, I want to explore in more detail the tensions that arose from seeking to combine these two distinct normative constellations. Proponents and organizers tied LETS' success to its ability to forge community labor, not simply as an *imagined* process but as an actualized one—where community would generate trading, and trading would build community. But this depended on the successful combining of two very different normative temporalities, a combining that failed to take place.

In common with other researchers, my interviews disclosed a range of difficulties facing community labor. These included the problems mentioned earlier: of inadequate resource time to participate fully (particularly as an organizer), the time involved organizing a trade, problems of no-shows and tardiness, and "unreasonable" travel time in getting to the one traded with. Other grumbles and difficulties included overexacting friends demanding jobs be repeatedly performed until "perfect"; purchasers absorbing and having to deal with damage caused by insufficiently skilled or negligent providers; parties not returning calls; and the confusion of social cues that sometimes arose over whether an invitation was a friendship-motivated gift or the first part of a trading-motivated exchange. Finally, interviewees grumbled about the problems overly homogeneous, sociality-based networks generated, with their limited diversity of offerings (see also chapter 8).

These problems were far from invariable or constant. For some members and some schemes, LETS realized (perhaps more than realized) its promise. Nevertheless despite the fact that pursuing community labor generated problems other than those relating to time,[14] interviewees commented frequently about time being wasted, given away, taken advantage of, or misunderstood, as different norms and expectations of signaling, tempo, duration, and rhythm collided. Why couldn't LETS' two normative temporalities meld, cohere, or at least more comfortably coexist? Without denying those instances when some kind of fusion or consensus emerged, three factors stand out: lack of a clear, strong organizing framework or design so that one normative framework would structure (or trump) the other; the expectation and requirement that *individual* members would manage competing temporal pressures; and the relationship of LETS time to times beyond its networks.

ORGANIZATIONAL DESIGN

LETS promotional literature ceaselessly asserted the compatibility and fusion of community sociability and trade. The LETS development agency LETSLINK U.K. described it as "like having a hundred friends," "access to . . . goods and services many of which are rarely available in the normal market," and "opportunities to turn your unused time, skills or resources into assets."[15] Yet when it came to the practical question of *how* this articulation was supposed to work, tensions to do with time rarely got elaborated. One striking aspect of the way LETS networks depicted the relationship between sociality and work—and the relationship between community and labor market time—was the lack of an ascribed hierarchy, particularly a consistent hierarchy, between the two. In the desired fusion of community with labor, neither side, nor its accompanying temporality, seemed intended or established as the instrument, terrain, component, or corpus of the other.

Lack of hierarchy may sound like a strange concern. However, LETS' assumption that community and labor would carry an equal normative weight distinguishes LETS from many other settings in the global North in which community and labor market values and time cohere in large part because design or expectations clearly establish one side as subordinate or functional to the other. We can see this process in two contrasting examples. In the case of the Toronto bathhouse labor market norms were clearly subservient to community ones (see chapter 5). While sex volunteers were supposed to be attentive to managing the time taken in any single encounter and to maintaining a steady through-put of (ideally) satisfied clients so as to avoid lengthy queues, sexual labor was unequivocally in aid of (and subordinated to) community. A very different logic can be found in the party selling of sex toys or Tupperware (McCaughey and French 2001; Vincent 2003). Here duration, rhythm, and tempo may *mimic* social gatherings—a group of friends, for instance, enjoying each other's midday company. However, while the temporal *aesthetic* of party selling is community-based, it is motivated, underpinned, and rationalized by commercial imperatives. The economic interests of the company (enacted through the role of the dealer and volunteer party hostess) structure and repeatedly intrude upon the party's rhythm, timing, and end point, as guests are shown items and encouraged to buy— not least so the host can earn herself a "party gift" as recompense for her labor and the venue she has provided.

In these cases, as with many others where community and labor market temporalities successfully combine, the integration of two normative orders proves intelligible—indeed the practice itself is *rendered* intelligible—because integration takes a very specific shape.[16] In different kinds of exchange, purchasers and providers know which aspects of the temporal order—timing, tempo, duration, rhythm, and so on—are governed by which normative framework. While there may be, and perhaps always is, some ambiguity or confusion of cues when norms of affinity and trading cohere in the contemporary global North, and while participants may exploit or play with this confusion, as Bird-David and Darr (2009) entertainingly describe in Israeli customers' rejection or attempted renegotiation of their retail "gift," usually one side or other dominates. In other words, people *know* whether it is a commercial transaction or a social one, even as this knowing may change at different moments or be complicated by various relations of overlayering. LETS' difficulty was that, in trying to give community and labor (or exchange) equal weight, not only did people not know (or else diverge in knowing) what the deal was, but organizational design failed to help. Oriented to an upward cycle of community labor, LETS' design did not give adequate attention to *how* the normative temporalities brought into play would cohere. Nor was sufficient attention given to the effects any lack of coherence might have on LETS' success.

In part, then, failure came from organizational design narratives simply missing the mark. Absorbed in LETS' promise and the need to explain LETS' monetary structure, designers paid insufficient attention to the challenge of actually *combining* community and labor market time in practice, an omission made worse by the fact that both temporalities were constructed as *normative*, that is, as defining proper (and, as importantly, *improper*) behavior. However, organizational neglect was exacerbated by a second problem: placing responsibility for trading norms on individual members.

INDIVIDUAL NORMATIVITY

While those LETS established by economic development workers (and governmentally funded) operated somewhat differently, in most schemes (and especially in LETSystems) members were left entirely (or almost entirely) responsible for the terms of trade — for determining when, for how long, and with what ethos and value community labor would operate.[17] Pricing was a major factor here. One northeastern coordinator commented, "A lot of jobs are between 6 to 10 [currency] an hour . . . and professional jobs like therapies would be more like 20 or 30 . . . an hour. We've left it like that. People can charge what they're happy with really. . . . We've had a lot of people discussing, saying, 'Well, all jobs are equal, aren't they . . . ,' but we've found that whoever is doing the work can charge what they like." Jill Jordan, in her inaugural LETS talk at Findhorn in 1991, commented similarly, "*You've* got to set the price, your conditions, your standards. . . . The LETS system . . . takes no responsibility for quality of trades, or the way the two traders get on."

Certainly in some cases, norms, including temporal norms, were shared as traders came to the exchange with similar expectations and compatible practices. However, divergence among members was pervasive, as those who saw in LETS a community-oriented means of connecting with others in conditions of temporal plenitude and relaxed timing (away from the obsessive measuring and credentializing of work time), came up against others for whom LETS was, fundamentally, a pathway into the economic mainstream or an affordable means of getting goods and services within a normative structure of disembedded providers approximating (as best they could) hegemonic market norms (see Cooper

2004: ch. 8). This divergence, left in its raw state by the absence of organizational intervention, had widespread effects on LETS' vitality. The range of problems and complaints participants described affected levels of trading and growth as many members reduced or terminated their involvement; it affected how members talked about LETS to nonmembers; and it affected levels of interest among potential new recruits.

Why didn't trading activity generate new norms, potentially hybridizing community and labor market time? In the light of work in legal pluralism on the bottom-up development of new norms (e.g., Kleinhans and Macdonald 1997), what is striking in this research was LETS' difficulty in actually *creating* temporal norms. One piece of the puzzle was the limited trading activity more generally taking place. In most LETS, only a small fraction of members were significantly active, and even they rarely traded more than a couple of times a month.[18] While norm-making does not depend on dense, repeat activity alone, minimal trading combined with member passivity—unsure of the terrain on which they were operating—worked to restrict the *creative* as well as the habitual dimension of establishing and settling new norms.[19]

New norms, however, do not only derive from successful practices. Elsewhere I have argued, in line with others, that mistakes, miscommunications, and breaches can also be norm-generating (Cooper 2009). Here, again, this did not appear to happen despite incidents of nonperformance, of delay, perfectionism, exclusion, unfriendliness, and undesirable (or unwanted) offers. One factor distinguishing LETS from other contexts, such as Internet communities or casual public sex spaces, where mistakes often lead to norm growth, was the absence of an audience or witnesses. At the Toronto bathhouse, for example, norm learning and norm development were enabled by misunderstandings being watched or overheard by others, by participants discussing their own and others' mistakes in the aftermath of bathhouse events, and by organizers' swift intercession—either on the night or subsequently (for instance, through new bathhouse policies, etiquette suggestions, or rules).

Despite being a highly irregular event, the Toronto bathhouse was very much a pedagogical site. LETS, however, demonstrated a much more ambivalent attitude toward member education. While in some respects LETS were pedagogic, particularly in relation to the idea of local currencies, they (and especially LETsystems) proved far more hands-off when it came to the terms of actual trading. Thus alongside limited levels of exchange, LETS' stress on autonomous individual exchanges led mistakes to be privatized. While there was some licit sharing of reputations within schemes—who to avoid, who provided a good, skilled service—and while many people assumed a responsibility to act ethically (see also chapter 5), when it came to knowing, defining, and building *shared* community expectations and entitlements, people stumbled around. When was slow performance, for instance, a legitimate target for complaint? When did complaint represent un-community-like impatience? With minimal institutional guidance, and with considerable divergence in member perspectives and preferences as to LETS' purpose (was it mainly to make friends, to live one's politics, or to trade?), too little consensus existed to consolidate what would count as a breach below a certain high threshold. While interviewees described a range of dissatisfactions, few suggested that new hybrid norms had emerged as a result.

What of the converse effect, of norm *differentiation*? Did the cleavage between community and labor market temporalities *intensify*, as practice (or at least expectations) solidified along contrasting normative lines? Such an argument is tempting, but my interviews don't clearly support this conclusion. It's not apparent that members became increasingly aligned with community or labor market temporal norms. Indeed many members continued approvingly to describe the virtuous cycle of community labor even as their actual involvement suggested otherwise. But in a context where exit carried far fewer costs than voice, unmet expectations led trading to decline as members pulled back or left. One former organizer and participant from the North Midlands remarked, "Say I'm trading with you and I do a job for you that isn't that good, and you're also caring-sharing. You want to say I've done a crap job, but you like me so much you can't actually bring yourself to say it. . . . You go away with a sense of dissatisfaction. Two trades down the road you think, 'I'm fed up with LETS and want to leave.'"

WIDER TEMPORALITIES

Central to networks such as LETS is their open, multilayered interaction with the world around them, a web of relations accentuated by the regular passage of participants to and fro (see chapter 1). Alternative currency networks are not spatially distant utopias involving long, arduous journeys. And for most LETS participants, getting there required little more than a bus or car ride, although for some participants even this proved too much. But geographical proximity (between participants) wasn't the only or even the most important kind of connection. LETS' contact with and proximity to other economic systems was also important. The operation and experience of LETS as a new kind of local currency network, including, specifically, its *temporal* operation, was shaped by and tied to the experience of other economic places. And as a supplementary rather than self-sufficient economic structure, LETS' success depended heavily on how it intersected with mainstream economic time.

This relationship was not wholly antagonistic. To the extent that particular LETS networks forged pathways into work, their temporal aspirations were compatible with mainstream economic norms even if, for the most part, such temporal norms remained inadequately actualized within LETS themselves. Local currency networks also proved compatible with mainstream temporal arrangements to the extent the latter created "spare time" envelopes for particular constituencies to participate in trading, often due to their enforced exclusion from mainstream work. Refugees, chronically disabled people, those without employment, and pensioners could, at least in theory, make use of LETS' opportunities to practice new skills, gain otherwise unattainable goods and services, and develop or sustain social networks (Seyfang 2001b; Smets and ten Kate 2008). Moreover when LETS were located in geocultural localities that shared their slower, relationship-prioritizing, consumption-reduced rhythm, they seem to have been more successful. As one organizer in southeast England commented, "When it really works and works well, is when it's in your life and it's in balance." Peter North (2007: 137) reached similar conclusions in his New Zealand research: "Green dollar exchanges worked for those who understood their rhythms; whose livelihood strategy . . . was strengthened through membership of the network."

Yet for the most part, in Britain LETS' combination of a loosely *actualized* community time and *unattained* labor market time placed networks in tension with the wider temporal norms members had either internalized or felt forced to accommodate as they tried to stitch LETS' threads into the not fully chosen temporal fabric of a much more complex life. Of course, sewing different temporalities together, or managing their interaction and copresence, is not inherently problematic. Carmen Leccardi (1996: 177) writes, "Qualitative, non-homogeneous different times coexist in a sort of constantly reconstructed equilibrium"; we can identify this coexistence in how people choose activities, such as leisurely dining or fast, high-adrenalin sports, for the contrasting tempo and rhythm they offer. Yet with restaurant eating and sports, timing and duration are, for the most part, relatively bounded and clear. Certainly some participants experienced and understood LETS also as a contained leisure activity, but LETS' own temporal structure was, as I've described, more ambitious. LETS required members to be available for work outside of "office" hours and to respond flexibly to requests as and when they came in. The LETS advocate Liz Shephard (1997: 25) commented, "You can fit LETS exchanges around a busy schedule." LETS asked members to repeatedly consider, and when necessary to revise, their offers and wants, to ensure trading happened—part of a shared, collective obligation to keep the local economy flowing.

Some participants no doubt appreciated the "other time" LETS enabled, even produced, with its more relaxed tempo and socially oriented attentiveness. But for many, LETS' slower, less clock-based working practices constituted simply another, voluntarily acquired, but nonetheless demanding "to do." Amid the complex planning, sequencing, coordination, and compression of daily life, this was a "to do" that only *created* time—in the sense of inserting new activities into the day—at some cost, as a LETS organizer from southwest England explained: "It came to a point where two of us who were on the admin team and had been on the admin team for ages just felt that it was time for us to stop and that it was taking too much of our time. And when the two of us pulled back, unfortunately nobody else came forward, and so I think that was kind of the beginning of the end."

Moreover while those members with more income and less free time may have applauded LETS for its community-building (rather than trading) potential, questions of time efficiency and effectiveness—not just in trading but also in *building sociality through trade*—emerged. For these members (and, even more, *potential* members), LETS time got carved out of the high pressured remainder of nonworking hours, and while trading *might* build social relations, it was not necessarily considered the best way of doing so. As a coordinator from northeast England commented, "People get quite busy and are quite happy to join in on a social basis. . . . They're not that bothered about the trading aspect. . . . We have a few members [who] just like the idea of LETS and don't actively trade." An organizer from the North Midlands similarly remarked, "I think people are either socially orientated—wanting to make friends; economically oriented—they want to trade; or politically orientated—they're looking for an alternative kind of lifestyle community-type thing. . . . The top two would be political or social so they're not actually bothered about trading; it's all a bit of an excuse to make friends or prove that they're doing a political thing. . . . We've all got a mixture of the three motivations, but trading is always a sad third, it's always Cinderella."

Concluding Remarks

In a context where LETS, through the momentum of community labor, seemed guaranteed to thrive, this chapter has considered why British LETS failed to grow, centering on the part played by discordant temporalities. In the inattention paid to time within LETS' design, in the reliance placed on individual members to establish norms of good conduct, and in the force of wider temporal pressures on LETS practice, we can find reasons why community and labor time did not cohere. But while discordant temporalities pulled against the virtuous cycle LETS' proponents promised, to what extent was community labor truly absent? Certainly as an idea, community labor was expressed in many forms and forums, verbal and documentary. And as an expressed idea, community labor had effects. The promise that trading would build community and that the social connections to result would, in turn, enhance trading was exciting and infectious; it inspired many people to join LETS. But, alone, however much this idea was expressed, it was not enough to sustain the optimistic interest and participation LETS required to grow. Something else (or more) was needed—namely community labor's *practical actualization*.

The suggestion of this chapter is that community labor, as an actualized cycle, failed to take shape. When we search for something resembling the claims LETS' advocates made, we cannot find it. But does this mistakenly assume that actualization will replicate what is desired or promised, in other words that conceptual lines are lines of resemblance? What if actualization necessarily differs from what is imagined, as Elizabeth Grosz (2005) explores? Certainly a version of community labor, resembling some of the claims made about it, was evident in practice. Those I spoke with described instances of friendly trading, and consistently people talked about trading happening far more between people known to each other. But if, for the most part, trading did not precipitate social connection leading to further trading in any extensive way, can we find community labor actualized in a different form, namely in its failure? Was community labor in some sense present in the patchy, thin character of the virtuous cycle realized, in the inability of such a cycle to grow, and in the actions LETS members took as a result of their networks' lack of lift-off?[20] In other words, did a form of actualization (that did *not* resemble the community labor imagined) exist, a form that generated new, intensified forms of imagining that, in turn, produced further practical efforts to do more? Finding community labor in this dynamic loop of increased effort reminds us that community labor (like other concepts) is not a freestanding finished state—an autonomous, self-sustaining phenomenon—but a *process*. As such, perhaps community labor *can* exist in the problems and challenges faced and in the urging, endeavors, and efforts repeatedly put by some into its achievement.

Yet while it is worth remembering that failure can be a kind of action, and certainly can be an action with consequences, identifying community labor's presence in such manifest failure begs the question: What follows? For the value of the community labor imagined and expressed lay in its promise that LETS would grow and flourish through the upward cycle assured. If community labor exists instead in a very different material form, for instance, as failure or as intensified effort, its effects are then quite different. While we cannot know what the effects would have been had the community labor actualized resembled its imagining, what did clearly emerge were the effects of community labor's *struggle* to take shape: in demoralization and participant withdrawal; in the difficulties that attempts to generate a significant influx of new members faced; in organizer fatigue; and in the spinning off of LETS socializing as members enjoyed the events and activities that organizers put on but felt no impetus (other than sometimes guilt) to actually trade.

This chapter has focused on the factors shaping conceptual lines, particularly the movement from imagining to actualization. In the chapter that follows I reverse direction as I continue to explore the life of concepts within everyday utopias. Focusing on a concept that was actualized, but in very different ways from how it was explicitly imagined, chapter 7 explores the community development work performed by property at a free school.

CHAPTER 7

PROPERTY AS BELONGING AT SUMMERHILL SCHOOL

It's my room, it's my space, and I have the right to say I don't want anyone here, or actually I'd like to talk to [name] who's an adult, or actually
I have [children's names] here and we're having a nice cup of tea. . . . It's
like if you lived on a street and you had people from across the street over
having tea . . . and then people walk down from three doors down and just
walk in to your . . . basically you invited *these* people for tea . . . and so you
just don't let anyone walk in off the street. . . . I'd say, "We're just having
tea. If you want to have tea, see me tomorrow."
Summerhill School teacher

In work on intentional communities, stories of property are common (e.g., Metcalf 1995; Sargisson 2010). Yet particularly in contemporary writing, these are often tales of anxiety and disappointment, as people misuse shared things, fail to work hard in
the absence of any material incentive, and feel overregulated, out
of control, and exhausted by the constant negotiation and debate
property's frictions generate. Metcalf's (1995) Australian collec-
tion is striking in its account of the gravitational pull toward individual ownership within many intentional communities as a way
of dealing with communal property's problems. But are there other
solutions? And how much is this narrative of collective ownership's
failure and private property's rise contingent on a particular conception of property?

This chapter focuses on property, what it is and what it does
within a residential, intergenerational community. In contrast to

the previous chapter, which explored the failure of imagining to take effect, as narrated conceptual lines were stymied from materializing, this chapter explores a concept, property, that did take effect, even as it failed to be imagined. Or, to put it more precisely, property was imagined, but the conventional form this took did not capture the more innovative and embedded ways in which property was actually practiced. Trying to render innovative social practice intelligible (or imaginable) is, as I discussed in chapter 2, a key dimension, but also a key challenge, for utopian conceptualizing, which doesn't start from scratch, but enters into the middle of conceptual lines already drawn from which it does its work. In contrast to those conceptual approaches that focus on the work concepts do when they are unrecognizable and unsettling, here intelligibility is oriented to creating forms of imagining that can re-present practice in ways that are empirically recognizable (the "ah yes" moment) even if unorthodox. My aim though is not simply to capture the property relations at work in the school—a capture that is intrinsically interpretive, selective, and purposive. I also want to explore what it is that the property relations I have identified actually *do*.

The stage for this discussion is Summerhill School, a predominantly residential, private school, established by the influential education theorist A. S. Neill in the early 1920s and still flourishing almost a hundred years later, on the outskirts of a small Suffolk town, Leiston, on the southern part of England's eastern seaboard.[1] With between sixty and ninety-five children attending at any one time,[2] Summerhill's fame (or notoriety) rests on two primary principles. First, classes are optional, and the decision whether or not to attend rests entirely with the child. Second, community rule-making and dispute resolution involve the school as a whole through its meeting, committee, and ombudsman structures. One striking feature of Summerhill is the extent to which children as well as adults use the school meeting to raise grievances and establish new "laws," whether these relate to others' behavior at bedtime, use of one's things, or getting the community's permission to be exempted from particular requirements (or prohibitions). Underpinning these principles of optional classes and community adjudication is Summerhill's foundational commitment to democratic self-government and children's freedom.

Summerhill School has often been dismissed by critics as a dystopic *Lord of the Flies* kind of place, where an infantile rule of tyranny and lawlessness prevails (see Jessop 2009). But it can also be read as an everyday utopia. Both readings frame the school as a place of self-regulating children and collective governance; however, what a utopian reading also emphasizes, in the face of dystopic characterizations of Summerhill as a place of chaos, is the careful, reflexive actualization of an ambitious dream about how children should be raised and educated. Summerhill has long been an iconic and inspirational site globally, despite being largely ignored by Britain's educational establishment. As the head teacher (principal), Zoe Readhead, commented when I interviewed her, "From time to time . . . South Korean education ministers will pop in, but English ones—never." Since its inception, Summerhill has also motivated other educators, internationally, to create schools along similar lines (see Ho and Hindley 2011), and pupils attend Summerhill from many places, including Israel and Brazil, as well as continental Europe, Japan, and South Korea (Korn 1990).

Together children and adults create and experience home life. As a residential community, Summerhill provides a place of dwelling in the commonsense meaning of the term: somewhere lived in, comfortable, and generative of multiple interpersonal attachments. For the teacher quoted at the start of the chapter, what Summerhill resembled most keenly was a small village, with its flows, casual interactions, and engendered sense of familiarity. Children and adults certainly pass regularly through the school gates (when going into town, out on school trips, or once they have finished their education or employment there), but for the period during which they are members their lives are lived in and around an old Suffolk house and its assorted buildings nestled in wooded grounds. In this way Summerhill differs from sites such as LETS, where community trading time occurs in heteronomous spaces and as such is dependent on what can be carved out of an already busy life. As a residential community, Summerhill establishes its own space and creates its own time divisions. Moreover with its family-like ethos, and strong boundaries between inside and out, the school contrasts with the other sites of this book. Yet in certain respects there are similarities. Summerhill is very much an *everyday* utopia, and, like the other sites explored, it operates through routines, laws, and ways of doing things that have sedimented over time in response to the many practical challenges of running a successful boarding school.

A criticism often made of community life is that it imposes sameness

The main school building, during the school's 90th birthday celebrations, June 2011. Image courtesy of Zoe Readhead, head teacher, Summerhill School.

upon members. As an empirical claim about Summerhill School, the allegation of homogeneity clearly misses the mark. Certainly the school has unifying elements in its development of strong attachments, shared values, and effective external boundaries. At the same time, the school is a space of variation. Not only is it home to children and adults of very different backgrounds, interests, and ways of behaving, but it is also a space strongly committed to what I refer to in this chapter as a *variegated social*. Summerhill is not organized around a singular mode of communal living in which all practices and relations, for instance, are public, visible, and accountable. Nor does it go to the other extreme and demand that members live lives of solitude, great intimacy, or individualism. Rather the school manifests a spectrum of relations, norms, and practices. These can be thought of as variegated in the sense that streaks of difference coexist; as Neill (1945: 33) remarked, "Everyone should be in a position to have . . . a community life and a private one at the same time. . . . I . . . have day dreamed of a school where every child could have a private and public life."

Yet building and sustaining a variegated social is no mean achievement in a close-knit intergenerational community. Drawing on field research diaries and interviews with school members,[3] I argue that a key factor in its accomplishment is Summerhill's property structure and practices. On the surface, Summerhill emulates the turn toward individual ownership and personal control within many residential communities as mentioned at the start of this chapter. Indeed one of the things that most struck me during early interviews at the school was the level of control that individual teachers had over their classrooms and the importance given to this control within the school's organization. Teachers established the rules, policies, and tone for their teaching spaces, with the right to exclude children who did not conform. One teacher told me, "It's very gratifying and nice to know this [classroom] is my space and I have a say over how it's used and by whom." While the classrooms seemed particularly subject to individual authority, managing space by making particular people accountable for its use seemed to have a more general application. Another teacher remarked, "There's times when the library was a communal space but there was no one responsible for it.... It was trashed, so if you assign someone as responsible for a space. . . . then people will respect it more because it's tied to the person responsible for it." Neill (1968: 133) makes a similar point about the care of communal *things*:

> I concluded that what was wrong was that the tools were used communally. "Now," I said to myself, "if we introduce the possessive element . . . things will be different."
>
> I brought it up at a meeting, and the idea was well received. Next term, some of the older pupils brought their own kits of tools from home. They kept them in excellent condition and used them far more carefully than before.

Yet despite these explicit assertions of the importance of individual possession and control, the way property works at Summerhill is not simply about belongings. Underpinning and woven through more conventional notions of ownership are other forms of *belonging*. Of course, these can be understood as something other than property. But the argument of this chapter is that recognizing their entanglement in and sometimes substitution for the more conventional, propertied subject-object form makes possible a more complex and fuller understanding of how Summerhill works. It also, importantly, provides a conception of property that challenges the disembedded, fungible, neoliberal form that dominates in the global North. In other words, reimagining property in terms of belonging can contribute productively to a transformative politics that has tended to get stuck in questions of property's distribution at the expense of rethinking its form (a limitation of equality thinking also; see chapter 4). However, property as belonging is not a new ideal; its limits are important also, as I explore.

Approaching property as belonging, I should stress, did not reflect the *explicit* ways ownership was discussed by those I interviewed. At the same time, it did cohere with school members' more idiomatic use of property and ownership's terms. In a sense, this more figurative resemblance is unsurprising. For it is in the idiomatic language of community members—in the drawing of concepts from other contexts and the hybridized creation of new ones—that the distinctive ways in which a particular community works can be identified. The nuance and attentiveness grasped through idioms contrasts with the more formal use of concepts, which (as here with property) betrays the power and influence of mainstream discourse.

A Property Framework

To understand property at Summerhill, I want to start with a rather different property paradigm, that of conventional private ownership. Here a single actor has (almost) unlimited control over a thing or land, with rights and powers that range from access and manipulation, to sharing, selling, and destroying. Conventionally such property is legally understood as a relationship between the owner and the rest of the world in terms of a thing (or space) that is recognized and protected by state law. Organized around exclusion or noninterference by others, this model of property ownership bestows the (absolute) right upon a human subject to determine how and by whom the thing is used and treated. Certainly in contemporary practice this Blackstonian model of mastery or dominion is complicated in all sorts of ways. There are limits on what we can do with the things we own, which vary according to what is owned; property rights are often divided, so one person might have rights of use, while another has rights to sell (or destroy).

Applied to Summerhill, a conventional model that incorporated the complexities and limits of contemporary legal ownership would tell us something about how property works at the school. In particular it would shed light on the power vested in individual forms of ownership, from school members' ownership of their personal effects to the school's ownership of their fees and the head teacher's ownership of the school. However, it would also miss a lot of what goes on. It would miss the legal orders recognized and enforced by the school (but disregarded by the state); it would miss the overlapping character of property rights, powers, and freedoms as rights variously granted by state, school, and community custom meet and fold over each other; and it would miss the ways relations of property and governance blur into each other. Approaching property at Summerhill in conventional terms would give us, in short, a disappointingly thin picture of school life, missing much that is innovative and effective about the school's practice. How else, then, might we think about property?

BELONGING

> According to the original sense of "property," the thing possesses me,
> I belong to it and am identified by it. But according to the modern sense
> of "property," I possess the thing, it belongs to me.
> — GRAHAM 2010: 27

While belonging is conventionally seen as descriptive of the *already* propertied relationship, as in "this house belongs to me," I want to treat belonging as central to the *formation* and assumption of property relationships, decentering in the process the pivotal role conventionally given to exclusion. But what kind of belonging is this? In this chapter, three variants are in play. The first is the one conventionally (and *exclusively*) associated with property. Here an object, space, or rights and freedoms over it, are held by (belong to) the owner. Property scholars often think of this form of belonging through the metaphor of a "bundle of sticks," in which the different powers and rights that property can bestow are imagined as discrete sticks; one stick might be a right of access or possession; another might be the right to sell or to destroy.[4] This approach means the range of sticks and the thickness of the bundle can vary depending on the nature of the belonging—in some cases near to "full-blooded" (Harris 1996), in other cases as much more limited.

What stands out about belonging as a bundle of sticks, for my purposes, is the ease of severability. Rights can be pulled apart, and both rights and the thing over which rights are held can be separated from the owner (see Penner 1997). This means sticks can be distributed among participants, including (as experienced at Summerhill) in interlocking and mutually dependent ways, where the use of one stick, such as a right of access, depends on others' use of their sticks also, including their rights to sell, improve, or destroy. But what this "bundle of sticks" form of belonging also suggests, in contrast to the two other sorts of belonging outlined below, is fungibility. The right or thing is replaceable, but so too, in a sense, is the rights' holder, since a change of owner is assumed not to lead *in itself* to a change in the right or thing that is owned. I shall refer to this first kind of belonging as *subject-object* belonging to highlight the instrumental, hierarchical relationship that is imagined between the actor and the severable right, thing, or space.[5]

Belonging, however, can take other, less instrumental and less obviously agentic forms. Part-whole belonging, for instance, identifies a *constitutive* relationship between two (or more) bodies, where the formation of each is dependent on the relationship itself, as when a child "belongs" to a family or a garden "belongs" to a residential dwelling. To talk about belonging as a constitutive relationship means something broader than Margaret Radin's (1993) "property for personhood," a formulation in which certain propertied relationships are deemed vital to the expression and development of self. Radin's influential approach largely centers on items already in the (potential) property category. By contrast, this chapter works from the premise that other *social* relations can be thought of in this way, including child-family, citizen-nation, and religion-cultural formation. While these forms of belonging often take an asymmetrical form, a child belongs to a family in ways that aren't quite reciprocated (Does a family belong similarly to the child?), what matters is that the relation is dynamic and mutually formative. In other words, each part takes shape in and through the other. In this way constitutive belonging has some resemblance to understandings of property as the attributes, qualities, or characteristics of a thing—that which allows it to extend itself into or imprint upon the world. Whiteness might be (and has been) read as one such property, indicating a social characteristic that gives some people power to act (or be in the world) in particular ways.[6] Other racialized positions might also generate other kinds of property, for what counts as property is socially dependent upon wider networks and relationships, as Sarah Keenan (2010) discusses.

The third kind of belonging, proper attachment, relates closely to constitutive belonging and is sometimes used to characterize the subject-object relationship. Here belonging (as in "I belong here," "my country belongs to me," or "he belongs with his mother") identifies a relationship of proximity, attachment, or connection. Floya Anthias (2006: 21) writes, "To belong is to be accepted as part of a community, to feel safe within it and to have a stake in the future of such a community of membership." We might think of this kind of belonging through the notion of proper or rightful place: where you belong, or what you belong to, is shaped by who else belongs. And, as I discuss below, through belonging organizations, nation-states and neighborhoods can hold property (or expectations of propriety) in their members. Yet attachments can also be forged counterhegemonically, through political projects oriented to generating new kinds of legal belonging. Campaigns, for instance, advocating lesbian and gay relationship recognition might be read as counternormative versions of the "we" that belong (legally, socially, emotionally) together, an attachment that can also generate property in the other — as critiques of gay marriage for privatizing welfare responsibilities attest (Boyd 1999; Barker 2012). In the rest of this chapter I will refer to this form of belonging as *proper attachment*.

RECOGNITION

Belonging may be central to property relations, but not all forms of belonging count. Working across the relations actualized at Summerhill School, as well as wider propertied imaginings, we can think of property's conceptual lines as requiring not just belonging but also authoritative practices. These practices, formal and informal, collective and individual, singular and routine, give recognition and entitlement to some relations of belonging, while ignoring, discounting, or rejecting others (Alexander 1998); indeed we might think of property's necessary recognition as the actualization of imagining based on imagining what is actualized.

Bestowal of recognition has both a formative and an entrenching character. It encodes things, relations, and claims as having *become* propertied, as well as confirming, through adjudicative and other practices, those relations of property deemed already to exist — even as such relations may be creations (back-filled) at moments of conflict or dispute. In other words, recognizing property relations may institutionalize or authorize informal past practices of collective or intersubjective property acknowledgment. They may also produce such propertied pasts as ontologically necessary, in the way some creationists claim God, like a set designer, created fossils to invoke a seemingly older world.

Yet while creationists focus on the one God, Summerhill practice suggests property recognition is far more pluralistic. I suggested earlier that to notice only state-recognized property relations at the school would miss a great deal. Consequently I want to approach property at Summerhill as a web of relations that hold a legally pluralist shape (see generally Griffiths 1986; Merry 1988; Tamanaha 1993; also chapter 6). The state may recognize property, in the sense of constituting or responding to certain relations of belonging (and their infringement). However, from the vantage point of the school, official state law is supplemented, displaced, and sometimes directly challenged by school bodies engaged in "legal" declarations or law-like practices. Such practices include unofficial, but still formal, declaratory acts by the school meeting or head teacher, as well as the informal, regular intersubjective sayings, doings, and expectancies that express and sustain the school's property ethos and culture.

The value of legal pluralism to opening up a more layered understanding of Summerhill's property practices can be seen in a few short examples. The first two highlight Summerhill's capacity and commitment to create and recognize property beyond state law; the third focuses on the relationship between different law-making bodies. Probably the most important property entitlement Summerhill members acquire when joining the school is a vote at its meeting, which takes place at various points weekly. While this property is obviously not recognized by the state and only figuratively identified as property by school members, owning one's vote is nevertheless central to Summerhill's ethos. Equally central are the constraints placed on what such ownership means; votes cannot be bought or sold. Readhead commented, "Everyone knows it's one man one vote." She went on, "One of the most serious things you can do is give people a hard time because of how they voted" (a reference to a case brought up at the meeting the day before).

A second example of property's establishment concerns not what the school allocates but what it recognizes as having emerged. In conventional schools, children regularly acquire presumptive property rights to the things they create, such as paintings, essays, and sculptures. But at Summerhill this liberal mode of property creation is taken further as children gain a form of locally recognized ownership over certain physical structures. One teacher explained, "Some kids built huts [in the woods], and they become the property of the builder." These kinds of rights are of course limited; they don't include the right to sell a hut to a non-Summerhillian or to retain it after leaving the school. However, within these parameters, the rights are recognized and internally justiciable. Indeed, claims to land can be "brought up" at a school meeting if they appear excessive.[7] One teacher described a case where a boy claimed possession of a part of the school grounds that he had cleared of nettles. He was brought up at a school meeting on the basis that the space he had recoded as settled was too large, its boundaries too expansive.[8] However, after discussion, the school meeting declared that the boy's labor and property assertion had transformed and redefined the space, which was now temporarily his.[9]

While Summerhill creates and recognizes property rights and freedoms far more fine-grained than those recognized by the state, its property framework is also affected by state law in numerous ways. Perhaps the most straightforward of these is the power given to school members whose property is officially recognized; the rights vested in Readhead, the school's legal owner, is one obvious example of this. A more subtle instance of how Summerhill ownership is affected by the state can be seen in the case of the school's laws. An important part of the Summerhill tradition is the ability of the meeting to vote down any, including *all*, of its laws and to live without them until they are gradually voted back in (see Appleton 2000: 112–15). In that context, I was struck during one research visit by the account of a recently arrived teacher who tried to abolish the laws and found it impossible because state-driven health and safety concerns meant many laws had to remain in place and could no longer be abolished. When interviewed, he commented on the frustration he thought children felt from having lost *ownership* (or perhaps authorship) of the laws. What remained to the school, he suggested, was mere ownership over the means of implementation.

CLARIFICATION, SIMPLIFICATION, AND DEFINITION

If property is about the authoritative recognition of different relations of belonging, processes of simplification become important as they work to clarify and define.[10] Simplification also takes shape through codification, as complex processes and networks get reframed to appear as things in relationship (Strathern 2004). In this sense codification flattens social life so it becomes intelligible even as a legally pluralist approach recognizes and works with multiple overlapping and intersecting codes. But property is not simply an intangible form of ordering. It also works as a coding that marks, from the fences around land that demonstrate ownership to the requirement in many boarding schools that children have name tags in their clothing (a policy that in its differentiated signaling of the school, family, and children's own identity gestures to the plural character of children's ties of belonging).

Coding simplifies and clarifies. It produces greater definition, establishing contours and boundaries around propertied things (Underkuffler 2003: 21–23), as well as around relationships to them. Gray and Gray (1998) comment that conceptual clarity and definitional boundaries are particularly important when property rights are understood as intangible abstractions rather than physically verifiable items — relations to others, for instance, rather than things. At Summerhill many relations and forms of belonging take on the solidity of property only when contestation or conflict causes definitional processes to become activated. These definitional processes aim to sort out and establish the contours and limits of the propertied relationship — how rights, freedoms, and responsibilities are distributed in relation to particular things and spaces. Nevertheless in the process, the familiar, habitual complexity of everyday school life comes into sharper relief.

POWER

If a central aspect of property is the social work it performs, power as a dimension of property becomes important. In other words, property's coding as object, attachment, or part depends on the capacity of such coding to make a difference. Gray and Gray (1998: 15) describe property as "an abbreviated reference to a quantum of socially permissible power exercised in respect of a socially valued resource." This does not mean that spaces, things, or relations are fully without power when recognition as property is denied. Nor does it mean that property's power is necessarily effective or accomplishes what is expected. Nevertheless the force that property relations and practices possess (or acquire) identifies an organized quality capable of generating both constitutive and more mediated effects.

At Summerhill, however, the nature of such effects when it comes to exercising power over the propertied things themselves is fairly restricted. From the perspective of the school (as opposed to the state), there are few contexts in which the owner is sovereign, with dominion over a sphere of indefinite and undefined activity, where little is prohibited. Teachers may have dominion over their classrooms, but they cannot sell or destroy them. Even in the case of personal possessions, when it comes to children's things, age-based restrictions limit the ability to sell, loan, or give them away, a strategy that protects, but also limits, children's property rights. Yet property's power isn't just about what can be done *to* propertied objects or the way power is expressed within the relationship itself. It also concerns property's "extroverted" power—its capacity to act on other processes and relations, as I explore below.

Intimate and Personal Life

As I suggested earlier, Neill (1968) saw private ownership as a way of promoting commitment and care in the use of things. Drawing on property as belonging, I want to consider property not as a means of maintaining well-looked-after things and spaces, or at least not entirely. Rather my interest is in the way authorized and defined relations of belonging (that is, property) contributed to Summerhill's character as a variegated social space, combining (in close temporal-spatial proximity) personal, public, and boundary relations.

For intentional residential communities, the challenge of combining privacy and publicity has often been fraught. While some secular communities may prioritize members' private life, more common to progressive twentieth-century communal living has been a championing of public norms (e.g., Kanter 1973a). Yet, as with common property, attempts to live publicly have given rise to community strain; kibbutzim are far from the only instances where, over time, the balance of living has reverted toward more private modes of living. Even where residential communities desire to sustain simultaneously both private and more public norms, doing so can prove challenging, particularly where people live, sleep, work, and play in the same contained space. As one Summerhill teacher commented, when discussing whether bedrooms were more private than other spaces, "My own bedroom has kids in it on a daily basis because we're watching a film or something." How, then, can intimate life be protected and enhanced when members live in close proximity to others? While mainstream property scholarship is attentive to property's many applications, when it comes to protecting and supporting intimate life, private ownership is depicted as essential. But within a property-as-belonging framework, how important is this individual subject-object relationship to maintaining an intimate life? Do other things do this work instead? Or is intimacy supported by conventional forms of property ownership embedded within wider networks of belonging?

BEING ALONE

> There's quiet withdrawal space everywhere. There's lots of places you can be alone.
>
> —ZOE READHEAD

While certain school activities are required to be undertaken privately (urinating and smoking, for instance, both involve restrictions on who else can be present), rights and powers over space can also be deployed to achieve a more *voluntary* seclusion. One such instance referred to by many I interviewed concerned the right of adults and older children to be alone in their bedrooms. One teacher stated, "It is the one place they can go to have some privacy and get away from community control."[11] For younger children, required to share bedrooms, such seclusion or alone time has to be achieved in other ways, such as curtaining off the bed or asking roommates to temporarily withdraw.

Yet while school members may attempt to use their recognized rights over bedroom space to achieve privacy and alone time, success is far from guaranteed. Children and adults I spoke with commented on the respect shown for each other's privacy; at the same time my visits witnessed several occasions in which children "brought each other up" at school meetings for unwelcome intrusions. According to Readhead, "Children are in and out of each other's spaces all the time, although there is always that right to ask someone to leave, and that's one of the main cases that come up regularly at the meeting, that people won't get out of my room."

Rights holders' adjudicative success on such occasions did codify the space as *already* theirs according to a subject-object relationship of belonging. At the same time, to the extent that challenges proved frequent, rights holders' *practical* ability to keep others out was more limited. Thus the practical accomplishment of seclusion often involved other kinds of space, bringing into play a more complex fabric of belonging than an entitlement to control or exercise dominion over a particular space or thing.[12] One such other kind of space was the school's wooded grounds. A teacher commented, "You can walk in the woods and imagine being lost. . . . The landscape allows being alone."[13]

Summerhill's grounds highlight the interlinked character of different forms of belonging. On the one hand, the grounds belong legally to the school's owner as part of her state-recognized property. At the same time, the grounds also belong *constitutively* to the school—in the sense of constituting and forging its symbolic and physical landscape. Children belong *in* the grounds because the grounds are *for* them, constituting their proper place as well as a legitimate, recognized attachment. In part, children's place and attachment come from their emotional connection and identification with Summerhill. But it comes also from members *knowing* what the grounds are, what they represent within the school's symbolic code.

Addressing seclusion as an effect of particular school spaces (or as emerging from a proper attachment to them) takes us away from the conventional propertied relationship between land ownership and privacy. Here, within the envelope of state law, it is not principally the legally recognized right of some to manipulate their soil or things that makes privacy possible. Rather being alone is, in Keenan's (2010) words, "held up" by a network of material and symbolic practices, forms of belonging that are defined, recognized, and empowered to generate effects.

AFFECTION AND DISLIKE

A second way individual property is conventionally deemed to support personal life is through its ability to create and signify partiality or affective distinctions: who is liked better or deferred to at any given moment, through the access and use they are offered in one's land and things. In this way property becomes a mechanism through which friendship, hierarchy, intimacy, hostility, and distance get forged and demonstrated. As a boarding school community, Summerhill members' ability to permit others to enter their bedrooms and to share or gift at least certain things provided a means of revealing not only long-standing affective distinctions but the ebb and flow of particular ones.[14] One teacher commented, "Obviously, there's the whole friend and not friend, and 'I don't like you at the moment so you're not going to get anything.' . . . It's quite an important way to define a social group here. . . . If you give a group of people free access to your skateboard lying around, and someone else still has to come and ask you, you're demarcating who's in your friendship group."

While saying no (or having the power to exclude) dominates academic accounts of private property, what was striking in my interviews with Summerhill members was the important role of permission. It wasn't simply that some were denied access but that some had to ask for it. One teacher remarked that new children and teachers had a difficult time managing such requests, feeling a social obligation to say yes and lend their stuff freely without knowing or seeking to find out the reputations of those who asked to borrow things. But while children and adults learned from the time they spent within the school community how to say no, strong norms of sharing were also remarked upon.

Tensions between the right to exclude and norms of inclusion highlight the ambivalent and complex relationship between commodified, constitutive, and attachment-based forms of belonging. On the one hand, property variously depicts things and spaces as belongings that also define who belongs where, while having the capacity to extend and mark attachments (that I belong with you because I let you belong in here with me). On the other hand, inclusion norms tie belonging to the collective "we." So bedrooms belong to the community both in the sense of forming a constitutive aspect of community life and in the sense that they are something Summerhillians (as people who belong together, if casually and sometimes with friction) will generally share. One effect of this, interviewees suggested, was that control over space and things was not much used to organize and disclose affective relationships in any stable or absolute sense. While "spite" chuckings-out reveal the temporary and transient use of dominion, school members commented on the importance of sharing things, and especially space, regardless of how well people got on. Thus rather than ownership and property rights being used to demarcate relationships, other practices did this work instead. One practice mentioned by several people concerned choices about who to socialize, play, or spend leisure time with; one teacher commented, "You surround yourself with the people you like. . . . In my free time I do choose [those] I'll hang out with."

According to many conservative and liberal property theorists, the contribution of ownership, possessions, and the power to manipulate or remake things and places in the production and expression of selfhood is a major reason for valuing (private) property. For Radin (1993), it is through the ongoing (creative) relationship with particular, meaningful spaces and things—through the control and the self that is vested in them—that people develop as persons. At Summerhill liberal conceptions of the possessive individual as proprietor of her person and capacities were regularly voiced, particularly when it came to children's control over their time and schedule. According to Neill (1968: 27), "The function of the child is to live *his own* life."[15] His daughter, head teacher Readhead, similarly remarked, "When you're not in class, you're your own person."[16]

In contrast to several of the other sites discussed in this book, particularly Speakers' Corner and the Toronto bathhouse, at the school wearing masks or fabricating the self is not encouraged (on the natural self, see also chapter 4). According to Stronach and Piper (2008), Summerhill is a place where you cannot pretend to be someone else. Others described how the school made it possible for children to find themselves, to realize what they liked and didn't like and what kind of person they were becoming. Readhead remarked, "I think it's being able to find that part of you which lets you be the person you really feel is you."

In supporting the development of selfhood through the establishment and protection of a sphere of personal autonomy, children's ownership of their bodies proved to be a significant aspect. This is clearly not ownership in the commodified sense; Summerhill children cannot sell their body parts, nor do they sell their labor. Rather what it identifies is property according to the two other senses of belonging: as a constitutive relation of part and whole and as a proper attachment. Children are encouraged to feel emotionally connected to, not alienated from, their bodies—a connection seen to derive from control, confidence, and practical activity. Thus Summerhill students have far more freedom over where their bodies can go than in most schools, including the freedom to stay out of the classroom. They also have freedom to partake in "risky pastimes . . . the sort of games which other children participate in outside school hours."[17]

A different area of corporeal belonging concerns rights of touch.[18] At Summerhill all members have the complete right to control who can access or touch their body. The entitlement of children to *deny* access to their bodies, whether to educators or to other children, is of course no longer educationally unusual. What stands out at Summerhill, however, is the right to *allow* touch. Indeed the school has long adopted the principle that nonsexual physical contact is an unexceptional part of school life, granted and initiated between adults and children at appropriate times. A school policy statement in 2002 commented, "Hugging, sitting on laps and other physical displays of affection are an accepted and much valued part of community life."[19]

Yet, notably, during the period of this research, physical contact had come under strain as the result of official pressure on the school to accommodate and respond to wider cultural child sexual abuse anxieties (see Stronach and Piper 2008; also chapter 4). Education inspectors in 1999, for instance, reported that "some of the physical contact between staff and pupils could be misconstrued and as such is ill-advised."[20] At least partly in response, the 2000 school staff handbook stated that staff visited by pupils at night must ensure that their door is open or that someone else is in the room.[21] The measures introduced by the school, alongside teachers' frustration at government policy,[22] highlight the contrasting understandings of propertied belonging at play. In a sense, state institutional fears about child abuse speak to a commodified conception of property in which children come to belong to adults inappropriately and as objects. In contrast, Summerhill expressed a conception of belonging far more rooted in notions of proper place and proper attachment, querying the idea that children at a school, where self-ownership, confidence, and democratic governance were affirmed, could become the commodified objects of adults' pleasure. At the same time, as this book has identified, when different conceptual lines come into conflict, certain lines may prevail. It would be too simple to say that the state's feared belonging trumped the school's more benign approach. However, the state's conception of children as at risk of objectification affected the school's ability to present—in both practical and documentary ways— children and adults as belonging together.

Producing Community Life

So far this discussion has suggested that, in contrast to liberal property claims, it is not primarily ownership (or control) over things and spaces that makes an intimate life at the school possible. From a property-as-belonging perspective, other kinds of relationships matter also. These include proper attachment: what belongs with what, as well as the constitutive relationship between parts and whole. Different kinds of authorized and recognized belonging come together to form intricate webs that are important to approach holistically rather than being split—as property jurisprudence tends to—into propertied and nonpropertied forms. But if belonging, rather than belongings, does much of the work of developing and sustaining a personal life within the school, what about that other main aspect of a variegated social world: *community* life? Property (or at least private property) is often placed in conflict with communal and public concerns, as if living in common undermines both individual ownership and the personal life such ownership is ostensibly there to protect. But if intimate and more communal ways of living are able to coexist (as they do at Summerhill), and even to support each other, what contribution, if any, does property make to building and sustaining this more collective dimension?

To understand the challenge of building such a collective life, we need to consider the kind of communal environment Summerhill sought to create. In contrast to some of the spaces discussed in this book, the dominant trope at Summerhill was that of family. According to a former teacher, Matthew Appleton (2000: 90), "The sense of being part of a huge family is a very strong one. For some kids it will be the place they have felt most at home in life. I have often heard older kids talk about their friends being like brothers and sisters." Adult Summerhillians I spoke with variously described the school as a family, a community, a village, and as a tribe. But did all children belong equally? What social factors might generate unequal forms of connection? When I asked adult school members, I was told, perhaps not surprisingly, that distinctions of national identity, class, and gender didn't impact significantly on children's relationship of belonging to the school. However, this didn't mean belonging wasn't seen as a *process*.

In the discussion that follows, I want to explore the process and place of *becoming* Summerhillian in relation to two principal dimensions of the school's community life: the development of a collective identity and the governing of public spaces and private activities. My focus is the contribution made by property rights and relations, as conceptual lines centered on belonging.

COLLECTIVE IDENTITY

At Summerhill School personally owned things can be used to establish collective identity in several different ways. One is through the visibility and informal territorialization that taking control of particular spaces with one's things makes possible. On several visits I was struck by the way younger boys used their skateboards and bicycles to structure and dominate the social economy of the forecourt. In the light of Neill's (1968) focus on young boys, I asked one teacher whether the boys' visible presence allowed them to capture Summerhill's collective identity. He demurred, remarking, "They're the most visible part of Summerhill. They're the ones that cause the most trouble. They're the ones you'll hear and see most of the time. . . . But the majority of the school are not those boys, and they also live their lives here."

A second way property can be used to establish a collective identity is when groups of children (again, often young boys), without permission, hide or ruin each other's or the school's things. These kinds of property infractions constitute a way of generating alternative, unauthorized, temporary networks of belonging; they also, importantly, provide rituals through which children (and sometimes adults) *become* Summerhillians (Neill 1968; Popenoe 1970). The school's response to property breaches, in turn, reestablishes a different collective "we." Adjudications at school meetings work to present a community that is utilitarian, nonpunitive, and inclusive, where members, importantly, recognize everyone at some point will break the law and where, through acknowledgment of wrongdoing and acceptance of a fine, Summerhillians are immediately reincorporated back into the polity.[23]

This sense of a community brought into being through practices such as adjudication establishes Summerhill as an entity that is held in common. At one level, certainly, the school belongs to Readhead; one teacher remarked, "I say [to Readhead], 'You're the boss, tell me what to do.'" He then went on to describe the difficult time teachers had who came thinking the school was a democracy: "This is a family-owned business. . . . It's not a workers' commune." At the same time, to treat the school as *only* a family business, or commodity, within a subject-object relationship misses not only Readhead's and her family's noncommodified relationship to the school but, more important for my purposes, the other relationships of ownership and belonging that exist. These might not be recognized by the state, but they are recognized by the school and form a key aspect of the school's identity as a democratic community. As Readhead commented, "Yes, it belongs to me, but it is the community that owns it. . . . When I'm talking to people . . . about the community, it is actually an entity, the community is *some* thing. . . . The meeting, to me, is us, and it's a tangible body. . . . The things that anger me a lot, in the school, are when pupils are not participating in that process on a regular basis. . . . Coming to Summerhill is . . . being a practicing member of the community." Another teacher similarly remarked, "[Children] need to feel ownership of the school to accept certain laws and limits on what they can and can't do."

Readhead's focus on the school as belonging to its current (and past) members was echoed by several people with whom I spoke. While Neill (1945: 35) himself wrote, "Summerhill is not mine: it belongs to a collective movement that embraces many," at the time of my research in 2011, this sense of a wider progressive educational community, to which Summerhill belonged, did not seem widely shared within the school. Teachers I spoke with commented on the lack of a broader supportive presence beyond occasional donations and help at times of crisis. Yet in ways that resonate with my discussion of giving in chapters 6 and 8, Readhead also described the school as "a *gift*; a working model of a very clever educator. . . . It's really important the school is here to show what actually Neill meant."

Thinking about those to whom the school belongs highlights the overlapping and intersecting character of different property formations; it is not a zero-sum relationship in which the property claims to the school by some detract from the propertied rights of others. But while propertied forms of belonging invariably raise questions of identification and attachment, they also go beyond this. It's not simply that school members are Summerhillians because the school belongs to them (or that being Summerhillians gives them property in the school). As important, if not more important, is what this propertied relationship is used to *do*.

One important dimension of this involves practices of stewardship. For official state bodies, it is Readhead who is the school's primary guardian,[24] a role teachers in the school confirmed: "Zoe still has the final word on things, so if she sees something happening that could damage the existence of the school, she can say no . . . it's not going to happen anymore" (teacher interview). But the school has sought to continue Neill's legacy in *collectivizing* (to some degree) this stewardship.

Children's participation in the stewardship of Summerhill has been an important element of the school's success. Indeed when I asked Readhead what children's ownership meant, her reply centered on what such ownership *did*: "They will defend the laws and they take on responsibilities beyond what they would like to do." But while stewardship is a propertied relationship that involves work, it is also a relationship that both produces and depends upon belonging. Children's stewardship is anchored in their attachment and deep knowledge of the school — in the ways they belong to it. But through belonging to the school as a constitutive part, the school also belongs to them as something precious and potentially fragile with which they are entrusted.

The trust and reliance placed in children's stewardship was demonstrated with particular symbolic clarity when the school appealed against the Education Secretary's "notice of complaint," which would have removed Summerhill from the private schools register.[25] Summerhill went to court to challenge the government's decision; the government proposed a compromise settlement,[26] and the school asked for time to consider it. They took over a courtroom and held a school meeting to determine collectively whether the government's offer should be accepted. Appleton (2000: 266) wrote, "There really is something extraordinary about this case in which High Court proceedings are stopped and government officials are forced to wait, while a meeting of children decide whether or not to accept their proposals." Of course, the decision to allow the school meeting to play this role lay with Summerhill's owners. But it should not be dismissed, I think, as an empty gesture. Asserting the school's signature character in the face of government attempts to make Summerhill less extraordinary, the decision also reflected a relationship of trust in which the school community, guardian-like, was enabled in holding that most valuable property: property in and property of Summerhill's future.

Beyond such external symbolic moments, children's stewardship of the school is perhaps most evident when it comes to governing its common spaces. For Summerhill, sustaining its identity over time as a democratic, self-governing community has depended upon groups of children playing this role; in those periods when responsible children have not existed in sufficient numbers, Summerhill has had temporary difficulties in maintaining its ethos and principles of operation (see Appleton 2000: 73; Segefjord 1970). For while some spaces and things are under the purview of particular adults, civic spaces and things tend to be governed by groups of kids. Organized by committee structures, Summerhillians manage the use of sensitive equipment and organize events, deploying differentiated property rights, including those of access, to do so.

Property rights also come into play in the governance of Summerhillians. Direct forms of governance can be seen in the health and safety committees, ombudsmen, "beddies officers,"[27] and investigation committees that are empowered to enter particular spaces to carry out norm-maintenance work. One teacher, discussing the investigation committee, remarked, "They have the right to search people's rooms. . . . We as staff couldn't go into people's rooms in the middle of the night . . . which the investigating committee can do." But alongside those rights of access tied to particular responsibilities are the more indirect ways regulation at Summerhill happens. Echoing Jane Jacobs's (1962) work on informal surveillance—her "eyes on the street" (although suggestively at odds with prevailing public management strategies which tend to keep older children *out* of areas, such as playgrounds, used by younger ones)— Summerhill has used access rights to keep older children *in* younger children's spaces. Yet the presence of older children who might act as a moderating force depends upon more than mere permission (or entitlement). As Readhead remarked, it may be insufficient, for instance, for older teenagers to feel common spaces *belong* to them as part of the school community, if other, more desirable spaces belong to them specifically.

Using property rights and practices to create visible subjects at Summerhill is mediated, at least in part, by subjects' *willingness* to be visible, as with the young boys skateboarding in front of the school de-

Summerhill School students hanging out in the school's woods, circa 2003. Image courtesy of Zoe Readhead, head teacher, Summerhill School.

scribed earlier. This does not mean only, or even primarily, creating an environment in which members *choose* to comply — a Foucauldian version of governing through the agency of subjects. What it means, in the Summerhill context, is giving members options, for the terms and conditions of students' belonging to the school is at odds with a policy of constant scrutiny. Against the conventional school logic of (potentially) untrustworthy subjects necessitating relentlessly visible, governable spaces, Summerhill *offers* members access to secluded time-spaces where unruly acts are possible, as well as to spaces of managed publicity. As one teacher remarked in relation to the woods, "We know what's going on in general terms but that's their place — they disappear into the woods, and then they come out." At the same time, he described the variety of indoor spaces that allowed children to access noisy, buzzy places as well as quiet, calm ones. Rights to access and, indeed, to shape particular spaces certainly make this kind of variegation possible. Yet central to the time-space distribution of activities is the forging of belonging. This is not the belonging emphasized in more conventional schools, where children *belong* at specific times in specific places. Rather it is the belonging of activities and behaviors to their own "proper time-space" as a property (or part) of Summerhill School—even as such allocations are periodically challenged, disregarded, revised, or overturned.

Boundaries

Summerhill is a place outsiders frequently enter. While a few outsiders come without license or permission, causing the school to invest in security measures to protect its spaces, things, and people, most enter invited. Education inspectors, other officials, tradespeople, and prospective parents are regular visitors. However, the group that I wish to consider involves those who attend purely out of a social, political, or educational interest in the school.

MEMBERS AND VISITORS

Outsider interest is something intentional communities regularly confront (Sargisson 2000; Skinner 1976), and communities have different means of managing it. At one extreme are those rare communities who deny an insider-outsider distinction. As Kanter (1973b: 402) describes, such communities "wish to be open to all comers . . . where everyone is welcome. . . . Some of these communes do not even make a member/nonmember distinction; whoever is there at the time 'belongs'." This approach, however, has proven less common in recent years as intentional communities work instead to differentiate between insiders and outsiders. At the same time, many communities remain keen to model their spaces, practices, and structures. Some incorporate visitors into their work schedules, thereby gaining some limited labor support while simultaneously enabling people to experience community life. A less committed mechanism (on both sides) involves scheduled visit days.

Educators, academics, and other progressives from across the globe continue to visit Summerhill, keen to witness its educational innovations firsthand. One-time visitors are formally welcomed on designated open days and looked after by a Visitors Committee member. However, in ways that echo the "limited common property regimes" described by Rose (1998: 139), which function as a commons within and a property regime without, a host of property rules work to mark, maintain, and communicate community boundaries (see also Blomley 2004a).

Management of visitors through property rules and practices is an important contributing factor in the reproduction of Summerhill as a defined and bounded community. During one set of visits, I noticed a large sign at the entrance informing visitors they could not have meals at the school, swing on the Big Beech, or use the swimming pool. Similarly school laws prohibit visitors from remaining after 5 p.m., going upstairs in the main building, or entering people's rooms without permission.[28] Undoubtedly the most symbolic marker of visitors' outsider status is the school meeting. Even repeat visitors have to wait behind the closed door of the large gathering space until their entry has been proposed by a school member and a successful vote taken.

The practical and symbolic demarcation between insider and outsider clearly has a host of effects. Yet at another level, it breaks down, unable to ensure the practical excludability it depends upon (Gray 1991). Once visitors are allowed in, spatial and temporal prohibitions can only partially cordon off sights and sounds. As a consequence, a reversal of belonging threatens in which visitors shift from being the excluded to becoming the subjects of the property relationship, with Summerhillians as their objects. This reversal, anchored in the permeability of boundaries (as well as, perhaps, being an inevitable effect of their production), reveals how subject-object and more co-constitutive forms of belonging may not only coincide but morph into each other. Inviting outsiders in and trusting supporters to enhance the school's mission unsurprisingly risk bringing into being more commodified forms of belonging, as permissions granted to sympathetic visitors to look, listen, and ask questions turns the school into an object of scrutiny. This commodified form of belonging is certainly unauthorized by the school; Summerhill does not institutionally recognize or underpin such visitor power. Nevertheless it cannot eliminate its effects. Alongside the impression a constant flow of visitors has had on the school community, wider effects are also apparent as filmmakers, reporters, educators, and academics extract and re-present the school's meaning and practices in ways that do not always coincide with the interests and agenda of the school.[29]

LEAVING THE SCHOOL

Asymmetries of access and use between school members and outsiders identify *who* belongs, in the course of determining *what* belongs and is available to them. However, equally central to the marking of boundaries are the property relations that come into play when Summerhill members leave the school grounds. Conversations with Summerhillians revealed a range of exterior market exchanges, from shopping, eating, and attending the cinema to using public transport and taxis. For the most part, these external transactions proved relatively formal, individualized, and self-interested, highlighting, as one might expect, the normative boundary members cross on leaving the school.

But while school members clearly exercise ownership rights when engaging in property transactions, does the school also exercise rights of ownership? Can children be usefully described as the effective property of Summerhill—a claim that resonates with the idea of "borrowing persons" that Marilyn Strathern (2010) explores? Unsurprisingly, when asked, members balked at the idea that they were property. And of course, the school does not meaningfully exercise ownership of its members in ways that would allow it to use, give away, or sell them. However, several examples arose in conversations about the ways children belonged to the school and the effects that followed from these recognized (if not always desired) modes of connection.

One instance concerned the harassment children feared from standing in for Summerhill. Echoing an older "siege mentality" history (Croall 1983: 187), students talked about the hostility they received in the local town of Leiston. Readhead likewise told me, "Inevitably, there are times when people can be hostile to Summerhill kids—particularly other kids, teenagers." She added, however, "I know the local tradespeople are very supportive of our children because they say what nice kids they are."

Making a good impression in this way indicates how children's belonging, enacted through representing the school, can lead to what we might call reflexive "property-limitation" rules, as children's self-management is mobilized to generate conformity to particular behavioral standards when out in town—standards that (unlike in many schools) differ from those governing behavior within the school itself. One teacher remarked, "When going into town . . . we have a whole set of laws about how they should behave. . . . They do become representatives of the school. . . . While the community cannot control their actions, you try to steer them to behave favorably towards the image of the school." Readhead makes a similar point, telling of a boy with unbrushed curly hair who set out to visit the doctor: "I said . . . 'You can't go to the doctors, they see that and they assume that we're not looking after you. You can't go with your hair in a mess. . . . Next time if you want to go to the doctor you have to clean up.' . . . It's not a school law but it's very acceptable for me to say. . . . And I'd be very happy to bring it to the school meeting. We're all aware of our image and the image we portray. . . . [Children] carry the responsibility of Summerhill with them and, certainly, ex-pupils feel that very strongly."

In these examples, children's mode of belonging to the school—as members of a community and, in some respects, as resources in a family business[30]—provides an important medium through which the boundaries between inside and out get drawn and mobilized. Undoubtedly the children are an essential, perhaps the most essential, part of what makes Summerhill distinctive, enabling and strengthening its wider brand recognition. At the same time, the distinctiveness of Summerhill as a community, along with children's felt sense of belonging to it, reveals the value of conceptual lines that stretch property beyond the subject-object relationship to encompass other kinds of institutionalized belonging. These other recognized relations of attachment, constitution, and place entwine with property's more conventional fungible form to shape how the division between inside and out will operate. As representatives—in the sense of being both delegates and reflections of the school—children extend Summerhill's presence and impact beyond the school gate, affecting perceptions of the school both positive and negative. But treating Summerhill children as belonging to the school suggests also, for the most part, that they do not belong to Leiston—just as local Leiston people do not, for the most part, belong at the school. In this way, as the school mobilizes property in its members, boundaries are not only recognized and deployed but brought into sharper definition.

Concluding Remarks

I opened this chapter with Neill and others' assertion about the importance of individual possession, an assertion heard regularly at the school, whether it related to Readhead's ownership of the school, individual items belonging to school members, or the spaces over which particular teachers or children had dominion. Yet my argument is that while conventional forms of ownership are asserted and undoubtedly matter, when it comes to understanding the work of maintaining a variegated social involving personal, communal, and external life at the school, these mainstream conceptions of property are too limited. Even if we add a legal pluralist dimension, conventional property frameworks still have us looking for mastery, dominion, exclusive control, or particular rights and powers over (or in relation to) spaces and things, if now extended to include those propertied practices authorized and upheld by community law and custom as well. Certainly including school laws and norms gets closer to the way property works (and is imagined) at Summerhill, but it still draws a line around a set of practices in a manner that places too much emphasis on exclusion and control, on the one hand, while seeming to disregard the embeddedness of practices (the network of relations and rights that belonging invokes), on the other.

Belongings undoubtedly are used to produce effects, as I have explored, but the subject-object connections between people, things, and spaces cannot be easily separated from the work of belonging as a constitutive relation of formation and as proper attachment. In this chapter I have sought to trace how a set of movements around belonging can come within property's gravitational orbit — indeed, more than this, can come to constitute a core part of how we might conceptualize property. Linking *belongings* to *belonging*, as complexly intertwined processes, is useful beyond its capacity to capture something of the governmental technologies through which Summerhill works. As a way of *imagining* property, belonging emphasizes the place of connection and relationship. Radin's (1993) "property for personhood" approach offered a step in this direction; however, it is limited by its tendency to restrict property to things and relations *already* imagined as commodifiable — understandable in the context of right-wing moves to make everything ownable. As such, and in tune with property law more generally, property for personhood works to extract certain law-like relations from a much wider web. The approach in this chapter, by contrast, has sought to *re-embed* belongings, extending and thickening property relations by reframing what property is understood to entail. At the same time, it does not treat all relations of belonging as property; recognition, power, and definition are also significant dimensions.[31]

As I suggested at the start, property has been deemed one of the most troubling issues for the development of a utopian attitude (see chapter 2). Not only is it a site of tension for utopian communities, but it is also a concept particularly subject to wishful thinking in contexts where idealistic imagining and actualization appear particularly far apart (as radical fantasies of its sought-after disappearance replace individual daydreams of personal accumulation). Yet despite the disjuncture between radical fantasies of what property could be and conventional experiences of actual property relations within the global North, these two perspectives also share common ground in that they presuppose a concept of property rooted in relations and practices of exclusion and control. The difference between utopian thinking (to the extent it eschews eliminating property altogether) and mainstream manifestations thus revolves around whether property is privately, publicly, or collectively owned and whether as a social structure it is deemed beneficial, inevitable, dangerous, or redundant.

In contrast to this conception of property, the conceptual lines communities such as Summerhill facilitate, oriented to belonging rather than to control, gesture toward other ways of approaching property, ways that may hold value in other contexts. This does not mean the conception of property developed here should be just extracted and applied elsewhere as if its conceptual lines were detachable from the specific practices of Summerhill School. While these lines are informed by property thinking and struggles in other contexts, especially in relation to indigenous people's land claims, squatting, and public land disputes, they also—like these other lines—have a specificity and location that is important. At the same time, Summerhill offers resources for property's reimagination. It also provides an example of how new property lines can be generated from a site whose main contribution to a transformative politics appears to be something quite different. Property as belonging is not intended to posit a new ideal (in part for reasons discussed in chapter 5; see also Cooper and Herman 2013). Relations of belonging for some are also relations of nonbelonging and conditional belonging for others. Property's need for authoritative recognition and clarity, even if undertaken by communities themselves in democratic ways, reveals too the inherent challenges in treating congealed forms of belonging as a source of power, as those relations and resources recognized as propertied are used to generate specific effects.

Yet approaching property as belonging does also make possible other, more critical reversals in how social relations are imagined. For if belonging constitutes the heart of property, does this not also mean that property is a key dimension of belonging? Posing this question encourages us to look at relations of belonging differently, whether the belonging in question involves a nation, family, community, spouse, ethnic community, or other kind of place (see Anthias 2006; Cooper 1998; Yuval-Davis 2006). It encourages us to look at the "rhetorics of territory . . . through which we are daily urged to construct our maps of loyalty" (Massey 2005: 185), and it incites us to inquire about the property that is granted subjects by such relations. This is not necessarily (perhaps not usually) property as commodity (although of course slavery is exactly this). However, it would be naïve to assume that those collective forms of belonging that are conventionally celebrated don't bear their own propertied nexus, whether it is the authorized right of a parent to control his child, of a spouse to alimony, of a state to conscript its citizens, or of Christianity to make claims on England's culture and laws. Exploring the kinds of property to which different relations of belonging give rise thus draws our attention to the agency that property grants those persons, entities, and also communities that attract and hold the belonging of others.

In chapters 6 and 7, I have explored in different ways how social economies generate (or don't generate) community. In chapter 8, the last of my six studies, I maintain this focus as I examine how "trading" words can generate and be integral to a community of strangers involved in pleasurable, sometimes risky, sometimes theatrical encounters. The chapter's focus is Speakers' Corner. Drawing on the well-established trope of a marketplace of ideas, I consider the relationship Speakers' Corner delineates and makes actual between markets and play, addressing how this relationship can take multiple coexisting forms with very different implications for thinking about the politics of the marketplace.

CHAPTER 8

MARKET PLAY AT SPEAKERS' CORNER

It's spitting rain intermittently, and Speakers' Corner is relatively quiet. About nine men are speaking, most on stepladders. One sings; another stands silently holding the Good News Bible. A woman rants at a large crowd. All I can hear is the same word over and over: *disgrace*. A younger Marxist talks about investment, strikes, profit, and the destruction of capital. A cluster of men listen to him thoughtfully. He pauses and asks for questions and contributions.

Field notes, June 19, 2011

Despite extensive use as a trope for open public debate and as a marketplace of ideas, Speakers' Corner has generated surprisingly little scholarship. Academic work that does exist tells the story of the most prominent Corner in London's Hyde Park (Coleman 1997; Roberts 2000, 2001, 2008) and the stage it sets for polyphonic speech (McIlvenny 1996a, 1996b; Roberts 2008). Elsewhere I have explored Speakers' Corner as a place of social contact (see Cooper 2006b), arguing that the prevailing academic focus on the Corner as a place of oratory and debate neglects the work such speech does in generating social relationships and unexpected stranger encounters. This chapter takes a different approach. Anchored in utopian studies' emphasis on improvisation, creativity, and play as key dimensions of change — in terms of the world that is sought, with its imaginative, noninstrumental pleasures, as well as how to get there (Sargisson 2012) — I want to explore Speakers' Corner as a place where play redirects and reframes how the market is manifested.

My reasons for doing so are twofold. First, in the light of narratives of the market's ever growing empire, I want to consider the way play might reorder and refashion how we think about the market. Left-wing writers and activists have long engaged in a very thoroughgoing critique of the market, including as a process, formation, and ideology, whose essence (despite appearances) is organized around commodities, exploitation, competition, and alienation. Jameson writes, "the rhetoric of the market has been a fundamental and central component of this ideological struggle [over social democracy], this struggle for the legitimation or delegitimation of left discourse" (1991: 263). Yet alternatives—particularly alternatives outside the traditional sphere of goods' distribution—have been more hesitantly posed, despite interesting work on the commons, cooperatives, and community economics (e.g., Gibson-Graham 2006b; North 2007). In chapter 6 I considered LETS as one small-scale economic alternative to mainstream market relations. This chapter takes a different tack. While it remains with traditional markets in the form of face-to-face embodied interactions, my focus is not primarily on the challenge of creating more egalitarian and fairer modes of generating and exchanging goods, services, and money. Rather I address what markets can do when located within another domain, namely that of play. I am not concerned, however, with how play has become commodified or subject to market relations. Rather, I am interested in what it might mean to recuperate the market, and specifically the marketplace, as a structure, ethos, and mode of interacting through play.

In doing so, and this is my second aim, I want to explore how concepts combine and articulate together. According to Mitchell Dean (2008: 26), "Concepts are terms within a network of differences, distinctions, and oppositions, and therefore do not make sense without each other." How concepts combine or interact becomes ever more complex once we recognize the material dimensions of this process; that conceptual articulations don't just happen in the realm of imagining. Chapter 6 addressed the difficulty of getting two concepts, community and labor, to practically combine. Here my focus is on two concepts that did. However, the combining of markets and play at Speakers' Corner did not take a single form but was simultaneously actualized in multiple ways. Or, to put it another way, rather than drawing a single conceptual line, as I did in relation to property at Summerhill, this chapter explores the multiple lines made possible when concepts are actualized, particularly when they are actualized in ways that remain relatively unformulated at the level of speech. In the context of Speakers' Corner, play functioned as a tool for attracting "customers." But it also provided a mode of interaction through which market relations could be critiqued and satirized, while simultaneously fusing with the market architecture of the Corner to produce a distinctive kind of enjoyable and stimulating social practice.

Recognizing the presence of different articulations is important to grasping the complexity of a site such as Speakers' Corner. But it is also important to understanding the power and effects of conceptual plurality, the way different conceptual articulations intersect, and— although this is beyond the scope of the chapter—how and when certain articulations come to dominate, impelling particular conceptual lines at the expense of others. To develop my analysis, the discussion that follows draws from a series of observational field visits to Speakers' Corner between 2003 and 2012, alongside conversations with different speakers (which ranged from banter to listening to debate) and about thirty interviews with regular participants, speakers, and one-time (or occasional) listeners.[1] The Corner was unquestionably one of the easiest spaces I researched in which to find participants wanting to talk (perhaps unsurprising since talk is what the Corner is about). In most cases, simply opening a notepad was sufficient to generate interest from regulars, who would ask what I was writing about. Regulars were also striking in their willingness to host me for short periods of time, taking me around the Corner, commenting on different characters present, and introducing me to those they thought would have something interesting to say (see also chapter 1).

Speakers' Corner

For many, Speakers' Corner constitutes a foundational, internationally recognized, liberal trope, a symbol of free expression and the marketplace of ideas. Yet this reading of Speakers' Corner, while influential, ignores the specificity of London's Corner as a geographical place, as it also risks ignoring Hyde Park Corner's radical and proletarian origins. Today many venues throughout the globe get characterized as speakers' corners, and at the turn of the twenty-first century open-air public speech spaces existed in Singapore and Sydney, among other places. Planners often design or promote speakers' corners, not necessarily with success, as part of revitalizing and rebranding delineated urban spaces. Speakers'

A crowd listens to a speaker at Speakers' Corner, Hyde Park, London, 2011.
Photo courtesy of SBImagery.

corners can also be found in the form of highly mediated and controlled "right of reply" outlets within the mass media. But the Speakers' Corner at the center of this discussion is the most famous. Located at the northeast corner of London's Hyde Park, the Corner covers a relatively small scrap of land, one that is easy to miss. However, on Sundays it is filled with speakers, hecklers, and crowds, listening, asking questions, arguing, observing, and using the venue as a place in which to meet others. On a warm Sunday there may be thirty speakers at any one time, and a thousand or more people — one-timers and regulars, Londoners and visitors — passing by in the course of a day, with a couple of police officers sometimes stationed in case of complaints or trouble.

Speakers' Corner signifies an everyday utopia in several respects. Like Summerhill School, it is very much a defined, physical place, whose spatiality allows it to create symbolic and practical boundaries that here come into play once a week.[2] While Speakers' Corner is largely subject to the same statutory prohibitions as other public spaces in terms of what can be said, it functions within the cultural imaginary as a place of free speech, where anything can be uttered. Yet in my view, what is striking about the Corner, in ways that resonate with the discussion of bathhouse sex in chapter 5, is its utopian norms of contact. At Speakers' Corner you can start a conversation with anyone. Against conventional etiquette, which suggests politics and religion should be avoided with strangers, at the Corner these form the heart of conversation. In addition, Speakers' Corner substantially disavows external status differentials. In ways that resonate with the norms of many twentieth-century U.S. nudist clubs, where occupational and status signifiers were supposed to be bracketed, at the Corner credentials bearing wider cultural capital, such as qualifications and occupation, carry little or no weight. As one speaker told me, "A rich person or someone who is somebody famous . . . can easily be put down by a homeless person in a meeting, so in that way there's an atmosphere that can undermine hierarchical power. . . . It's a very leveling atmosphere." In this respect, Speakers' Corner might be read as a utopian public sphere, a place that rejects the credentials and professional capitalization of expertise that pervade contemporary middle-class publics.

Yet the Corner is far from flawless. Aside from the relentless, ubiquitous abuse routed through scatology, Speakers' Corner is a venue where right-wing, sexist, and xenophobic remarks form a regular part of the mix. Arguably the fact that a space is right wing does not exclude it from operating as a utopia, and various scholars have written on conservative utopias (or collective longings; e.g., Fitting 1991; Herman 1997). However, given this book's orientation toward the *progressive* qualities of the spaces examined, my discussion of the Corner centers on the *critical* marketplace it established, even as its libertarian discursive ethos makes it an uncomfortable domain, and one that is often hard to like as more extreme versions of everyday prejudice get freely voiced. Speakers' Corner is also a very male space. Most speakers and almost all the hecklers are men, and the style and content of discussion is structured according to conventionally gendered norms of aggressive, combative debate and what is deemed appropriate *public* conversation (Cooper 2006b). One speaker told me, "There's a lot of male egos about, and the male ego is pushy, upfront, and penetrating," adding (for reasons not altogether clear), "So is the male penis."

Yet while homophobic, xenophobic, and sexist remarks, often uttered deliberately to provoke, seem to gesture toward conventional, if not fully authorized opinions, in other respects Speakers' Corner constitutes a space rooted in social and cultural marginality. For many regulars (although not all), Speakers' Corner offers a place of debate, proselytism, recreation, networking, and socializing for those who for reasons of economic, national, ethnic, or political powerlessness, or mental ill health, have less access to more established or conventional spaces. Regulars

I spoke with commented that the Corner provided a weekly home for eccentric characters and for people (largely men) with mental health problems. While some alluded to "crazy people" generating a spectacle that others came to watch (and consume), interviewees also remarked that the Corner was an important place for solitary, lonely, or unwell people to experience camaraderie, support, and attention.

The culture and social accessibility of the Corner, in large part due to its central location within the capital, has also facilitated its use by migrants and refugees. One speaker I interviewed, one of very few women to give regular orations, told me that in the 1940s German refugees met there. In contemporary times, groups of young Middle Eastern men gather. While some listen and engage with the more theatrical public orators, many use the space as a place for serious deliberation. These semiprivate conversations, involving small clusters of men, are a feature of the Corner usually ignored by commentators (and in the public imaginary) since they trouble the Corner's iconic portrayal as a place of *public* oratory and debate. Yet it is in these smaller gatherings that more serious speech happens, as one regular explained: "The most quiet meetings are where you get intellectual stimulation; the bigger crowds are fluff and nonsense. If you want to gauge this place, look at the small meetings."

Speakers' Corner is a complex, contradictory place. In some ways it appears to be a typical site of male camaraderie and casual misogyny, yet simultaneously it is a place where those lacking social capital or other forms of recognition have gathered. With its Hyde Park base,[3] the Corner is rooted in a long history of dissent. In his account of the Corner, Coleman (1997: 4) locates its origins in the scholars (or fools) who wandered through towns and villages in the Middle Ages, "making witty observations about ecclesiastical and secular orthodoxy." Later, Coleman argues, the radicals of the English Revolution made for the streets, forging "a key part of the founding of the outdoor speaking tradition in Britain" (6). But the specific siting of Speakers' Corner at Hyde Park's Marble Arch originates with Tyburn, an infamous place for public hangings until 1783. Before people were killed, they were allowed to address their final words to the gathering crowd (25–30). While this was expected (and indeed was often used) as a chance to repent, some offenders took the opportunity to defiantly defend their actions. John Roberts (2008: 107) writes, "During the seventeenth and eighteenth century . . . 'last dying speeches' at

Hyde Park became a place for public dialogue about diminishing customary rights against the growing imposition of capitalist social relations and the rule of private property."

For the discussion that follows, it is important to recognize the location of Speakers' Corner within a history of popular, diffuse challenges to capitalism. According to Roberts (2000: 281), "The carnivalesque behaviour of the condemned, the mocking of the law, the transgression of governance, the inversion of codes and conventions, in short, scaffold culture, repealed the sober nature of an emerging bourgeois law." From 1783, public executions were relocated away from Hyde Park to the far less observed environs of Newgate Prison. However, the late eighteenth and nineteenth centuries witnessed a series of changes and developments that brought the modern Speakers' Corner into being, as Hyde Park itself became increasingly used as a space of protest, with fiercely fought, sometimes internationalized conflicts taking place there around the franchise, economy, and statehood. The struggle to gain Hyde Park as a place for lawful expression of popular dissent was also part of a more general nineteenth-century movement to sustain open working-class spaces of assembly, speech, and protest. According to Antony Taylor (1995: 394), "Agitations for rights of access [to spaces such as Hyde Park] were conducted almost entirely outside the sphere of contemporary liberal politics. . . . In this sense they represented a genuine expression of the long-standing, independent, metropolitan radical tradition and demonstrate the uniquely plebian nature of the concern for public space in London."

Beginning in the mid-1870s, with the passing of the Parks Regulation Act in 1872, Hyde Park's Speakers' Corner emerged as a legally recognized and important site for public debate. Yet while its origins lay in the struggles of radical forces to express dissent effectively and lawfully, as a modern venue the Corner has faced other challenges. According to Coleman (1997), at one time any politician wishing to be successful in the electoral marketplace needed to present his or her views at mass meetings held in indoor and outdoor venues such as Speakers' Corner. But the status and significance of open public speech spaces changed radically with the advent and subsequent ubiquity of radio, television, and then the Internet. Speakers' Corner survived while other national, open-air venues fell into disuse. But even at the Corner, use contracted to a Sunday event at which a limited range of public politics would get aired. Many Corner advocates I spoke with described its decline from a "university of the working class" to a space of triviality, mockery, and cheap entertainment. Elsewhere I have questioned this dichotomy (Cooper 2006b). Here I am interested in addressing a different dimension of the Corner's political potential, one not based on the erudition of what is said but on the Corner's ability to manifest and open up more critical conceptions of the market (or marketplace) by articulating markets to play. I want to start with the kind of market the Corner enacted, and then consider how it got tied to play. My discussion draws on four forms of cultural expression that got assembled at the Corner (and through which the Corner itself took on shape): carnival, tasting, contact zones, and edgework. These forms provide the mediating practices through which market play, in quite different ways, was both enacted and expressed.

A Marketplace of Ideas

A man in his early thirties stands on a crate; the audience is packed tight around; in the front are two older male hecklers. The speaker reads from typed, large-font pages about the movement of industry to China. "What injection have you taken?" one heckler shouts. The speaker ignores the interruption and, swaying slightly, asks his audience, "Does anyone agree with this theory?" The heckler says he does, that his earlier objection was based on a misunderstanding. "Bring back plastic toys," he calls. The speaker announces, "I'll go back to my first point." "Oh no," says the second heckler, "not again; you're on a continuous loop." Later the second heckler says it makes a change to hear a sensible speaker, but that he should put down his pages and stop reading. The first heckler sees that I am writing notes and calls out, "Why are you taking the speaker so seriously?" The audience laugh.

—FIELD NOTES, FEBRUARY 26, 2012

When I asked speakers if the Corner was a marketplace, they largely thought it was not, since nothing was bought or sold. Nevertheless the concept of a marketplace where ideas compete, without necessarily being or becoming commodities in any conventional sense, has proved an enduring one. Accounts often start with U.S. Supreme Court Justice Oliver Wendell Holmes Jr.'s famous dissenting opinion in *Abrams* v. *United States*; there he stated, "The ultimate good desired is better reached by

A speaker talking to a regular attendee at Speakers' Corner, 2010. Photo courtesy of SBImagery.

free trade in ideas. . . . The best test of truth is the power of the thought to get itself accepted in the competition of the market."[4] Truth, on this reading, is not harmed from being surrounded by falsehood. Rather it is in the competition between ideas, in the presence of speech's worst offerings, that truth will emerge and become known (see Peters 2005). This valuation of ideas battling against each other resonates profoundly with defenders of Speakers' Corner. Many agreed that the tussle of ideas would enable the truth to win and that "bad ideas" or false claims should be deliberatively crushed rather than politically suppressed.

Advocacy of a marketplace in ideas is not restricted to the claim that bad speech brings stronger good speech to the surface. Other arguments in its favor relate to moral rights to self-expression, societal improvement and education, and the benefits individuals gain from being able to access not only the goods they need and want but the ideas they need and want also. Yet it is in this analogy between a market in ideas and one in goods and services that many critiques of the former are situated. Over some decades scholars have questioned the value (and reality) of a free marketplace in ideas, noting the legal restrictions that invariably exist in relation to certain kinds of speech as well as the harm or trauma some speech can cause (Lawrence 1990; Matsuda et al. 1993). Writers have questioned the assumption that markets in ideas lack transaction costs,[5] given that even neoclassical economists acknowledge goods and services markets have such costs; they have highlighted the inequalities of power and visibility among those who generate and consume ideas; they have questioned whether "good" ideas actually benefit from being surrounded by bad ones; and they have challenged the notion that all that good ideas need is a permissive environment (e.g., see Blocher 2008; Brietzke 1997; Ingber 1984).

Yet while legal writers, in particular, have extensively debated the normative claim that a free marketplace in ideas is possible and advisable, they have paid far less attention to the actual form and character such a marketplace might assume. Certainly there are commercial marketplaces transacting in ideas, and these have received some attention, but if the marketplace of ideas extends beyond the commercial realm to include other spaces where ideas freely compete, how should we think about these kinds of markets? In contrast to the dearth of writing on the character of marketplaces wherein ideas are traded for free, a rich vein of writing exists within geography, tourism studies, social anthropology, and sociology on other kinds of sociable marketplaces.[6] Such work has considered the distinctive character of local markets as informal places where interpersonal contact happens and community is forged; the particular camaraderie of casual rather than more intense or intimate interactions; the economic regeneration and tourist flows of staged or festive marketplaces; and the way class and ethnicity cohere in trading sites that range from suburban malls to indoor flea markets and bazaars.[7]

Speakers' Corner shares many features with such goods-based marketplaces. It is a regular, weekly event in a defined place, facilitating lively face-to-face interactions. It involves a diverse array of speech-based "products," with different speakers competing for attention and interest. Like street and community marketplaces, the Corner reveals considerable diversity in the ethnic, educational, and economic capital of its users, who include one-timers, occasional attendees, and regulars. And like many other marketplaces (or spaces of exchange), the varying regularity and intensity of participants' presence shapes the quality and quantity of attention received in return (see also chapters 5 and 6). Moreover, in common with other markets, Speakers' Corner has a strong self-regulating dimension. Although it is formally governed by state law, the character and ethos of the Corner owes much to its own evolving norms, even as, like other marketplaces, it is not a fully compliant or orderly space. Despite restrictions on particular kinds of speech — such as swearing, blasphemy, sedition, and hate speech—transgressions occur. Similarly prohibitions on selling pamphlets and other materials are breached, as are, occasionally, prohibitions on physical assault.

Yet despite some similarities, Speakers' Corner, in common with liberal jurisprudence's imagined marketplace of ideas, reveals one major distinction from the marketplaces that social anthropology and social geography conventionally explore. At the Corner, for the most part, no formal trading takes place. Certainly other marketplaces aren't solely concerned with things exchanged or sold. Thomas Tiemann (2008: 475), writing about the social quality of farmers' markets, talks about "old-timers" who come with little to sell but who are able to "add much to the conversation." Crewe and Gregson (1998: 41) also comment, "We thus need to move away from a utilitarian view of exchange, to see consumption as a social experience as well as an economic transaction; as exploration as well as exchange; as full of fun and sociality." However, what kind of marketplace can it be where *no* trading takes place at all, where there is no payment, transactional moment, purchase, or withdrawal from circulation of the acquired thing?

Certainly, examples exist of markets without paying customers; the transformation of British welfare provision since the 1980s is one prime example (Clarke and Newman 1997; Newman and Clarke 2009). Alongside the influx of private, commercial service providers, the development of public markets forced state providers to compete for clients and users (against other public providers as well as, increasingly, commercial for-profit bodies). The intelligibility of these arrangements as markets suggests a *direct* transaction involving payment is not necessary for a field to be imagined as a market. But if markets are imagined within mainstream thought as encompassing more mediated forms of exchange, where individual recipients don't directly purchase a service but payment comes instead from another (usually state-based) source, can markets (or marketplaces) meaningfully operate when no payment takes place at all? Chapter 6 considered the case of LETS, a trading structure that has been characterized as gift-like despite its use of local currency payments. If gifting can happen when things are paid for, can a market exist even when things are given away?

In William Morris's ([1890] 2003) utopian novel of the future, *News from Nowhere*, markets have become little more than distribution points for food and other produce (see also Levitas 2013). The notion of markets as places where goods are collected, without payment, offers one way of reimagining what marketplaces might *become*. But does a lack of payment or direct exchange necessarily mean that nothing comes back in return? Approaching the concept of the market through Speakers' Corner, we might look beyond the direct encounter to other, more mediated forms of circulation and return, resonant of the circulatory and reciprocal structures explored within scholarship on the gift (e.g., Hyde 1979). When I talked with Corner regulars about what they received back, one speaker wryly remarked, "People do give — quite a lot of grief." While audiences do not pay for the privilege of listening to or of engaging with the speakers, and while they do not offer gifts in return, it would be wrong to ignore what they contribute. We might point to the spread of new ideas, the way audience members enable particular words to traverse Corner space, bringing worth to the speaker in terms of reputation and recognition (see also Schroeder 2004). In a more general and extended sense, audiences are also essential to the Corner's viability and vitality, providing listeners, potential new speakers, hecklers, converts, and the energy that comes from physical movement and a flurry of cross-conversations.

But whatever comes back to the orator cannot be measured against the speech that is given. Unlike LETS, where local currency is used to calculate the relative value or contribution of different people's goods and labor in order that people should have a fair bundle of transactions over time, Corner exchanges are not formally governed by norms of equivalence. At the same time, in ways that parallel the place of reputation at Summerhill School, the asymmetric value of what different speakers in particular bring to the Corner is marked by the size of crowds and re-marked upon by regulars, several of whom also remarked that they preferred to speak with people who were their "equals" to ensure a commensurate or at least worthwhile exchange.

Thus to the extent that giving away involves a deferred, undetermined, or nonequivalent transaction, it resonates with the idea of a marketplace in which ideas are exchanged and spread. But does giving away have to involve something flowing back to the one who gives? In his challenging and provocative reading of the gift, Derrida (1992b: 12) writes, "For there to be a gift, there must be no reciprocity, return, exchange, countergift, or debt. If the other gives me back . . . there will not have been a gift. . . ."[8] In the discussion that follows, I want to follow the conceptual line of a marketplace in which organized orderly forms of reciprocation are unimportant. This does not mean there are no exchanges or returns of value to those offering up their wares. However, what is important about the exchanges that take place, and about the relations between marketplace participants, eludes conventional forms of accounting or value. But if the marketplace is not structured by trading and equivalence, what might take their place? I want to consider here three other core characteristics. They are: selection, diversity, and tension.

Selection and choice are important dimensions in mainstream conceptions of the market. While usually tied to payment or exchange, both public welfare markets and the marketplace of ideas suggest selection and choosing can be separate from both (Newman and Clarke 2009: 79–82). Yet different market sectors understand the process of selection very differently.[9] While regular street marketplaces may not usually entail the agonizing of some public sector markets, particularly when the good to be chosen is a school, a hospital, or home, research on everyday marketplaces foregrounds the thick and diverse interactions that selection entails. Goods may be chosen equivocally or with certainty, happily or anxiously; they may be fingered, tasted, or fully consumed, actively tested or passively absorbed. And selection is not simply the act of the one who buys. Stall holders also select customers, particularly in conditions of time scarcity or when other pressures mean only "good-quality" customers are sought. Producer-led selection was certainly evident at the Corner, where speakers exercised a considerable degree of choice. While orators on a stepladder or box could not explicitly exclude people from listening, they did make a series of calculated and deliberate decisions about which questions they would recognize or answer, who they would insult or play with, and how much attention they would give to different participants.

Tied to the question of selection is that of diversity. For the former depends on the presence, or at least the *perceived* presence, of the latter. And as the experience of local trading networks makes clear, building vibrant, sustainable economies can be difficult if only a narrow range of wants are met (see chapter 6). What diversity means, however, varies. Markets may be specialized and, as with Speakers' Corner, deal in only one thing, such as speech. However, if all stall holders had identical goods, if differentiation and judgment (however fine-tuned) proved impossible, there would be little interest in circulating, and if all those circulating engaged with offerings in identical ways, stall holders might lose interest or at least stop paying attention. The ennui of this kind of marketplace can be imagined in the unlikely hypothetical scenario of a place filled only with McDonald's restaurants. Certainly this degree of uniformity was far from present at the Corner; however, several regulars expressed concern that isomorphic tendencies were leading to an excess of religious speakers and far too few political ones (see also DiMaggio and Powell 1983).

The third dimension we might locate in the trade-less market is that of tension. In ways that resonate with Tsing's (2005: 5) discussion of friction as the necessary "grip of encounter" in the context of awkward and conflictual global interactions, we can think of market tension as something like the tautness of a rope when subject to countervailing weights or forces. We can also think of the market shifts that emanate from the interplay of tension and ease, somewhat akin to the coordinated tension and release of sexual power play (Newmahr 2011) or when playing erotically with strangers (see chapter 5). At Speakers' Corner tension emanated from the unpredictable and singular experience of encounters. One regular speaker commented on this, as we sat on a bench having tea, watching a family enter the Corner: "What they're going to encounter in the next minute or two minutes, it's unique. . . . Who knows who they're going to meet now or if they're going to stop or not stop." While play also invokes tension as Huizinga (1970: 29) describes, what the conceptual lines of the marketplace, in particular, mark out is the centering of tension in the *selected* encounter. This may seem to highlight the meeting or exchange that actually *happens*, but equally important, and certainly foregrounded in experiences of the marketplace, is the encounter (or exchange) that's avoided or missed: the quality customer who gets away, the time-waster who got in the way, the desirable item that isn't spotted or is sold out, used up, or gone. Thus an important aspect of market tension is caring, in the sense of something mattering or being at stake, where an outcome, livelihood, or feeling is on the line, even if only for a moment (see chapter 5).

Taking Speakers' Corner as my anchor, this discussion has traced some of the elasticity in conceptions of the market within the global North. But how do these different dimensions of the market—of exchange, giving, selection, choice, and tension—interrelate? How do Corner practices, particularly of play, support and give rise to particular forms of market imagining? Focusing on play has several benefits for a utopian enquiry into the contribution markets might make to a transformative politics beyond their more familiar terrain of resource allocation. It allows us to consider how markets work to enhance pleasure in domains not conventionally read as economic, and how markets are worked, how they provide structures for creativity and invention, and how they can be expressed and critiqued. Thus I am interested in those practical articulations of market play that reconfigure the market in more progressive ways, as well as those articulations that work to illuminate and critique how neoliberal markets operate.

Market Play

At first glance, play and markets may seem conceptually some distance apart, one a voluntary leisure practice, the other an instrumental structure for meeting interests or needs. Yet this apparent polarity has been undermined in several ways. Alongside accounts of marketplaces and other marginal exchange spaces that emphasize the pleasure and playfulness of these spaces (e.g., Gregson and Crewe 1997), market play has also become institutionalized. From "playing the markets" to economic game theory; play as a commodity or consumer experience; the insertion of markets within play worlds, such as the cyberspace world of Second Life (Boellstorff 2008); and markets as dramaturgical structures, involving staged, sometimes spectacular performances (Agnew 1986; Giesler 2008), it is clear that play and markets cohere and combine in multiple different ways. Yet in thinking about Speakers' Corner as a market play space, it is important to note how many orators approach it seriously, intent on conveying religious and political opinions, even as others may find their performances entertaining. One speaker remarked, "Some of these people think they're serious . . . these Christians and such, but frankly they're a joke." At the same time, approaching play through the Corner troubles any simple equivalence between play and jokes or trivial amusement.

Following the conceptual line between play as imagined and its Corner actualization (see chapter 2), I want to approach play as an activity and attitude that involves creativity, some quality of pleasure, concentration, and absorption as it pulls participants out of their ordinary worlds into one with different rules, norms, moves, and concerns (Huizinga 1970). As Henricks (2006: 1) remarks, "To play fully and imaginatively

A regular speaker at Speakers' Corner, 2010. Photo by Kathy.

is to step sideways into another reality, between the cracks of ordinary life." In this way play involves improvising as well as rituals. It also involves invention, which may include inventing or reinventing the self—taking up, removing, or varying who one is (Schechner 1985: 300) as quotidian social relations, buying, selling, or getting professional advice are enacted in another key (Henricks 2006: 161). Yet in the course of play, the threat of ordinary life's intrusion remains ever present, trumping the largely noninstrumental character of play with more purposive activities and goals. As a result, one of play's main challenges can become keeping the game in play (Caillois 1961; Huizinga 1970), ensuring players are sufficiently matched in terms of skill that success (or defeat) is neither too swift nor too certain. For part of the pleasure of play comes from not knowing what the outcome will be, and heavily unequal matches are often uninteresting. But not all play is adversarial. The pleasurable disorientation and delight often associated with play can also come from unexpected encounters or from testing or experimenting with one's own skill, luck, and courage. In the discussion that follows, I explore four cultural assemblages that mediate play's relationship to the market. Exploring them reveals the very different purposes to which the market can be put as a social practice and structure. It also reveals the multiple lines and forms of imagining that the articulation of markets to play can produce.

CARNIVAL

> It's very hot and sunny, with fewer speakers but quite large crowds.
> A man stands still with Jamaican-styled armbands, a Jamaican flag, and what looks like New Orleans Mardi Gras beads on a foot-ladder. He's completely still—waiting for what? The Christian atheist is present again, with a placard around his neck saying "Christian atheism."
> —FIELD NOTES, JULY 13, 2003

In his hugely influential book *Rabelais and His World*, Bakhtin (1968) explores the changing nature of the historic European carnival. Central to his discussion is the medieval carnival, a defined and delimited time in which norms of decency and etiquette were put aside, secular and religious authorities mocked, relations of power temporarily inverted, and the body foregrounded as a sexual and digestive domain that was open, fertile, and porous. And there in the midst of the carnival was the marketplace (Bakhtin 1968): "the place where the city provisioned itself [was] the place where it envisioned itself" (Agnew 1986: 33).

In recent years scholars have taken up Bakhtin's image of the carnival to explore resonant qualities within contemporary sociocultural practices and institutions (e.g., Gregson and Crewe 1997; Langman 2002; Smith 1993).[10] While some work focuses on those contemporary events actually characterized as carnivals, much writing addresses other practices in which a bawdy, folk-based, joyous, often transgressive inversion of power and authority are evident (e.g., Ferrell 2001). Yet the widespread use of carnival to affirm a diverse range of contemporary practices has been criticized on several grounds. While some, such as James Twitchell (1992), object to the affirmation of vulgarity and bad taste associated with "carnival culture," others, like Chris Humphrey (2000), have more methodological objections.[11] As a result, recent scholarship has moved to highlight historical and contemporary carnival's more contradictory and ambivalent character. As such, carnival is not only a place where folk culture and "an alternate conception for the ordering of human society" are expressed; carnival also provides "a bulwark of authority, built into the fabric of communal governance . . . [one that was] permitted, even fostered, by those very authorities" (Ravenscroft and Gilchrist 2009: 37).

Speakers' Corner is not a carnival space in any simple sense. Its weekly character, participative unevenness (many come simply to observe or as a pleasant short-cut through Hyde Park), and value for some speakers as a place of serious or proselytizing argument temper its carnival qualities (Cooper 2006b). However, I want to explore further how carnival as a cultural formation delineates a particular set of articulations between markets and play.

At the Corner the disavowal of formal politeness and the bawdy irreverence associated with carnival are immediately evident. Regulars, familiar with Corner norms and practice, will approach strangers, leaning in close to ask questions, to elicit reactions, or to make claims. Talk, particularly when performed for an audience that is incited to talk back, is deliberately vulgar, hyperattentively concerned with the sexual and digestive body. Two well-worn Corner insults, for instance, are "Stand back a bit, that breath is getting worse" and "I was homosexual, then I saw you, I changed my mind" (McIlvenny 1996a: 53).[12] Speakers' Corner also shares with carnival an emphasis on the standpoint of the people (with all its biases and exclusions), the valuing of good argument and quick wit, and the use of masks, costume, and dramatic performances (Cooper 2006b). More resonant with the bathhouse, perhaps, than with other spaces in this book, such as Summerhill School and nudism (given their ostensible privileging of authentic contact and naturalistic presentations), Corner orators use theatrical devices to gain attention and, more generally, to create the "distance from the self" that Richard Sennett (1992: 264) suggests is necessary for play with strangers to happen.[13]

If Speakers' Corner brings into being relations and practices that resonate with those of carnival, how does this structure the articulations the Corner actualizes between markets and play? At its simplest, we might think of carnival as a kind of market strategy, in which speakers attempt to capture listeners' attention through the use of outlandish garments, flags, and other paraphernalia. Bawdy talk, jokes, and insults play a similar role; speakers use these techniques in calculated and often highly skilled ways to draw a crowd, and then to retain their interest once gathered. But carnival indicates other market play forms, which cannot be reduced to audience hooks.

One market play form that maintains the contingent relationship be-tween markets and play (as two separate practices) treats carnival as a playful register through which an "exterior" market is satirized and cri-tiqued. Carnival here may highlight the location from which critique takes place as "the people" take aim at the elitist interests of corporate global capitalism. Or carnival may gesture to the place of wit, laugh-ter, and skilled imaginative performance and costuming in *leavening* the critique. But play and markets can also combine in other ways. For in-stance, the market may be playfully, if unsettlingly, simulated by the sus-tained competitive circulation of nonsense speech. Paralleling Agnew's (1986: 37) discussion of the festive forms of medieval marketplace life, Speakers' Corner offers a place in which the market's negative associa-tions with unequal exchange, rivalry, and exploitation can be replayed in heightened tones as speakers bully and ridicule their audiences. At the same time, while mainstream market relations may provide a shadowy norm against and in relation to which Corner play takes place, during my research visits economic market relations were not overtly flagged as something to be parodied. What was more explicitly signaled was the combination of market and play as a particular type of *playful* prac-tice that drew on the architectural scaffolding of the marketplace. In ludic battles between speakers and hecklers, in the mock seriousness of speakers disclosing their wares, and in the flow of those attending as they traded in and moved among participants discharging accusations and in-sults, carnival at the Corner provides a mode of cultural expression that mediates and thus gives shape to play. This is play as an exuberant, im-provised, open-ended, and *irreverent activity*, enacted in and through the tense, selective formation of a competitive, exchange-based (but non-monetary) marketplace.

Yet while carnival may structure how market play is actualized (using the marketplace format to organize play), what carnival produced most keenly was a particular form of uncertainty.[14] Were jokes funny or insult-ing? Was the outlandish costume or bizarre sign wit or insanity? Were as-sertions to be taken seriously or played with? While audience members sometimes interpreted orations in ways that worked against the grain of what was said, treating serious remarks as entertaining and witty re-marks as insulting, what speakers intended often remained oblique. This sense of being toyed with, familiar to many Corner attendees, gestures to something that lies at the heart of the uncertainty generated: the question of worth. Earlier I considered markets as places where things are given away in conditions where reciprocity or giving back may be required or, conversely, disavowed. The enactment of carnival at Speakers' Corner manifests the ambiguity (or ambivalence) over return in the Corner's multiply folded relationship over what is given and given back. Tony Allen (2004: 43) captures this in his account of a summer spent orating at Speakers' Corner: "Paul [another speaker] . . . reckons that nothing changes here. The speakers have nothing to say and they are saying it to people who aren't listening."

While the *political* calculation involved remains uneven and largely unstated, as a place of playful giving, in which the conventions of market exchange are both troubled and impersonated, the economic value of what is given is repeatedly remarked upon. At the same time, such value is regularly and determinedly misassessed or denied, as the worth of what is bestowed (moving in all or any direction) remains contested and in doubt. For if speakers don't take themselves seriously, what value, if any, inheres in their speech? Does the oratorical form, with its implication that something of substance is being bestowed, misleadingly encase worthless material? Speakers frequently decry others' dismissal of the Corner as a place of mere triviality, insulting an audience who, they imply, have received something but given nothing in return. Yet underpinning this allusion to an unfair exchange is the sense of a joke played out on the bodies of the audience who expect to receive a good and instead are deliberately given (or may feel they have received) a worthless, and therefore gift-less, gift.

TASTING

If carnival primarily signals the culture and ethos of a site engaged in market structured play, tasting addresses the individual experience. Tasting is a common activity in marketplaces where sellers attract prospective customers by offering a sample to try. It has also become increasingly popular as both a specialized and mainstream tourist activity, most prominently for wine. While vineyard tourism has become especially popular (Hall et al. 2000), other venues also encourage visitors to try out the goods on offer. At farmers' markets cheese, olives, jams, and oils are commonly sampled, as those attending browse different stalls.

Ideas of browsing, tasting, and sampling suggest the emergent aspect of wants and desires, where consumers don't know what it is they truly seek until they find (or taste) it. Indeed in ways that echo the bathhouse participants discussed in chapter 5, browsers *hope* to be surprised by the piquing and accentuation of desire stimulated by the unexpected find. In the process traders assist (or enable) the development of consumer wants and agency as consumers become coproducers of an experience that is enhanced by the (developing) expertise or skillful knowingness—the calculation and judgment—of the one who tastes (see generally Callon et al., 2002; Petrini 2001). Such norms and rhythms of discernment—the attentive pause of a sensory assessment—are prominently mobilized in contemporary wine tasting, with its investment in the challenge of what can be learned (or told) from a single sip. In contrast to public play norms that depend on a distance from the unknown other (Stevens 2007: 47), in tasting intimacy and proximity come to the fore as what is other gets ingested and incorporated into the self (see chapters 3 and 5).

Powers of taste have long been associated with class and other biases (Howes and Lalonde 1991), as well as with the accumulation of a cultural capital that can then be deployed within other markets and spheres. At the Corner playful forms of tasting express and generate their own non-elite expertise.[15] Regulars contribute to the production of Corner goods as they take advantage of the Corner's participatory structure. But the coproduction of one-timers is also important as they sample what's offered, asking questions, commenting, soliciting the views of others, and providing marginal annotations (as they turn to a neighboring listener) and as they clap, laugh, or risk a heckle.

To think of Speakers' Corner as a place of tasting and browsing indicates ways play can be used to entice passersby to stop other than the more flamboyant, attention-demanding hooks associated with carnival. Speakers do not have to rely on the audacious, provocative, or outlandish gesture; those attending can be pulled in by the opportunity to taste what's available—a pleasurable way for onlookers to sample without commitment. But tasting is not simply a form of consumer capture; it also suggests a way of thinking about market play as a fused or hybrid formation quite different from the mockery and ambivalent distance of carnival play. Certainly tasting and carnival overlap. Tasting (like carnival) can involve competition between stall holders (as it can also involve competition between audience members in their response or representation of what is tasted). And both tasting and carnival are hugely sensory, with their direct (and implied) appeal to sights, sounds, and smells.[16] But tasting also suggests a distinct kind of pleasurable engross-ment or attention (see chapter 5). One dimension of this is tasting's re-lationship to uncertainty and novelty as a new or untried offering — from a different seller or from a different harvest — is sampled by those whose palate can appreciate what is tasted. Such appreciation is an important feature of Speakers' Corner play, made more challenging by the dis-avowal of credentials within the Corner's talk-based economy; the hard-to-map character of many speeches; and the idiosyncratic character of many speakers. The ability to swiftly recognize orations — to know where they're coming from and where they're going, at least in part to lob an effective argument back — is highly rated, even as the skilled orator may play with her or his audience by making such knowing extremely diffi-cult.

One claim made in play studies is that the spoilsport is more disrup-tive than the cheat (e.g., Huizinga 1993). The latter simply tries to win in illegitimate ways; the spoilsport challenges (and undermines) the entire premise of play. Although this point is often associated with role-playing or rule-based games, it also has salience for tasting-based forms of play. Tasting benefits from variety, not only in what's available but also in the preferences of different tasters, and disliking what's been tasted is cer-tainly an acceptable response. However, while sampling or tasting does not require that everything be liked, it does depend on valuing the tast-ing process, being willing to try stuff, and not assuming in advance that everything sampled will be useless or worthless. At Speakers' Corner, similarly, tasting doesn't mean valuing the Corner in particular ways, for instance, as a space of free expression; nor does it depend on valuing par-ticular speech acts within it. But it does rely on treating Speakers' Cor-ner as having some kind of worth against the spoilsport's dismissal of the space as too inconsequential, boring, or crazy to bother with.

Tasting as a cultural mediation of the market's relationship to play suggests possibilities for new conceptual lines. Rather than the market, as conventionally understood, structuring the kind of play taking place, playful tasting, such as that actualized at the Corner, opens up more utopian ways of imagining the market. It is not simply that the Corner creates a pleasurable marketplace. Rather Corner tasting, as it inclines Speakers' Corner toward other market spaces where browsing and sam-pling also happen, suggests ways of rethinking what markets *might* be. Beyond the enjoyable aspects of some commercial, competitive trading environments, the delight in tasting—with its invocation of trust, selection, and ingestion—carries with it the potential to drive reimaginings of the market as a sensory, attentive structure, where things sampled are discussed, where new things are tried and tried out, and where the one who offers recognizes her gain in the interest and appreciation that others show in what she has brought to the market.

CONTACT ZONES

> I listen to a fundamentalist Jewish speaker talking to a small pro-Palestinian group that has gathered. No, my mistake, he's not Jewish but a messianic Christian. . . . The discussion is heated, but moderately good-natured. A child walks through the cacophony with her hands over her ears.
>
> —FIELD NOTES, JUNE 22, 2003

I take the term *contact zone* from Mary Louise Pratt (1991, 1992), who, in turn, draws it from linguistic accounts, where the idea of a contact language referred to the improvised lexicon that traders from different places often used to communicate. According to Pratt (1992: 6), a contact zone is "the space of imperial encounters . . . in which peoples geographically and historically separated come into contact with each other and establish ongoing relations, usually involving conditions of coercion, radical inequality, and intractable conflict." The notion of a contact zone is an interesting one for Speakers' Corner, highlighting the space's global reach even as it foregrounds the Corner's location within the colonial heartland. It also complicates the Corner's other sociality frame, that of a "third place." Ray Oldenburg (1989), who developed this latter term, identified third places as supplements to home and work, where people (usually men) forged acquaintanceships and became mates. At third places men do not pursue intimate relations or overly personal conversation. Talk is in groups and usually concerns impersonal matters or the affairs of nonparticipants, and while particular individuals can become nodal (or prominent) figures, the emphasis is on the fluctuating collective rather than individual members or friendships. Elsewhere I have considered Speakers' Corner as a third place (Cooper 2006b); here I want to think about how Corner encounters constituted and took shape through the site's enactment of a contact zone and the kinds of market play realized as a result.

Contact zones may suggest spaces of asymmetrical heterogeneity at the periphery of an empire and so some distance from the third places of the global North. However, as a particular kind of marginal space, Speakers' Corner bears witness to "the interactive, improvisational dimensions of [unequal] encounters so easily ignored or suppressed" (Pratt 1992: 7). While the notion of third places speaks to the camaraderie among regulars, the Corner is more than a place where regulars gather. As a contact zone, located within a city that bears the human and physical traces of its colonial past and contemporary position as a major thoroughfare, London's Speakers' Corner also provides a permissive, sometimes stimulating, often challenging space of conversation among people not only unknown to each other but who dwell in geopolitical regions where contact between them (perhaps for reasons of religion, nationality, or class) might be prohibited, difficult, or practically impossible. One experienced speaker commented, "If you wander over there now, you'll hear five or six conversations between people taking place who simply wouldn't be in communication otherwise. I don't think there's any doubt."[17] Most such conversations are horizontal, in the sense of being between audience members. However, they are often vertically facilitated by speakers or other regulars. The familiar camaraderie among regulars, common to third places, is important in making a contact zone at Speakers' Corner possible, even as the energy and unpredictability of a contact zone, in large measure due to one-timers' presence, which others play off of, provides much of the stimulus for regulars' presence as well (Cooper 2006b).

Thinking about Speakers' Corner as a contact zone resonates easily with notions of the Corner as a marketplace (in which exchanges take place among a circulating, selecting crowd) but less clearly coincides with notions of play. Indeed Somerville and Perkins (2003) use Pratt's idea of a contact zone to talk about a *discomfort* zone, "an unresolved space" where "intervals of differences" are preserved (262) through what Tsing (2005: 4, xi) describes as "the awkward, unequal, unstable, and creative qualities of interconnection . . . where words mean something different across a divide even as people agree to speak." Certainly this discomfort is apparent in many Corner conversations and debates, as, for example, when American tourists find themselves compelled to justify, defend, or apologize for their nation-state's global geopolitical actions. Yet on another level, even these awkward exchanges can be read as a form of play. Observation suggests they are absorbing and noninstrumental, an end in themselves that engages skill, tension, and uncertainty. While they may not always be fun, they are voluntarily chosen and appear on some level satisfying. Unlike the serious clashes that take place between unequally situated people within other contact zones, at Speakers' Corner clashes get reperformed as verbal sparring. One Corner speaker remarked, "The argument is preferred over the chat. . . . Those in the audience who are arguing with each other . . . have their eyes on other people surrounding them. . . . They're doing it *in front of others*. . . . It's a *public* argument." Often hosted or incited by the provocative wit and taunts of speakers and hecklers, clashes at the Corner take shape in a nonphysically combative key. It's not simply that they are enacted verbally rather than as a fight; more than this, the wit of observing regulars works to regulate and contain a conversation that might otherwise get out of hand.

Whether conversations across the contact zone take the form of verbal sparring or more serious debate, like other forms of play such conversations are temporarily and spatially bounded. In this sense Sundays in a small, crowded, graveled corner of Hyde Park, surrounded by railings, with heavy traffic flowing close by, provides a space of almost magical disinhibition where people can talk to others about matters and in ways that would not be tolerated in most other public places. Thus play as a form of verbal touch, based on the proximity and attentiveness of bodies to each other, is enabled by the marketplace Speakers' Corner enacts, even as the (neoliberal) market also provides a discursive focus for many such temporary encounters. In ways that resonate with the circulatory publics discussed in chapter 4, the market structure of the Corner, with its constant movement, provocations, exchanges, and encounters, enables unlikely forms of pleasurable stranger contact. And like the bathhouse, Corner interactions provide a lattice or network through which the touch forged by verbal attention can, as a kind of gift, circulate.[18]

EDGEWORK

I don't belong to your world, where everyone is a friend.
— SPEAKER TO HECKLER, FEBRUARY 26, 2012

I have considered the contact zone as a space principally organized around horizontal relations; however, at the Corner, it also takes another, far more asymmetrical form. In this we can see the cultural enactment of edgework as a very particular kind of play. The term *edgework* comes from Hunter Thompson (2005 [1972]) and has since developed to describe sporting, voluntary risk-taking that explores or plays with various edges, including sanity/insanity, life/death, and lawful/illegal. Edgework is often associated with extreme sports, where approaching the edge brings pleasure and satisfaction as well as risk (Lyng 2005a: 4–5). This complex sensory and affective encounter with danger that edgework articulates has led it to be set against a modernity characterized as rational, safety-obsessed, and instrumental, a modernity that leaves little room, in Lyng's (2005b: 21) words, for the "vibrant experience of unexpected and unimagined sensual realities."

Yet in other ways, edgework is, if not modern, then certainly contemporary in its focus on individual control, self-responsibility, skill, and risk-taking (themes explored in relation to the bathhouse). According to Jeff Ferrell (2001: 84), "Edgework embodies . . . the anarchy of autonomy and self-invention." In some respects, it parallels too Caillois's (1961: 24) description of *ilinx*, a type of play in which vertigo is pursued. Through scary torquing physical movement, perceptual stability is temporarily destroyed. Quentin Stevens (2007: 41) suggests vertigo provides an escape from normal bodily experience and normal perceptions of the world. Yet while edgework may seek to approach the edge or limit, it is not in search of death. And it is here that the skill and technique of the player become centrally important. Johan Huizinga (1970: 29) suggests that play tests a player's "courage, tenacity, and resources." In the case of edgework, this is particularly evident. Ferrell (2005: 76) describes how edgework involves precision, even as it also plays with the vertigo of abandonment.

At first glance, edgework may appear to be a strange concept to find actualized at Speakers' Corner, a place dedicated to the art of talk rather than physical risk. Yet surveys indicate that public speaking is more commonly feared than death (e.g., Miller and Stone 2009). And, as with other markets in which bargaining requires "skill, perseverance and steely nerves" (Buie 1996: 227), edgework can be found in the voluntarily acquired, and to some degree *pursued*, risks of unscripted, unconventional discursive encounters between people. These edges can arise in conversations between people hailing from adversarial geopolitical locales, as they can also arise in conversations among people with vastly different political perspectives or backgrounds. But in the horizontal encounters of the contact zone, getting close to the edge, taking risks, and the free fall of disorientation are not necessarily what makes such contact play. For play here resides in other factors, which bring participants up against the risk rather than dwelling within it.

Instead it is in the *vertical* exchanges between orators, hecklers, and audience where edgework appears most apparent, including as a source of thrill-seeking pleasure.[19] While risk might take shape in the shy audience member who pushes herself to ask a question and thus straddles the edge of her own comfort zone, more commonly edgework is performed by hecklers and orators. In this sense, as a form of emotional risk-taking whose boundaries vary according to individual participant sensitivities, edges take three, often combined forms. In the first, speakers toy with risks to themselves, for instance, by making claims that cannot be substantiated, through jokes that fall flat, and at a more heightened level by speaking publicly and very *visibly* to an audience that may fail to materialize. Tony Allen (2004: 45) evokes the fear this last challenge elicits: "There is a nightmare scenario and it goes as follows: Stood on the ladder with no-one listening, everyone sees me with no audience — alone and friendless . . . and assume that I'm deranged or deadly boring."

In the second form, the edge is extroverted. Like the sex play Staci Newmahr (2011) discusses in her interesting ethnography of a sadomasochist community, speakers create disorienting, emotionally risky play for others through insults, sexualized slurs, and deliberately provocative remarks about national identities and race (which, unlike sexist remarks, get played out in all directions; see also McIlvenny 1996a).[20] However, in this relation of challenge and response, with its dares and tests, the speaker on the stepladder is not necessarily the one who exerts control. Sometimes hecklers and audience members will dare or provoke the speaker to take further risks or to walk the edge of losing control, as Allen (2004: 27) describes. Challenging self and other also produces a third edge, of the gathering or venue of Speakers' Corner as a whole: How near can an argument get to a fight without tipping over? What skill is required to get close while keeping the fight from happening? One speaker commented, "You can abuse someone . . . and that happens, that's one of the most regular features — an abusive discourse without a fight. . . . [It's] the influence of the crowd and the concept of free speech. . . . You can push parameters beyond the norm."

In thinking about market play through the mediating structure of edgework, what appears to be central is the exchange: the feared or actual exchange of my first two edges and the more general exchange-based architecture of the third. While exchange appears to foreground the transaction, emphasizing exchange moves away from the conventional premise of neoclassical economics that market exchanges should have minimal costs; indeed exchanges should be already over (with resources allocated to their best use) since energy expended in the process of exchange is inefficient. By contrast, in edgework as a form of market play, exchange is the very site of pleasure. The centrality of exchange is also present in relation to carnival, contact zones, and tasting; however, what edgework in particular emphasizes is the pleasure that comes from a difficult, risky transaction. Unlike LETS, the exchange that edgework enables is not one of friendly sociability, a shared pot of tea while one LETS member performs domestic tasks for another. In edgework the pleasure of the exchange is closer to a pugilistic model of play—of play as battleground rather than marketplace. But while fighting-play involves skill and technique to defeat the opponent, in edgework skill and technique are deployed to *sustain* the other, whether this is to keep the exchange going or to make future or other exchanges possible.

Concluding Remarks

Speakers' Corner has long been known as a marketplace of ideas, as it has also increasingly been tagged as a space of entertainment, if not play; however, these two terms, *market* and *play*, are rarely combined in this context. In this chapter, I wanted to explore how markets and play might assemble together as part of a project of transforming what markets might be understood to be. Speakers' Corner offers a productive site for thinking about markets. As a culturally rich site, where formations established elsewhere, such as carnival and the contact zone, get reassembled, the Corner enacts the market in several different ways. My focus has been on those modes of enactment involving play. In part, this is because play provides a key register through which the market at Speakers' Corner is performed. But play is also important politically, beyond its heavily criticized investment in parody and pastiche (e.g., Ebert

1992–93). It provides a form for collaborative experimentation and invention that motivates and generates the energy and attention needed for creating new practices; it provides a way of enacting concepts, such as the market, that twists and reshapes what such concepts can become; and it provides a mode of critique that draws people in.

In this chapter, I have focused on three ways that play and markets combine. The first, play as a market tool, places play within a marketplace as stall holders use play deliberately, and with calculation, to gain attention, clients, or followers. This use of play was the one Corner orators most frequently identified. Sporting varying degrees of gravity and humor, speakers saw themselves as competing for an audience; entertainment, wit, and cleverness were used strategically and tactically to attract and keep it. Yet while play as a market tool proved the most deliberate application, in its instrumentality and investment in market competition it is the least interesting for my purposes. Of more interest is the second articulation, in which market and play fuse. Such fusion at the Corner took various forms, from the competitive fun of carnival to the pleasurable discernment that tasting and browsing items offered, the verbal sparring and intense debate of the market-structured contact zone, and the risky, disorienting exchanges and transactions that edgework relied upon. In these diverse forms, the market can be seen as providing and variously moving between offering an ethos, architectural structure, flow, and set of encounters, around and through which play takes place.

But *actualized* as market play, the concept of the market can also shift. The market (or marketplace) may identify combat and competition, but it can also signify selection, tension, and variety. In this sense Speakers' Corner generates a reading of markets that ricochets off dominant understandings and practices. As market play, it works with prevailing conceptions of the market and marketplace; as a noncurrency-based form of sampling and tasting, where skills, pleasure, and the assessment of produce are shared, it also functions as a micro-assault on the tenacity of what the market means and does. This was particularly apparent in the Corner's tasting practices, with their emphasis on the pleasures of an attentive, evaluating encounter, and in the skillful, tense exchange between speakers and audience. In both cases, trust functioned as an important feature. While conventional markets have been criticized for their exploitative, self-serving features (even as others emphasize their collaborative qualities), market play as tasting and as edgework depends on trusting oneself and the other to avoid real harm (see chapter 5).

The equivocation between replicating key features of mainstream markets and replaying the market in a different key is evident in market play's third main articulation. Here the two terms are not conjoined to identify a distinctive form of activity. Instead play presents an empowering, pleasurable, and largely safe structure through which markets, and particularly the market structures of global capitalism, can be critiqued. This may take shape explicitly—the play of satire, for example. However, it can also work in more subtle or nuanced ways. At Speakers' Corner carnival provides a mediating structure through which worthless exchange can be generated (and posited), parodying market relations in the process. Here the market is not recuperated as a progressive structure but is signaled, in its conventional appellation, through a critical (if not always deliberately intended) form of replay.

This chapter has been animated by a methodological and conceptual interest in exploring what markets (and marketplaces) can be, going beyond those approaches that make this question purely ideational or abstract or something that can be answered in a single unitary fashion— that *this* is what the market or marketplace *is*. For reasons discussed in chapter 5, my objective is not to determine the *best* market concept. Rather, in a context where debate on the left over the market has largely been oriented to comparing capitalist markets to economic alternatives, including public ownership, cooperatives, and the commons, this chapter has sought to spin the market around, to face the world of play rather than economic growth and resource allocation. This is not to discount in any way the importance of restructuring economic relations. However, it may be through reorientations such as this one that not only other conceptions of the market but also other uses can be found.

In chapters 6, 7, and 8, I have explored the possibilities for more progressive conceptual lines in relation to markets, property, and trading. In different ways, each of these chapters begs questions about the ability of change to take place. My discussion of LETS addressed the challenges faced in actualizing the imagined virtuous cycle of community labor. This chapter on Speakers' Corner, like that on Summerhill School, has worked from what is actualized (an actualization, of course, that depends on particular forms of imagining) in order to explore new ways of thinking about markets. But establishing and embedding new imaginings is a complex task. What contribution can everyday utopias make to it? More specifically, how does the conceptual richness of everyday utopias relate to wider processes of change? This question drives my final chapter.

CONCEPTUAL LINES AND THE
TEMPORAL PLACE OF CHANGE

Actual utopia . . . signifies that utopian possibilities are established in the concreteness and openness of the material of history. . . . This is the objective — real possibility which surrounds existing actuality with tremendous latency, and affords the potency of *human* hope its link with the *potentiality within the world*.

Bloch 1971: 172

In her essay on paranoid and reparative reading, Eve Kosofsky Sedgwick (2003) takes issue with the tendency of many progressive and critical academics to engage in paranoid readings, which persistently seek to uncover the socially damaging structure, effects, or unjust motivations underpinning even the most seemingly benign actions. Of course, critique is important, as is a skeptical attitude toward the claims of the powerful and a readiness not to take everything at face value. At the same time, if everything is wrong, if yesterday and tomorrow are just like today, corrupted by politics' relentless (if far from original) sin, investing energy in action to pursue a transformative politics seems pointless.[1] Thus underlying Sedgwick's essay is the importance of considering the effects of academic scholarship — not just what scholarly work says but what it does.

With its emphasis on longing, hope, and desire for another, better world, contemporary utopian scholarship is some distance from the paranoid readings of social life that Sedgwick critiques.

Yet writers such as Levitas, Bloch, and, from a somewhat different trajectory, J. K. Gibson-Graham are not interested in advancing an unbounded wishful thinking. Rather they seek to engage with material and artistic practices anchored in the real possibilities of the social conditions of their time. This book is situated within a similar current. As innovations forged and in formation, everyday utopias perform quotidian acts of governance, appearing in public, having sex, trading, learning, and debating in challenging, inventive ways. More than a flash in the pan, they form richly productive and important sites for social change politics, even as they also reveal the compromises, accommodations, and practical dilemmas of counternormative ways of living.

In a context of growing interest in socially experimental practices and a rapidly expanding body of scholarship on the utopian, this book has explored the conceptual contribution everyday utopian sites can make to a transformative politics oriented to more democratic, equal, and free ways of living. But how does such a contribution happen? Indeed, has it already happened? Or is it still to come? And if it remains before us, what work, what effort, might be required for such an everyday utopian contribution to take place? Everyday utopias support modes of thinking that posit change as lying ahead (and as such, make change conditional on specific mediating activities); however they also, importantly, pluralize and complicate this forward direction, challenging as they do so the notion that change lies *only* ahead. The complexity and multidirectionality of change is particularly evident in relation to everyday utopias' conceptual lines, and understanding it is crucial both for a utopian conceptual attitude and for thinking politically about everyday utopias.

Orienting Forward

> The problem about contemporary utopias is not that it is difficult to produce imaginary maps of the future, but that it is difficult to produce adequate maps of the present which permit images of a connected but transformed future.
> —LEVITAS 1993: 257

Contemporary utopian scholarship, like many areas of recent social theory, is drawn to the change that lies ahead (whether it lies ahead of the academic writer or ahead of the text or practice discussed). Consequently much work focuses on the relationship that utopian practices have to a desired or imagined future. For some, the utopian provides the aspiration, ambition, or dream that motivates and directs present struggles. For others, the work performed by utopia is prefigurative, materially enacting in the present a future that is longed for in order to both gain the benefits of this longed for future and hasten its arrival. Other work, meanwhile, focuses on what is latent within established practices and texts, identifying here the seeds or kernels of something that is (still) to happen, as Marx ([1871] 2001: 84) famously commented in his address on the Paris Commune: "The workers . . . have no ideals to realise, but to set free the elements of the new society with which old collapsing bourgeois society itself is pregnant."

This book has explored the forward orientation of conceptual change in two primary respects. The first concerns the movement from imagining to actualization as a temporally extended movement that requires work. In a sense, this conception of change is the one most commonly associated with the utopian, with its premise that once dreams of a better society have taken imaginative shape, their material fulfillment can then be pursued. While Marxist utopians, such as Bloch, emphasize the importance of dreams being embedded in what is possible, this book has taken up this trajectory to explore the challenge that is involved in moving from imagining to actualization. One instance of this difficulty was addressed in chapter 3, in relation to casting equality. While governance bodies may depict state touch as benign, concerned to make contact with the dispossessed and hard to reach, far more is required than documented words to make it so. A different instance of this difficulty in manifesting what is imagined can be seen in efforts to actualize community labor within LETS. While proponents of Local Exchange Trading Schemes dreamed of community labor as a virtuous cycle in which trade and community would each build the other, attempts to operationalize this fantasy foundered.

At the same time, the difficulties—and sometimes searing impossibility—of moving from dreams to practice (a process which of course reshapes imagining in turn) reveals not so much the pointlessness of dreaming as the difficulty in shaping and directing the process of change. This is the difficulty Levitas alludes to, and it is one that has been explored by theorists within and beyond utopian studies, as they consider the political implications of a far more contingent and uncertain political movement "forward" (e.g., Garforth 2009). Uncertainty here is not simply the result of opposing forces or social obstacles; rather it comes from a radically revised view of time and change in which the future is no longer solidly and predictably connected to the present but erupts suddenly and without notice (see Grosz 2005: 110).

In this book the contingent character of change has largely been explored through the frame of conceptual potential—the temporally extended process of moving beyond concepts as they currently are by imagining what they might become. Focusing on potential, particularly in unexpected places, reveals something of utopian scholarship's optimistic character; its hopeful attitude toward a world that in many respects appears so unpromising. But potential is not just about what *could be*. Drawing on Agamben, Muñoz (2009: 9) suggests that reading gay love into a poem written in the 1960s identifies a potential "that is present but not actually existing in the present tense." This book has been attentive to similar glimpses, exploring the potential that resides within different nows as they gesture toward different futures. One example of this is the latent potential within public nudist practice to bring forth new ways of imagining equality. Potential here is not simply about what equality as a normative organizing framework could be (or even do) but as well what it could come to *mean*. Yet unlike the virtuous cycle of community labor, whose positive and expansive future was perceived to be self-generating according to its own internal logic (even if the movement from imagining to actualization required work), potential suggests a future that needs with effort to be identified, imagined, and pursued. While the practice in which potential is found may have some self-realizing force, potential cannot be relied upon to simply roll out along some linear, temporal continuum. Rather potential draws (on) a complex and contingent relationship between temporalities, as it also draws (on) a complicated relationship between what is actualized and what is imagined. Potential may inhere within the present, but only because a future is imagined and brought to bear on imagining and guiding what is manifested in the now.

The capacity of innovative and progressive practices to drive (or at least to support) new forms of future imagining is at the heart of a utopian conceptual attitude that foregrounds materiality and does not treat utopian change as emerging from dreams and fantasies alone. As understanding, a utopian attitude emphasizes sensation and affect—that concepts can be known in nonlinguistic ways—and it recognizes the different ways imagining and actualization entwine. A key argument of this book has been that there is no single conceptual line that captures what practices mean within a given context. Particular practices make a multitude of different conceptual lines possible, and, as I explored in relation to market play at Speakers' Corner, this goes for the articulations between concepts as well.

In this book, I have argued against an intellectual politics oriented to seeking out or forging flawless concepts. A utopian conceptual attitude does not mean building a future in which idealized normative concepts are realized. At the same time, from a progressive perspective not all conceptions are of equal worth. While the conceptions that prove productive may depend on the specific conditions faced and the task at hand, property as belonging seems preferable to property as exclusion or objectification, for instance, with its orientation to noncommodified attachments and the co-constitutive relationship between parts and wholes. Yet property as belonging is still premised on relations of nonbelonging as well as on the capacity of *recognized* relationships (to things, people, or places) to express the interests of some (rather than others) and to impress upon the world and to make a difference. Likewise while a conception of equality oriented to undoing social distinctions, including (but not only) the nudist/textile divide, may challenge relations of unequal power far more substantively than the mere redistribution of permitted spaces, this is not intended as a perfect rendition of what equality should entail. The conceptual contribution of everyday utopias to transformative politics does not depend on investing in particular concepts or conceptual lines, hunkering down, and defending the concept against all threats upon it (see chapter 5). Aside from the fact that notions of perfection have been thoroughly questioned as ideals, including within utopian studies, the very materiality of the framework adopted here works against the drive to idealization (which is easier to sustain—although still problematic—when concepts are treated as generated by thinking alone). As I argued in relation to public nudism, approaching equality as something *manifested* means recognizing the ways conceptual lines are structured by practice—how, in this case, the equality that public nudism expresses absorbs surrounding norms, including norms of separation, legitimacy, contagion, and the proper. For everyday utopias are neither temporal nor spatial islands. Their proximity to mainstream life is a defining feature of their existence, of what they are capable of achieving as well as the constraints under which they operate. Certainly, we can speculate about equality's potential to mean something utterly different than it currently does, but to the extent it is a potential anchored in the present (and of course new conceptual lines can erupt without warning), we cannot ignore the other norms that structure its existence and as such may condition its (imagined) futures too.

Relating to the Past

Certainly, the conceptual lines explored in this book have largely been oriented forward, to those new forms of imagining or practice that the conceptual instability generated by oblique and queer encounters makes possible. But everyday utopias also face what is passed and do so in several ways.[2] They may pursue a "cut-off" past, refusing or blocking conceptual lines in order to hand them over to a previous time, from the body modesty that the Toronto bathhouse sought to dispatch to the disciplining of children, which Summerhill School sought to eliminate. Producing boundaries between what we do now and what they did then is a common theme in utopian literature, often marked by the dialogic relationship (or interior dialogue) of visitors and utopian hosts. Visitors remark on the novel practices they encounter, seeking to make sense of the utopian present through the norms and knowledge of their own (past) society, while those they meet express a range of feelings, from disbelief and shock to alienation, fascination, and sometimes utter noninterest in those earlier, archaic practices now left behind. Unlike the future-oriented worlds of fiction, however, which promise or stimulate desire in the reader for a life wherein much of what is now taken for granted has vanished, in everyday utopias it is the making-*past* of conceptual lines that needs working. Histories of particular sites may suggest such pasts have been achieved, but for many sites the production of what is past is an ongoing (and contested) project, as illustrated in the persistent conflicts around how to treat sexed bodily distinctions at the Toronto bathhouse.

A transformative politics does not have to mean creating road blocks or ditches behind us, however, as if to ensure the past does not catch up as we travel the temporal highway into the future. Many writers have commented on the ethical importance of maintaining a relationship to past injury and trauma, citing what is owed to the ghosts of the dead for a progressive or critical politics to develop (e.g., Derrida 1994; Gordon

1997; Valverde 1999). And in the case of everyday utopias, the past is not always identified as what is wrong; indeed it may also be what needs recuperating. Regulars at Speakers' Corner spoke longingly about a time when the Corner was a "university of the working class." Likewise promoting community time within LETS asserted a conceptual line that involved drilling down through a less than satisfactory present to recover past modes of neighborly generosity as conventional imaginings of Britain's past were deployed to help steer and stimulate new forms of contemporary practice. But the past can also work to legitimate the present. In the British governance project of casting equality, reimagining the past in the terms of the present was used to justify and support equality work. Equality became conceptualized as something always already there, as the remarks of the Equality and Human Rights Commission chair, Trevor Phillips, exemplify: "The principles which continue to provide the essential character of the relationship between individuals and the state . . . fairness, respect, equality, dignity and autonomy— have been developed and enriched in Britain over the centuries."[3] While many would seriously doubt Phillips's words, the struggle to secure and validate everyday utopias' present is a centrally important theme, one often lost by placing the change to which everyday utopias contribute as lying someplace else.

Securing the Present

As experiments in living that necessarily involve prefigurative practice (in the sense of enacting today that other world which is sought, a world that may reside in the future but also may not), everyday utopias assert the importance of maintaining and sustaining what is, rendering the pursuit of further change secondary to securing and protecting existing forms of innovative practice. This emphasis on maintenance is an important dimension of everyday utopias and other experiments in living. For those who feel the current world falls far short of what they desire, it is tempting to locate change for the better in some other and—usually for optimistic projects—future time. This impetus, however, can undermine the importance of protecting and maintaining more progressive practices and organized networks that already exist, practices that may be largely oriented to sustaining and insulating their present against current or future threats, as Summerhill School found themselves doing as a result of the turn-of-the-century Labour government's insistence that they change key, signature aspects of their practice.[4] Indeed when I asked Zoe Readhead, Summerhill's head teacher, about her long-term ambitions, she replied, "We can't really have ambitions more widely because we don't really have the time or the money . . . so really it's still about survival. I think for Summerhill it's about ticking along, and doing what we do, and having the number of kids that we have, and making sure the school survives because it's such an important place."

The emphasis on stability, clearly, is not only about concepts. However, the conceptual dimension of this process is important lest the conceptual lines of everyday utopias be seen as *only* geared toward what lies "ahead" (or "behind") as new forms of actualization or imagination drive change. Community labor in relation to LETS provides one example of what we might call a continuous or sustained present. While the movement from imagining to actualization invokes a future time, and while the logic of the virtuous cycle, as imagined, stretches and expands into the time to come, the concept of community labor itself depends on sustaining a momentum in which *present* values and good practice endure, albeit in ever more intensified form. More commonly, perhaps, sustaining and protecting the present works through concepts in which imagining and actualization appear to converge. Closer inspection may suggest that they do not in fact converge or that we cannot really ever know quite how or whether they do (see chapter 2). Nevertheless stasis appears present when neither imagining nor actualization impels or provokes the other (or are impelled or provoked themselves) into significant change. This may be because each has sufficient elasticity to absorb changes in the other or because no mediating practices have intervened to redirect or rupture relatively stable conceptual lines. We might read Summerhill's general approach to democracy and to pupil self-governance as two such areas. Both have played a major role in maintaining continuity in school practice and belief, despite (and perhaps also because of) the challenges they have faced. While the imagining and actualization of democracy and self-governance are open to being pulled apart or pushed in different directions, and while both can be interpreted in ways that center upon their mutual divergence, the school has gained legitimacy and stability from the fact that the movement between imagining and actualization appears to be mutually reinforcing. In other words, practices such as the school meeting reflect, shape, and consolidate notions of democracy organized around responsible (at least in the long run), engaged children and adults prepared to abide by (and work within) majority decision-making processes. Voluntary lessons reflect, shape, and consolidate notions of self-governance organized around the rational, self-possessed child.

It is tempting to treat this present-focused orientation to sustaining what *is* as inherently conservative, regardless of whether it is the continuous present of dominant social formations or the already transformed present of everyday utopias. And indeed there is a conservative dimension in the resistance of many of these sites to engaging with new political currents and movements, as there is also a hegemonic dimension in the conceptual lines that prevail, even within everyday utopias, over others. At the present time, public nudism, for instance, within the global North appears more likely to express an entitlement to equal spaces rather than an undoing of the nudist/textile distinction; state touch appears more likely to revolve around top-down forms of contact than attentive kinds of feeling. Observers may be able to draw an infinite number of conceptual lines from particular social practices as my discussion of property at Summerhill School and markets in Speakers' Corner makes clear (even as an infinite number of other lines will remain unthought or implausible). However, the capacity of concepts to condense the movement between actualization and imagining means some lines will socially triumph over (potential and actual) other ones.

Yet while there may be a conservative dimension to everyday utopias' orientation to stable conceptual lines, to dismiss out of hand the significance and value of the continuous present ignores the precarious character many organized experiments in living (and governing) face. For controversial ventures with little security or power (including those ventures, like casting equality, whose power is vulnerable to withdrawal), the legitimacy, distinction, and intelligibility that comes from stable conceptual lines is crucial as what is imagined and what is done reinforce each other.[5] But if this is the case, if practice and imagining cohere in ways that are functional or purposive, what risks (or, conversely, benefits) lie in activities that destabilize such lines? If Summerhill, for instance, deliberately and consciously deploys commonsense notions of property and ownership in order to create a better governed, more manageable school, where children treat others' belongings and spaces with respect, knowing the penalties of not doing so, what is at stake in advocating new conceptual lines oriented to a wider, transformative politics?

New Conceptual Lines

An important premise of this book has been the conceptual creativity of a multitude of spaces as the conceptual lines of everyday utopias are forged and mediated by practices, forces, and actors in many different places. Social movement activists, for instance, may identify themselves strongly as being outside of the state, but their actions may also come to shape the state — in terms of how it is imagined and how it is materially actualized.[6] At the level of conceptual creativity, there is no simple dichotomy between inside participant and detached observer without a perspective, able to view all. I have said that there is no single perspective or conceptual line. This is important when it comes to the criticism that forging new imaginative lines undermines existing functional ones. If many different conceptual lines can coexist, this means not only that property at Summerhill, for instance, can be understood in multiple simultaneous ways, but that these multiple ways can simultaneously do different kinds of things. So, the school can practically deploy notions of individual ownership, while at the same time providing a site from (and through) which other more radical kinds of property can be imagined.[7] But what happens to these other, more radical lines? Stable lines may consolidate the practices of everyday utopias in ways that have wider effects. But if innovative forms of practice are to generate or drive new forms of imagining, where do these forms of imagining go?

Contemporary utopian studies has tended to pay most attention to questions of critical distance, focusing on the capacity of (temporally, spatially, and aesthetically) remote (or estranged) sites to provide a location from which the status quo can be interrogated. By contrast, this book has paid more attention to relations of critical proximity. The sites I have explored do not exist in some other, distant place, but nearby and near to hand. Everyday utopias' closeness to (even, at times, their nestled place within) the mainstream may affect the capacity of sites to develop new, radical conceptual lines (in terms of what they imaginatively express as well as what they actualize). At the same time, it is this proximity which facilitates the development and movement of lines across different spaces (rather than remaining the exclusive undertaking of particular utopias themselves) and which has the *potential* to give new conceptual lines force.

This force is not guaranteed, of course. How particular conceptual lines travel, indeed whether they travel at all or remain as phantom lines that loop around and go nowhere, depends on their take-up, what holds them up, channels, thwarts, and redirects them (see Keenan 2010). For the reach of concepts depends on what they do and on how they travel—how, for instance, the playful markets of Speakers' Corner can impress on other markets, a process that may indeed defer explicit questions about how markets are imagined in the course of generating more material effects. Or market play, as an explicitly cultural concept, may travel, if it gets supported in its capacity to pollinate—generating new life, which will also be a different life, elsewhere.

The effects of conceptual lines—their force and limits—are shaped by many factors. For those conceptual lines anchored in the innovative practices of the everyday utopian spaces discussed, these factors include the systems, procedures, rhythms, and rationalities of wider social life. Nevertheless in considering the power new conceptual lines can exert, the recognition they receive—whether from social forces or institutional bodies—also plays a part. And here I mean recognition of everyday utopias as well as of the conceptual lines everyday utopias establish and incite. The approach adopted in this book—with its orientation to different mediations, to critical proximity, and to the conceptual lines that get forged collaboratively, interactively, and in ways that draw, pinch, and poach from what is around—is geared, perhaps foremost, to such recognition and the challenge of its strengthening: how everyday utopias and other experiments in living and governing can be given their due. Recognition of adventurous social spaces, and their power to effect what we can imagine, as something that goes beyond the "ah yes" moment shown toward the accomplishments and innovations of others, takes many forms. It can involve regard or attachment; it can involve creative participation in building and experimenting with new conceptual lines; it can involve skepticism and distrust. But fundamentally it is about *noticing*, about identifying the conceptual lines of everyday utopias as relevant to the project (which is, of course, an ongoing project) of forging a social justice politics of change.

NOTES

1. Names have been changed to maintain interviewees' anonymity.
2. Everyday utopias aren't restricted to the global North; however, the backdrop of particular kinds of national social formations—here liberal postindustrial nation-states—is important to understanding the relationship everyday utopias have with where they dwell, as well as to understanding the particular kinds of conceptual pathways that get generated.
3. Scholarship on such sites includes work on agricultural cooperatives (Gibson-Graham 2006b), the World Social Forum (Fisher and Ponniah 2003; Santos 2006), protest camps (Butler et al., 2011; Roseneil 1995), and alternative festivals such as Burning Man (Doherty 2004) and Michigan Womyn's Music Festival (Browne 2009).
4. See also Michael Gardiner (2006: 2), who draws on the intersection of "everyday" and "utopia" to indicate "a series of forces, tendencies and possibilities that are immanent in the here and now, in the pragmatic activities of daily existence."
5. See Russell Jacoby (2005: xiv–xv), who draws a distinction between "two currents of utopian thought: the blue print tradition and the iconoclastic tradition. . . . Iconoclastic utopians . . . dreamt of a superior society but . . . declined to give its precise measurements."
6. To "teach desire to desire, to desire better, to desire more, and above all to desire in a different way." See Abensour (1973: 330), quoted in Thompson (1977: 791).
7. This is not always performed consciously. It can also take shape through the potential that inheres within the practices themselves; see also chapter 4.
8. Drawing on Louis Marin and Thomas More, Fredric Jameson (1977: 9) explores the process of neutralization, the way utopian texts "point-by-point" negate the world of their author, an "entity . . . understood as a sub-text, itself constructed (and then neutralized) by the Utopian text itself." While everyday utopias may be founded and developed as a critique of particular dominant practices, such as

the critique of mainstream education by A. S. Neill, the founder of Summerhill School, their critique may be less comprehensive or "point-by-point" than those proffered by utopian literary texts.

9. This may seem less true for equality governance, which has become a pervasive dimension of state government discourse in Britain and other countries. However, its fundamental tension with other, more powerful state projects suggests it is likely to be disregarded and ignored as a meaningful aspiration (even if deployed as a rationalization) when it comes to other state action.

10. As Felski (1999: 16) writes, "Everyone, from the most famous to the most humble, eats, sleeps, yawns, defecates." On the everyday lives of nonelites, see Highmore 2002. Even during crises or transitions, customary, regular, habitual activities and sensations bind people to what once was, and to what is coming, as Śliwa and Riach (2012) explore in relation to the evocative power of smell in transitional, postsocialist Poland.

11. Bhatti and colleagues (2009: 62), for instance, in their discussion of gardening, remark that "everyday life is full of enchanting encounters that work to provide creativity, emotional attachments, and prosaic pleasures."

12. While the sites discussed have their moments of unexpected action, in which a conjuncture of events disrupt and transform what is planned, the account offered in this book focuses on patterned, organized practice—that is, with regularities of action and with cyclical rather than disjunctive time.

13. For further discussion, see Ruth Levitas 2013.

14. A similar account is given by Barthes (1977: 17) in relation to Sade's novels, in which he relates everyday utopianism to very detailed, organized, and orderly space and to "an economy of the passions" carefully and attentively instituted. He writes, "For the mark of the utopia is the everyday; or even: everything everyday is utopian: timetables, dietary programs, plans for clothing, the installation of furnishings, precepts of conversation or communication" (17).

15. This does not negate the significant ways in which the sites also invoke wishfulness. Sites such as Speakers' Corner and Summerhill School have a wider symbolic power that can generate forms of desire and longing—to speak freely, to be educated in a democratic school—which take shape at a distance (spatially, physically, affectively) from the sites themselves. However, the focus of this book is not on the wider circulation of social dreams or ambitions that the sites discussed symbolize, though these are important, but on their practical, tangible experience.

16. These themes have also been extensively explored outside of utopian studies; for example, see Comaroff and Comaroff (1992: 7) and Thrift (2008: 14).

17. For a critique of the distinction between fast and slow food and on class bias in relation to organic food, see Guthman 2003.

18. This nostalgia, however, does not mean that the everyday utopias in question are conservative in the sense of seeking to sustain hierarchy and inequality, as Michael Gardiner (1992: 23–24) suggests.

19. These include heterotopias, Temporary Autonomous Zones, real utopias, criti-

cal utopias, and concrete utopias; see Bey 2003; Bloch 1986; Hetherington 1997; Moylan 1986; Santos 2006; Wright 2011.

20. This does not mean actualization and imagining are in fact identical, for reasons explored in chapter 2. However, it suggests that they *appear* to resemble one another.

21. All interviews were carried out by me with the exception of two sets of structured interviews with LETS members in 2007 and 2010, carried out by Ryoko Matsuno and Stacy Douglas respectively, along with earlier introductory interviews carried out by Jenny Smith. Some interviews were face-to-face, some by phone; some, such as those with passersby at Speakers' Corner, were short, on-the-spot and hurried, and others were set up in advance and far more leisurely.

22. It is also important to remember, as others have discussed, that government documents are creative assemblages produced in specific ways for specific purposes. See Bedford 2009; Freeman and Maybin 2011; Hunter 2008.

23. There are similarities here to Gell's (1999: 34) "sustained thought experiment" in working with conceptual lines that do not already exist but that are in the process of being forged and built. What is important here is the work of particular mediators who, through different kinds of collaborative formations or interdependencies, bring social practice and imagining into a particular relationship with each other (see chapter 2).

24. The conceptual creativity and innovation of nonacademics also forms an important dimension of this book. As I discuss in chapter 2, theoretical work often dismisses the intellectual contribution of nonacademics to concepts' development, treating them instead as merely passive, unaware concept users or, to the extent participants themselves become the academic focus, the field of study from which concepts are academically abstracted or to which concepts generated elsewhere are practically applied. This book, by contrast, starts from the premise that we all do conceptual work, albeit attuned to different concerns and problems in different time-spaces, and people involved in establishing or taking part in experimental social spaces are especially active in this regard.

CHAPTER 2

1. Utopian studies approaches method and epistemology in various ways. While I draw on a number of scholars, the approach adopted in this book is particularly indebted to the work of Ruth Levitas. Levitas (2010) has developed a method called the Imaginary Reconstitution of Society, which has three modes (see also Levitas 2007, 2013). In its *archaeological* mode, it seeks to uncover, critique, and debate implicit notions of the good society within different political positions and programs; in its *architectural* mode, it seeks to construct alternative models of what society could be like; and in its *ontological* mode, it seeks to establish different ways of being. While this book does not work explicitly with these three different modes, it is influenced by Levitas's overall ambition of developing academic methods that combine analysis with reconstruction, based on the speculative premise (and promise) of society imagined otherwise.

2. The work of "opening our theoretical imagination" is often associated with philosophy, including in its more adventurous forms (e.g., see Colebrook 2002: 14–17). Two iconic figures in this regard are Gilles Deleuze and Félix Guattari, who identify philosophical concepts as being somewhat autopoietic creations, distinct from the concepts of everyday life. Deleuze and Guattari (1994: 22) write, "The concept . . . has no reference: it is self-referential; it posits itself and its object at the same time as it is created."

3. Emphasis added.

4. In the global North, this frequently means tracing terms from classical Greece and Rome through Christian Europe in ways that establish terms as the offspring of very particular places, conjunctures, and thinkers.

5. Although Chakrabarty continues, "When we translate them . . . into our languages and practice, we make them speak to other histories of belonging, and that is how difference and heterogeneity enter these words. Or, in thinking about them and self-consciously looking for places for them in life-practices we have fabricated using them, we sometimes rediscover their own plural histories in the history of European thought" (Dube 2002: 865).

6. Patton's discussion of this point relates directly to Derrida's work on justice, apology, gift, and hospitality. However, for the purposes of my argument, I want to depersonalize the method to capture something of its wider conceptual resonance; for an interesting use of Derrida's work on hospitality in relation to commercial hospitality, see Bell (2007).

7. Utopian scholarship also concerns itself with dystopia. On the complexity of the relationship between blueprint utopias and dystopia, see Jacoby (2005: ch. 1). Moylan (2000) explores "critical dystopias," creative mediums that contemplate what escalating horror might look like, yet leave the reader or viewer with some hope of how to transcend or avoid it (Geoghegan 2003). For discussion of the interconnections between dystopia ánd eutopia (the "good" society), see Sargisson (2012).

8. For discussion of dystopic and utopian themes in Agamben's work, see Salzani (2012) and Whyte (2010); on Bauman's dystopian thought, see Featherstone (2010).

9. Warnings of approaching calamity are also used strategically and calculatedly by states to justify (military) intervention; see Carr (2010).

10. Narratives of dystopia in the present have also been commonly deployed to counter what were perceived as more idealistic, often naïve portrayals of particular societies and states. This was a dominant feature of critical accounts of so-called socialist states in the twentieth century.

11. From outside feminist standpoint epistemology, Paul Gilroy (1993: 3–7) argues strongly for the importance of recognizing how knowledge and understanding are syncretic, being hybridized through people's intercultural social location and multiple relations of belonging.

12. On understanding the body, see, for instance, Ahmed 2006; Cohen 2009; Gatens 1996; Grosz 1994; McRuer 2006; Shildrick 2008. On understanding property,

see, for instance, Blomley 2004b; Peñalver and Katyal 2010; Staeheli and Mitchell 2008.

13. Thanks to Courtney Berger for clarifying this point.

14. Although see Jacoby (2005: 33) in relation to an iconoclastic, largely Jewish-inflected utopianism: "They did not visualize the future, they listened for it. They did not privilege the eye, but the ear. . . . If they were against images of the future, they sought hints of it in music, poetry, and mystical moments."

15. For a selection of relevant contemporary texts that usefully explore these themes, see Gardiner 1992; Levitas 2013; Moylan 1986.

16. For discussion of other approaches that explore the nonconceptual or material dimension of concepts, see Bernstein 2001; Cook 2005; Martín Alcoff and Shomali 2010.

17. Presence or actualization does not have to involve "real" life; concepts can be actualized through other kinds of practice, such as in utopian literature. However, for this to be a form of actualization rather than simply the expression of imagining, manifestation needs to exert some separate and distinct conceptual force or traction that comes from the process of materialization rather than being co-identical with the imagining that produced it. This materiality largely comes from the real material conditions of the utopian creator's world, but it can also get inflected through the process of trying to combine utopian design with a dynamic narration of events; see also Jameson (1977: 16–20).

18. An additional challenge is the impossibility of fully accessing either how concepts are imagined and actualized or how one dimension drives or shapes the other. The movement between imagining and actualization can take different forms; indeed critical work is often about revealing how lines that present themselves as lines of truth (where imaginings accurately represent what is) are instead lines of mystification, distortion, legitimation, or denial. Yet how do we know what these lines actually are? Technologies of estrangement may provide some needed distance from the process, but it is impossible to get behind either imagining or actualization to observe what it is they do, as if they are capable of being viewed from some detached exterior position. These difficulties highlight the value of utopian studies' emphasis on the speculative (see Levitas 2010). This book approaches the way concepts are actualized, and the force this has on imagining, by means of the "middle," through speculative tracings of conceptual lines, and through the mutual enfolding of imagining into actualization (and vice versa).

19. The pressure on conceptual lines, however, can also work against the established or emergent hegemony of new utopian spaces and practices. Both accounts of imagined places and actual social experiments are attentive to the challenge of dissidents who express new, antinormative (or counternormative) ideas or develop new oppositional practices.

20. Indeed there is something of the fractal or Russian doll effect, in the way each bequeaths the other in an endless, increasingly microscopic process of refinding or refounding.

21. The imaginings of actors that affect how the state is actualized are of course not

restricted to public officials but includes as well the numerous other actors whose fantasies and dreams of what the state is (and could be) have an effect upon it. For discussion of this theme in relation to social movement actors' engagement with the state, see Gill 2010.

22. This does not mean sensations of sourness are experienced as objective facts unmediated by imagined categories and ideas, but that things can be *conceptually known* in ways that are not purely linguistic.

23. Although, as conceptual art explicitly reveals, concepts can be expressed in many other ways.

24. While some of these processes depend on conceptual lines that are lines of difference, in other cases conceptual lines seek to represent what is (and is evolving). Yet even with such representational strategies, importantly, there are choices. And mediators will pursue certain lines over others as an interpretive but also as a more material process, oriented to particular tasks and purposes.

CHAPTER 3

1. Of course, much state scholarship implicitly concerns questions of touch; however, writers tend not to locate their discussion within a wider touch literature.

2. Department for Communities and Local Government, "Creating a Single Equality Scheme for 2010–2013, Consultation" (London, December 2009), 9.

3. Government Equalities Office, "Making Progress: Delivering the Equality PSA" (London, October 2009), 2.

4. *Haptic* comes from the Greek word *haptesthai*, meaning related to the sense of touch or tactile sensations. For further discussion, see Paterson 2007: 4.

5. For further discussion on this point, see Derrida's discussion of Husserl 2005: 168–71.

6. See also Mbembe (2003: 37), who explores the power of proximity in relation to suicide bombing, a technique that depends on coming as near as possible to the body of the enemy.

7. In addition provisions were introduced protecting people from discrimination on grounds of marital (and civil partnership) status, pregnancy, and maternity.

8. Within weeks of the Equality Bill's becoming law, the Labour government of thirteen years was thrown out of office and replaced by a Conservative-led coalition, which brought into force the more conventional, consolidating aspects of the Equality Act 2010 provisions but made it quickly clear that certain innovative aspects, such as the socioeconomic equality duty, would be explicitly "scrapped" while the dual discrimination provision was indefinitely postponed.

9. Government Equalities Office, "Turning Policy into Action Business Plan 2010–2011" (London, March 2010), 22.

10. Government Equalities Office, "A Fairer Future—The Equality Bill and Other Action to Make Equality a Reality" (London, April 2009), 30. For further discussion of the embodied equality state, see Cooper (2013).

11. Equality and Human Rights Commission, "Cohesion and Equality: Guidance for Funders" (London, October 2009), 9.

12. For example, Black, Asian and Minority Ethnic Women Councillors' Taskforce Report, October 2009; also Equality and Human Rights Commission, "Cohesion and Equality Guidance for Funders," 4, 7, 14.

13. At the same time, as with Josipovici's (1996) discussion of secular relics, being hard to reach suggests not only physical distance (or being out of sight) but also the intangibility (untouchable because not fully touched) of constituencies that remain tantalizingly just beyond the boundaries of governmental order.

14. Government Equalities Office, "Working towards Equality: Achieving Equality for Women and Men at Work" (London, October 2009), 19.

15. Government Equalities Office, "A Fairer Future," 15.

16. A small sample of interviews with national policy officials and NGO leaders was carried out for this chapter. However, the main source material for this chapter is publicly available government documents.

17. Government Equalities Office, "Working towards Equality," 16.

18. Department for Communities and Local Government, "Tackling Race Equality: A Statement on Race" (London, January 2010), 17.

19. Equality and Human Rights Commission, "What Our Plans Mean for You" (London, October 2009), 7–8.

20. Equality Bill Impact Assessment Version 3 (House of Commons Report Stage), November 2009, 34.

21. Government Equalities Office, "A Fairer Future," 9.

22. Equality and Human Rights Commission, "Our Strategic Plan: 2009–2012" (London, June 2009), 14.

23. See Equality and Human Rights Commission, "Cohesion and Equality: Guidance for Funders," 7; Equality and Human Rights Commission, "The Public Sector Equality Duties and Financial Decisions" (London, March 2009), 5. "Under the Gender Equality Duty, public authorities must consult staff, service users and other relevant bodies. Under the Disability Equality Duty, authorities must promote disabled people's participation and involve disabled people. Involvement requires much more active engagement of disabled stakeholders than consultation."

24. See Nick Johnson and John Tatam, Institute of Community Cohesion, "Good Relations: A Conceptual Analysis" (London, autumn 2009); also Equality and Human Rights Commission, "What Our Plans Mean for You," 24. For discussion of the cluster of terms surrounding community relations, social cohesion, and good relations, see Forrest and Keans 2001; Lewis 2005; Worley 2005.

25. Department for Communities and Local Government, "Tackling Race Inequality: A Statement on Race" (London, January 2010), 9. See also Cook et al. 2010.

26. Institute of Community Cohesion, "Good Relations," 39.

27. See Government Equalities Office, "Turning Policy into Action Business Plan 2010–2011," 11; Government Equalities Office, "Equality Bill: Assessing the Impact of a Multiple Discrimination Provision" (London, October 2009), 2; also Government Equalities Office, "Turning Policy into Action Business Plan 2010–2011," 10; Dickens 2007.

28. See Equality and Human Rights Commission, "Positive Action Briefing Note" (London, July 2009), 9; Trevor Phillips, "Poor White Boys Are Victims Too," *Sunday Times* (London), April 27, 2008.

29. An example of this is the pie chart "diversity wheel" of the community organization Olmec, in which six different inequalities are placed as contiguous slices (Olmec, "A Guide to Equality and Diversity in the Third Sector," London, June 2008, 15). For a more sophisticated framework, see Equality and Human Rights Commission, "Developing the Equality Measurement Framework" (London, 2009), xiii: a three-dimensional matrix involving (1) inequality (of outcomes, process, and autonomy), (2) across ten domains of social life and activity, and (3) involving eight social characteristics, including class.

30. For a very useful discussion of the relationship between touch and geometry, see Paterson (2007).

31. There are parallels here with Didi Herman's (2011) discussion of judicial "wayfinding."

32. Equality and Human Rights Commission, "Our Strategic Plan: 2009–2012," 20.

33. Equality and Human Rights Commission, "Developing the Equality Measurement Framework" (London, 2009), 404.

34. See also Equality and Human Rights Commission, "What Our Plans Mean for You," 20.

35. This discussion begs the question whether tentative knowing by state actors is always beneficial given the way state actors use *not knowing* as a deliberate and calculated political tool. Not knowing may relate to acts of state violence or collusion, but it can also relate to minority sexual and religious identities, where knowing suggests not only responsibility but also contamination (Cooper 2006a; Herman 2011; Lamble 2009).

36. Sara Ahmed (2004a), among others, has usefully explored the circulation of feelings and their effects. Her work challenges the assumption that emotions come from within and move out, arguing instead that emotions gather, impress upon, and shape subjects.

37. Department for Communities and Local Government, "Fairness and Freedom: The Final Report of the Equalities Review: A Summary" (London, February 2007), 6.

38. For a contemporaneous example, see the British government's expression of regret following the Report of the Bloody Sunday Inquiry on British soldiers firing and killing protestors in Londonderry in 1972. "Bloody Sunday Report Published," BBC News Northern Ireland, June 15, 2010, http://www.bbc.co.uk/news/10320609 (accessed November 29, 2010).

39. See, for instance, Trevor Phillips, foreword to Equality and Human Rights Commission, "Our Human Rights Strategy and Programme of Action: 2009–2012," 1.

40. Equality and Human Rights Commission, "Cohesion and Equality: Guidance for Funders."

41. Equality and Human Rights Commission, "Cohesion and Equality: Guidance for Funders," 3–4, italics added.

42. See *R (on the application of Kaur and Shah) v. London Borough of Ealing* [2008], EWHC 2062, judgment of Moses LJ that Ealing Council was in breach of their duty under the Race Relations Act 1976. The EHRC was an intervenor in this case, and their subsequent report (discussed here) can be interpreted as simply explaining the law given the decision in this case. At the same time, reports have a tone that conveys (or produces) particular feelings.

43. See, for instance, Equality and Human Rights Commission, "Cohesion and Equality: Guidance for Funders," 7, where it instructs bodies to "assess . . . the equality impact of activities and functions from [disadvantaged groups'] perspective."

44. Equality and Human Rights Commission, "What Our Plans Mean for You," 19.

45. One interesting account to explore these themes is Thomas Dumm's (1999: para. 15) exploration of Bill Clinton as a touchable president. According to Dumm, "Clinton has been a touchable president, in a variety of ways. . . . The most famous phrase associated with him is 'I feel your pain,' even though as it turns out most of us have been forced to feel his."

46. Casting equality, as an everyday utopia, may of course be criticized for aligning social justice with the augmenting of state power and dominant interests, working through social movements' attachment to the state and equality state projects' proximity to other state projects in ways that necessarily forgo any critical edge. As such, some might dismiss casting equality as nothing more than a means by which reactionary states can defuse or absorb the vitality of progressive politics. While this argument can be made, it assumes a high degree of coherence and integration in what states are and can do; for a similar argument see Newman and Clarke (2009: 70–73). Given this book's focus on the progressive tendencies and potential of everyday utopias, it is not the approach I take; see also Cooper 2013.

47. A multi-identity state framework not only provides a different understanding of what it means for the state to come in close; it also challenges the commonsense view of a clear boundary between state and society since it suggests that bodies, people, and forces are variously integrated, constituted, excluded, and at the borders of diverse state identities in complex, intersecting, and changing ways (see Mitchell 1991; Painter 2006). So the borders of the state as nation may not map neatly onto the borders of the state conceptualized as a network of governing apparatuses or as a regulatory web.

48. One premise of this discussion is that new forms of actualization, when it comes to state practice, can generate new ways of thinking about particular states as well as imaginings of what it is to be a state more generally.

49. This discussion builds on earlier work also driven by the challenge of state equality initiatives. See Cooper 1995, 2002, 2006a; Cooper and Monro 2003.

50. Department for Communities and Local Government, "Creating a Single Equality Scheme, 2010–2013 Consultation" (London, December 2009), 11.

51. Government Equalities Office, "Working towards Equality: Achieving Equality for Women and Men at Work," 21; Government Equalities Office, "Turning Policy

into Action Business Plan 2010–2011," 15; Government Equalities Office, "Working towards Equality: A Framework for Action" (London, February 2010), 11.

CHAPTER 4

1. Translated as "A Little Tenderness for Crying Out Loud!" See Judith Mackrell, "I Didn't Want Any Wobbling," *Guardian* (London), May 31, 2011.
2. Judith Mackrell, "In Your Face—but Lacking in Focus," *Guardian* (London), June 4, 2011.
3. World Naked Bike Ride U.K. website, http://www.worldnakedbikeride.org/uk/ (accessed July 5, 2011).
4. "Brian Coldin, Nudist on Trial in Bracebridge, Gains Support," *Huffington Post*, September 4, 2011, http://www.huffingtonpost.ca/2011/07/05/brian-coldin-nudist -trial_n_890818.html (accessed March 3, 2012).
5. See §174 of the Criminal Code of Canada.
6. I include in my discussion both nudism and naturism. Historically and geographically the two terms have been used to designate differences of ethos, culture, political orientation, and body appearance (e.g., see Bell and Holliday 2000: 128). However, as use of the two terms is not consistent in the literature, nor specifically relevant for my discussion, I use *nudism* to embrace both terms as well as to include other forms of public nakedness.
7. See "Naturists Lose Their Fight to Go Naked on the Beaches," *Independent* (London), April 28, 2009, http://www.independent.co.uk/news/uk/this-britain/natur ists-lose-their-fight-to-go-naked-on-the-beaches-1675185.html (accessed March 28, 2012).
8. See Daniel Johnson, "Beyond Safe Havens: Oregon's Terri Sue Webb," *Nude and Natural*, Spring 2002.
9. Nudism is not restricted to the global North. Alongside other histories of undress and clothes, including the coerced wearing of clothes colonially imposed, associational nudism exists in many other parts of the world, including India, Argentina, and Brazil. See International Naturist Federation, http://www.inffni .org/ (accessed April 6, 2013).
10. My focus in this chapter is the norms and anxieties present within the realm of public nudist practice, but as a conceptual line equality is also affected by those norms and anxieties that condition its academic thinking also.
11. In using a wide array of media, my aim isn't to *substantiate* my account through news stories. The stories cited come from media sources with a wide range of agendas and interests, including the production of sensational or entertaining accounts. However, the stories illustrate what nudism in public *might* entail.
12. Abbey House Gardens, venue website, http://www.abbeyhousegardens.co.uk /events.php (accessed May 27, 2011); Renee Chapple, "First All-Nude Flight from Miami Makes History," About.com Miami, http://miami.about.com/cs/nudists naturists/a/aa011603a.htm (accessed March 3, 2012); Maria Court, "Prepare for Take-off," *Dorset Echo* (U.K.), February 4, 2008, http://www.thisisdorset.net/news /2017891.0/ (accessed May 18, 2011).

13. World Naked Bike Ride U.K. website, http://www.worldnakedbikeride.org/ (accessed March 28, 2012); Kristi Ceccarossi, "Nudists Seek Harmony—Town Asked to Solve Downtown Issue," *Brattleboro (Vt.) Reformer*, August 22, 2006, http://www.freerepublic.com/focus/f-chat/1687615/posts (accessed March 28, 2012); Daniel Barlow, "Board Tackles Nudity," Rutland (Vt.) Herald.com, September 3, 2006, http://www.rutlandherald.com/apps/pbcs.dll/article?AID=/200609 03/NEWS/609030355/1003/NEWS02 (accessed March 28, 2012); Body Freedom Collaborative website, http://bodyfreedom.org; Kathy George, "Exposed and Stark Naked—on Purpose," *Seattle Post-Intelligencer Reporter*, April 6, 2003, http://www.seattlepi.com/local/116207_nude07.shtml (accessed March 28, 2012).

14. John Cloud, "Nude Family Values," *Time*, June 25, 2003.

15. During this period nudism was also associated, to differing degrees, with *lebensreform*, or life reform movements; these linked nudism to vegetarianism, alternative medicine, and healthy living, according to a back-to-nature ethos. For discussion of the movement in Belgium, see Peeters (2006). For accounts of this history, including the tensions and rivalries between different cultural and political strands of the movement, see Cleminson 2004; Jeffries 2006.

16. For further accounts of early- and mid-twentieth-century European nudism's relationship to racism, anti-Semitism, and eugenics, see Jeffries 2006; Kenway 1998; McLellan 2007; Ross 2005. For examples of racialized attitudes among earlier pro-nudist writers, see also Hartman et al. 1970; Merrill and Merrill 1931: 162; Parmelee 1929: 173, 235–41; Warren 1933.

17. Nudism's value in this respect may have proved more salient a hundred years ago than today. However, nudism's historic emphasis on fit, able-bodied women clashes with several progressive contemporary agendas, troubled by the pursuit of exposed, "complete," "unblemished" bodies. Alongside the disability politics at stake, widespread contemporary attacks on Muslim women in the global North for veiling and the attacks on "covering up" to advance a European xenophobic politics make nudism's continued celebration of the "naturally" revealed body troubling. At the same time, nudism raises the question of possible alliances between different kinds of stigmatized bodily appearance, or between people committed to a far more pluralist and open approach to bodily dress (and undress) that might also take in struggles against compulsory school and employee uniforms as well.

18. In relation to class, it is important to recognize the different economies at play in relation to organized nudist clubs and more radical initiatives oriented to free public spaces. See, for instance, Body Freedom Collaborative's strategies and approaches, listed on their website.

19. Contemporary gay nudist environments certainly exist, including the sauna and beach (e.g., Hughes et al. 2010), but the ethos of mainstream nudism continues to emphasize heterosexual family culture (Holmes 2006). For an account of a white, mainly middle-class, and heterosexual beach culture, see Obrador-Pons 2007.

20. For reference to "nude-phobic" violence, see *British Naturism*, Spring 2008, 46.

21. Severin Carrell, "Naked Rambler Faces Mental Health Checks after Breaking

Down in Court," *Guardian* (London), August 23, 2012, http://www.guardian
.co.uk/uk/2012/aug/23/naked-rambler-mental-health-checks (accessed August
29, 2012).

22. See, for instance, "Nudist Not a Public Nuisance," BBC News, January 10, 2011,
http://news.bbc.co.uk/1/hi/uk/1110330.stm (accessed March 3, 2012); see also
Terri Sue Webb, American activist prosecuted for nudity, supra note 8.

23. See, for instance, "The Naked Gun," Mailonline, October 14, 2010, http://www
.dailymail.co.uk/news/article-1320369/Florida-police-Taser-naked-jogger-Antho
ny-King-wearing-swim-goggles-super-powers.html (accessed March 28, 2012);
"Police Taser Naked Man in Streets of Kelso," TDN.com, September 7, 2011,
http://tdn.com/news/local/police-taser-naked-man-in-streets-of-kelso/article
_9a7c356e-d9bb-11e0-9849-001cc4c002e0.html (accessed March 28, 2012).

24. Samantha Epps Anderson, "Prayer Rally, Community to Focus on Naturists," In
dependentmail.com, October 19, 2006, http://andersonindependent.com/news
/2006/oct/19/prayer-rally-community-to-focus-on-naturists/ (accessed March
28, 2012); "Nudist Group Stripped of Service Claims PayPal Exposes Ignorance"
[concerning the Federation of Canadian Naturists], *Western Star* (Canada), March
25, 2008, http://www.thewesternstar.com/Business/Employment/2008-03-25
/article-1462601/Nudist-group-stripped-of-service-claims-PayPal-exposes
-ignorance/1 (accessed March 3, 2012). Also see the ban on naked children under
eighteen at the nude recreation site, Hippy Hollow (near Dallas, Texas); "A Brief
History of Nudism and Naturism in America," Southern California Naturist Association, 2006.

25. For an interesting historical account of the development of domestic American
suburban nudism, see Schrank (2012).

26. See Body Freedom Collaborative website, bold type removed.

27. For one illustration of tensions, see George, "Exposed and Stark Naked — on Purpose."

28. The significance of *showing* nudist writers beside their articles is briefly discussed
in *British Naturism*, Winter 2007, 7.

29. For a related instance, see the American town council hustings meeting held at
a nudist community. Again, through the candidates' political interactions with
naked prospective voters, naked bodies got incorporated into the democratic process in a far more vital way than if the candidates had simply deliberated on pro-
nudist texts. See "Town Holds Clothing-Optional Political Debate," Democratic
Underground.com, http://www.democraticunderground.com/discuss/duboard
.php?az=view_all&address=389x337447 (accessed March 3, 2012).

30. "Tunick's Naked Pictures of Me," *Manchester* (U.K.) *Confidential*, July 19, 2010,
http://www.manchesterconfidential.co.uk/Culture/Arts/Tunicks-naked-pictures
-of-me (accessed March 3, 2012).

31. See, for instance, British Naturism's legislative submission regarding "indecent
photographs of children," Select Committee on Culture, Media and Sport Written
Evidence, January 2008, http://www.publications.parliament.uk/pa/cm200708
/cmselect/cmcumeds/353/353we08.htm (accessed April 6, 2013).

32. For an extensive and rich discussion of orientation, see Ahmed (2006).

33. See Mike Lewis, "Under the Needle: Nudists Fight for Rights at City Pool," *Seattle Post-Intelligencer*, May 11, 2008, http://www.seattlepi.com/local/362641 _needle12.html (accessed March 4, 2010).

34. A theater audience might briefly become a circulatory public by discussing the play afterward or by passing something on, whether an object, hand wave, whisper, song fragment, or something else — a gesture sometimes, although usually lightly, invoked at particular performance events.

35. For example, see "Naked Couple Go for a Stroll" [treating open-air diners to a fifteen-minute naked parade], Metro.co.uk, January 28, 2009, http://www.metro .co.uk/news/world/508052-naked-couple-go-for-a-stroll (accessed March 28, 2012); "Naked Man Tasered 'in the Ass'" [having stripped at a university concert], Metro.co.uk, November 12, 2007, http://www.metro.co.uk/weird/75324 -naked-man-tasered-in-the-ass (accessed March 28, 2012).

36. This parallels claims of several theorists that (public) stranger contact needs mediating objects or signifiers of distance; see Arendt 1958; Sennett 1992; Zerilli 1995.

37. For an illuminating analysis of machinic and aesthetic perspectives on skin within early twentieth-century German nudism, see Möhring 2005.

38. For an interesting account of different tactile cultures among contemporary German and French nudists, which also sports some curious observational methods, see Smith (1980).

39. Dressing up pets when taking them outside also speaks to clothing's power as a signifier of public appearance, alongside the desire to make animals into public subjects. Thanks to Didi Herman for raising this point.

40. Historically street nakedness, as in Australia, has been proscribed, in explicitly racialized ways, to suggest the "not yet civilized" of improper public performance. See Watson 1998: 7.

41. Failure to appear properly in public may cause the public appearance of unhappy others to break down also. The town of Brattleboro, Vermont, illustrates this point. There, for a few summers, young people gathered naked downtown. According to reports, frustrated locals in response not only turned to law for remedy but exercised a form of resistance themselves, as public norms, such as "civil inattention," "civility towards diversity," and the pleasures of people watching, were abandoned. See, for instance, Ceccarossi, "Nudists Seek Harmony." For a useful general discussion of contemporary American norms of public engagement, see Lofland (1998).

42. Especially in formal sites such as courts or government offices. See the Court of Appeals' (Scotland) rejection of the "naked rambler's" appeal over a contempt of court finding. Lord Gill commented that appearing in court naked was unquestionably contempt. "Judges Turn Down Appeal by Rambler," news.scotsman.com, November 8, 2007, http://news.scotsman.com/nakedrambler/Judges-turn-down -appeal-by.3478376.jp (accessed March 3, 2012). See also Duncan Heenan, *British Naturism*, Autumn 2008, 23.

43. "Bay City Police Used Taser to Kill Teenager, Previously Used Tasers against a Naked Man," Mediamouse.org, April 9, 2009, http://www.mediamouse.org/news/2009/04/bay-city-police-taser-naked-man.php (accessed March 3, 2012); "Prosecutor Charged with Parading Naked in Office Complex," *North Country Gazette* (N.Y.), October 11, 2006, http://www.northcountrygazette.org/articles/101106NakedProsecutor.html (accessed March 3, 2012).

44. For example, see "Naked Tourist Shocks City" [regarding a man who ostensibly thought walking around naked in Germany was tolerated], Reuters U.K., May 22, 2007, http://uk.reuters.com/article/idUKL2245467620070522 (accessed March 3, 2012). One important exception to the rural/urban divide is the city beach where nudity may be permitted and legitimated (e.g., see Valverde and Cirak 2003); my discussion, however, focuses on non-beach city spaces.

45. For work on urban and public space and the organization of sensation and touch, see Adams et al. 2007; Edensor 2007; Voskuil 2002. Juhani Pallasmaa (2000) has also written on the need for open-ended, touch-based, flexible, and experiential architecture. His account parallels several themes discussed here.

46. Thus, equality functions as both a presupposition of public nudism as well as a mode of expression underpinned by other presuppositions.

CHAPTER 5

1. Interviewees included a mix of attendees, volunteers, and committee members, and ranged from one-time attendees to regulars. In terms of demographics, those I spoke with varied in terms of gender, sexual and ethnic identity, and occupation but were largely in their late twenties to mid-forties and predominantly Canadian.

2. Initially known as the Toronto Women's Bathhouse (or Pussy Palace), the increased drive to fully include transgendered participants led to the Pussy Palace becoming the Pleasure Palace in 2010. The name Toronto Women's Bathhouse changed in various ways over time to emphasize transgendered people's welcome participation. Since the majority of interviews were carried out before the change of names, and with women, I use the name Toronto Women's and Trans Bathhouse to reflect the original primary focus as well as the growing inclusion of and attentiveness toward transgendered participants. On the history of Canadian lesbian and gay community activism, particularly in relation to the state, see Adam et al. 1999; Grundy and Smith 2005; Herman 1994; Kinsman 1987; Ross 1995; Smith 1999; Tom Warner 2002.

3. Cate Simpson, "Sugar Shack Stirs Desire," *Xtra: Canada's Gay and Lesbian News*, April 24, 2008, http://www.xtra.ca/public/Toronto/Sugar_Shack_stirs_desire-4671.aspx (accessed February 23, 2012).

4. Participants I spoke to described very different practices in relation to viral risk. Dams and condoms were described as widely available, but several participants indicated that use was limited.

5. Some interviewees described being insufficiently attentive at the moment of parting and thus losing an opportunity to see someone they liked again.

6. For discussion of the socially contingent and contested character of need, see Fraser 1989; Waldron 1996; White and Tronto 2004.

7. We might see the bathhouse as illustrating Nancy Fraser's (1989: 300) notion of a "leaky" or "runaway need", one that has escaped (or is being encouraged to escape) its conventional institutional home, here domestic life, for more liberating pastures.

8. Emphasis added.

9. For critical engagements with care ethics more generally, see Bauman 1993; Beasley and Bacchi 2005; Cloyes 2002; Cockburn 2005; Cooper 2007.

10. See, for instance, Engster's (2007: 29) account of when a particular action — here baking or buying a cake — constitutes an act of caring.

11. Moralities can be inculcated in many ways, and rule-based frameworks itemizing what can and can't be done, in isolation from other techniques, may prove relatively unsuccessful. Nevertheless, at the bathhouse, interviewees suggested rules were an important technique of governance as well as a means of clarifying the site's moral (and evolving) foundations. For further discussion of the bathhouse as a self-governed space, see Cooper (2009).

12. The "weighted" part highlights the fact that something matters or is at stake. It also identifies the emotional or expressive spectrum that mattering can denote; so things may matter to different degrees or according to different registers of pleasure, anxiety, rage, jealousy, calculation, and so on. Indeed one of the aspects of the bathhouse deemed by many participants to be most refreshing was the way it reframed (and so sometimes *minimized*) mattering when it came to body shape and size.

13. FCE is also located within wider debates as to when attentiveness becomes over-identification with the other (as immersion or engrossment) in ways that jeopardize the individuality and needs of the caregiver, while also hindering the caregiver's capacity to recognize and the recipient's capacity to express the latter's distinct, not fully knowable needs. See generally Benhabib 1992: 168; Dahl 2000; Young 1997.

14. This equivocation resonates with Derrida's (1995: 147) work on the undecidable: "It is when it is not possible to *know* what must be done, when it is not and cannot be determining that a decision is possible as such . . . otherwise the decision is an application."

15. This is to some extent an open question. If actors don't treat rules or laws as demanding compliance toward which they have no choice but to defer, the dilemma that ethics invokes remains.

16. Organizers, of course, could not control and direct ethical conduct, as the term is understood here, since ethics depends on the possibility of choices, decisions, and practices going in different, undetermined directions. At the same time, organizers were conscious that their own collective ethical decisions affected participants' *moral* obligations.

1. Thanks to Eva Hartmann for highlighting this point. Members who tried to offer "less essential" goods, lessons in political theory, for example (as one ex-colleague described doing), found themselves with little business and scrabbling around for more popular skills or goods to offer.

2. Jill Jordan, speech at Findhorn Foundation, October 1991.

3. See Michael Linton, email interview, August 21, 2000, quoted in Lee et al. (2004: 603); also Michael Linton and Ernie Yacub, "Open Money," Subsol, http://sub sol.c3.hu/subsol_2/contributorso/lintontext.html (accessed June 15, 2011). LETsystems saw LETS as one money system interacting with others rather than as a substitute or replacement. See Lee et al. 2004: 604.

4. Closure did not leave a lasting vacuum within the British world of alternative economics and local currency systems. Even as LETS were winding up, other initiatives emerged, including Time Banking and freecycle. In Time Banking mostly nonprofessional neighboring activities were offered in exchange for bankable (spendable) time credits (Gregory 2009; Seyfang 2004; Seyfang and Smith 2002). Freecycle is an Internet-based system coordinating the gifting of things no longer wanted. Freecycle networks operate in various countries (on U.S. freecycle, see Nelson et al. 2007) and have been particularly popular in Britain. See the website http://www.uk.freecycle.org/ (accessed June 7, 2011).

5. Interviews were carried out by myself, Stacy Douglas, and Ryoko Matsuno, with additional introductory interviews by Jenny Smith. Interviews varied by age, gender, ethnicity, and occupation and were chosen to elicit a range of perspectives including both urban and rural LETS, as well as general LETS and more specialized (or targeted) LETS networks. For general British data on LETS demographics, see Williams et al. (2001).

6. Other studies examining the relationship between economic transactions and sociality include research on "mass gifting" by supermarkets, party selling, commercial bribes, and the less than fully instrumental sociality of long-term business relationships (Bird-David and Darr 2009; Macaulay 2003; McCaughey and French 2001; Smart 1993; Vincent 2003). Writing has also focused on the social dimension of more explicitly ethical economic activities—from fair trade commerce and farmers' markets to new modes of gifting and exchange, such as freecycle and local currency-based exchanges—the focus of this chapter (see for instance, Moore 2004; North 2007; Raddon 2003; for other writing on social exchanges in the marketplace, see chapter 8).

7. In the light of contemporary work on postsocial relations, attentive to the interactive relationship between economies and objects (Cetina and Bruegger 2000, 2002), I should stress my focus here is the reciprocal interaction between human communities and trading, even as the embedding of economies within local sustainable environments also proved to be an important aspect of LETS' community commitment. For other recent work centering the agentic and analytical force of objects, see Bennett 2010; Coole and Frost 2010.

8. Some schemes found that people traded only at trading fairs. This also meant trades were more likely to involve things rather than services.

9. See, for instance, "LETS: An Introduction," LETS Forum (for southwest England), http://www.letsf.co.uk/index.php?module=htmlpages&func=display&pid=1 (accessed August 1, 2011); "What Is LETS?," Coventry LETS, http://coventry.let system.org/WhatIsLETS.htm (accessed August 1, 2011).

10. "LETSystem Dorchester and South Dorset," Sustainable Dorset, http://www .sustainabledorset.org.uk/organisations/letsystem-dorchester-south-dorset -local-exchange-trading-system (accessed August 1, 2011).

11. See also Michael Linton, "Open Money Manifesto," Openmoney, http://www .openmoney.org/top/omanifesto.html (accessed June 7, 2011).

12. Although see May and Thrift (2001: 19), who argue that claims of a relatively uniform acceleration within modern capitalist societies are overstated.

13. The emphasis on community time as social time also created, in some LETS schemes, a calendar of special days, involving annual or more frequent happenings. These not only provided practical spaces for social contact to occur but functioned symbolically to develop and enhance individual schemes' distinctive character and relations of attachment.

14. The complexity of combining sociality and trade was eloquently described by one interviewee: "If you ring someone out the yellow pages, and you get them to do a job and it's not very good you can go back and complain. You won't offend them because they're complete strangers. . . . I had something fixed for me the other day [through LETS] . . . a zip in my anorak. . . . I really appreciate the work . . . but she had left eight inches and I had to finish the eight inches off myself, but I wouldn't tell her. . . . If it was a shop I'd have probably taken it back and said that's not good enough. . . . [Member's name] is lovely and I enjoy trading with her and she's given me some good work. In fact sometimes she pays me half in sterling and half in credits, which is great 'cause I'm stint, and she's doing a lot for the core group, so all these factors make it a complex picture . . . a web of interactions. . . . But that same web can make it awkward sometimes" (ex-organizer and participant, North Midlands).

15. "The Benefits of LETS," LETSLINK U.K., http://www.letslinkuk.net/practice/posi tives.htm (accessed July 20, 2011).

16. Thanks to Kate Bedford for clarifying this point.

17. In other contexts, particular agencies or bodies might play a mediating role. See Hope (2009) on the way capitalism's conflicting temporalities were (temporarily) stabilized by the state.

18. For a summary of research on LETS' limited economic utility, see Evans (2009); also on trading levels, see Aldridge and Patterson (2002); Seyfang (2001b).

19. Arguably, establishing new LETS trading norms happened in other areas, not directly to do with time. Reasons for this difference are worth considering but beyond the scope of this chapter.

20. This also suggests that community labor was expressed in more-than-linguistic ways through participants' acts, expectations, disappointments, and departure,

which responded not simply to what was imagined but to the *particular* lines drawn between imagining and actualization.

CHAPTER 7

1. Summerhill School's fees for boarding and day pupils are generally low for a private school. On the website the school states, "We try to keep our fees as low as possible so that more families can afford it. . . . The A. S. Neill Summerhill Trust aims to provide bursaries for the school so that a greater number of families with financial limitations may apply." Factsheet on the school, updated January 2009, http://www.summerhillschool.co.uk/QAs-2009.pdf (accessed April 3, 2012). For accounts of Summerhill School, see Appleton 2000; Croall 1983; Gribble 1998; Neill 1937, 1945, 1967, 1968; Stronach and Piper 2008.

2. See school website, http://summerhillschool.co.uk.

3. Field research diaries recorded observations from seven two- to three-day visits between 2002 and 2011, alongside interviews with twelve teachers, nineteen children, and two with Zoe Readhead, the school head teacher. Interviews varied in formality, length, and style. Some were conducted with teachers between classes or when no one had shown up for a lesson. Discussions with children ranged from one-on-one conversations in a quiet space to group discussions that children joined and left as their interest waxed and waned or other needs or preferences arose. Because conversations with children were deliberately informal (and so not taped), this chapter quotes directly only from adult school members. With the exception of Readhead, all contributions, as in the rest of the book, are anonymized. This was not possible for Readhead given her distinctive position as the school's principal, Neill's daughter, and the owner of Summerhill as a family business.

4. For discussion and critique of the "bundle of sticks" (sometimes referred to as "bundle of rights") approach, see Arnold 2002; Freyfogle 1995; Penner 1996.

5. For a good account and critical discussion of this approach to property, see Davies (1999).

6. For work on whiteness as property, see the seminal article by Cheryl Harris (1993). This article has been taken up in many different ways; see for instance, Davies 2007: 43–44; Grabham 2009a; Keenan 2010; Roediger 1999.

7. Being "brought up" is a commonly used Summerhill term for the process where one person brings a case against another.

8. The resonance of this account with Locke's labor-based ([1821] 1988: 288–91) approach to property is striking.

9. As told, this narrative did not, unfortunately, include details of what possession in this case meant.

10. The legal geographer Nicholas Blomley (2008b) usefully explores the labor that goes into simplification (and the difficulty in creating a single, coherent narrative) in his study of a property boundaries dispute involving the movement of the Missouri River.

11. Although in other respects, no child's bedroom is fully theirs; as one teacher said,

"They can be moved around if new kids come, and of course older kids have had that space before them."

12. Seclusion is also not just a solitary activity. Groups of friends will find spaces on the grounds and in buildings to get away from others.

13. Other teachers interviewed were more skeptical about the ability of the school grounds to offer seclusion.

14. Using things to express differentiated intimacies is restricted by the "property limitation rules" different kinds of things receive. Some things cannot be used with some kinds of people to denote attachment or trust—giving younger kids cigarettes or pornography, for instance.

15. Italics added.

16. Zoe Readhead, in conversation with Jerry Mintz, *Education Revolution* 29, spring 2000, p. 24, http://lib.store.yahoo.net/lib/educationrevolution/aero50.pdf (accessed April 8, 2013).

17. Summerhill General Policy Statement, June 11, 2002.

18. For an interesting discussion of Summerhill's relationship to touch, see Stronach and Piper (2008).

19. Summerhill General Policy Statement, June 11, 2002.

20. Ofsted, *Summerhill School: A report from the Office of Her Majesty's Chief Inspector of Schools* (1999), Reporting Inspector Mr N Grenyer, para 31.

21. The commentary to the policy declares that this may feel intrusive of relationships with children, but advises that behaving otherwise would put the school and individual at risk if something perceived as inappropriate or harmful happened; Summerhill School Handbook, Child Protection Policy, June 13, 2000.

22. One area of conflict concerned the school toilet. The school argued that all children and adults should share toilet facilities as they would in any home, disputing the notion that the toilet was a threatening space (see Summerhill General Policy Statement, June 11, 2002). Several institutional authorities criticized the school's policy of having boys, girls, and adults share toilets. See Ofsted, *Summerhill School* (1999), paras. 12, 73.

23. Members can also ask a subsequent meeting for fines to be revisited and reduced.

24. See for instance Ofsted, *Summerhill School* (1999), para. 58.

25. This followed concerns raised by the 1999 Ofsted inspection. Removal from the register would have been drastic, making the school's survival impossible.

26. See "School Attacks Ofsted 'Vandals,'" *Guardian*, March 21, 2000.

27. These are elected school members who are responsible for making sure children go to bed and are quiet at the appropriate time (which varies with age) and also that they get up in the morning.

28. These laws relate to January 2003 and have been altered since.

29. See, for instance, the controversy following the screening of the Channel 4 documentary *Summerhill at 70*, broadcast in March 1992, and the account of it by the teacher Matthew Appleton, "Summerhill at 70—A Personal Perspective," *Friends of Summerhill Trust Journal* 8 (Spring 1993).

30. See also Neill (1948: 35), where he refers to a potential loss of income from students swearing in front of prospective parents.

31. Recognition and definition, arguably, have the effect of extracting property relations as they get separated out from their wider context; for further discussion see Cooper and Herman 2013.

CHAPTER 8

1. This chapter also draws from the weekly radio show *Voice of the People* and from other accounts of the Corner, such as Tony Allen's (2004).

2. Some speakers gather at the Corner on other days, but Sunday is the main day when people attend to hear speeches and to debate.

3. Hyde Park was initially established as a fenced-in space by Henry VIII to hunt deer. It was opened to the public in 1662. Over the subsequent centuries, it was used by diverse populations in diverse ways. See Leslie Jones, "Hyde Park and Free Speech," SpeakersCorner, posted May 4, 2010, http://www.speakerscorner .net/articles/hydeparkandfreespeech (accessed March 16, 2012).

4. *Abrams* v. *United States*, 250 U.S. 616, 630 (1919). For judicial use establishing the "market place of ideas," see Justice Douglas, *United States* v. *Rumely* 345 U.S. 41, 56 (1953); also Justice Brennan *Lamont* v. *Postmaster General*, 381 U.S. 301, 308 (1965).

5. There is an interesting contrast here with gift economies where the transaction is expected to be costly; indeed the exchange itself may entirely consume the use-value of the gift. See Hyde (1979: 10).

6. See, for instance, Ahluwalia 2003; Anderson 2004; Besnier 2004; Buie 1996; Crewe and Gregson 1998; DeFilippis 1997; Sherry 1990; Stillerman 2006; Watson 2009; Zukin 1995.

7. Ibid.

8. Italics removed.

9. Markets also vary in the extent to which competition is central. Although competition is conventionally associated with economic markets (including public sector ones), the many conceptual lines of the market drawn from Speakers' Corner do not all foreground competition. To the extent that the Corner market is about *discursive* exchange relations, the capacity to have a plurality of exchanges augments any given exchange rather than detracting from (or competing with) it. Speakers do not necessarily lose out from attention paid to other speakers, and audience members do not have to compete with others listening or with the speakers that they engage with. Certainly, there is competition at the Corner as I discuss. But it isn't structured by relations of scarcity, except for those imposed by limits of time.

10. For a useful discussion of the utopian dimensions of Bakhtin's carnival, see Gardiner (1992).

11. Humphrey (2000) suggests contemporary scholars are inclined to rely too heavily on Bakhtin's narrative in ways that neglect more recent scholarly work on the medieval period; that they overstate the socially oppositional character of

early festivals; and that, by omitting the intervening period between medieval and modern carnival practice, they neglect the social conditions out of which contemporary carnival activities have arisen.

12. The first was heard on *Voice of the People*, March 19, 2003; the second was heard on *Voice of the People*, April 9, 2003.

13. Speakers also commented that a degree of *physical* distance from the audience was important for play, even as a densely packed audience might contribute to reducing inhibition.

14. For instance, see the website for Terminator 24, a regular Corner speaker, http://terminator24.blogspot.co.uk/ (accessed August 13, 2012).

15. It is less clear whether the development of such Corner expertise is translatable into other contexts. It certainly does not seem to produce any obvious social or cultural capital that can be deployed elsewhere.

16. The particular sensory character of the Corner, the density of bodies, and the importance of being able to read intonation, expression, and emphasis within debate were reasons one speaker gave for why the Corner could not adequately be replicated on the Internet. He commented, "You don't get the satisfaction you get from standing up in a park and talking to people."

17. There are similarities here with Elijah Anderson's (2004: 28) discussion of the "cosmopolitan canopy" at Philadelphia's Reading Terminal Market, in the opportunity provided "for diverse strangers to come together and be exposed to one another."

18. In this sense, Speakers' Corner provides an interesting counterpoint to LETS, where exchange of goods and services was largely unsuccessful as a means of binding community.

19. Yet in coming close to the edge, a major difference with the edgework of extreme sports becomes evident. At Speakers' Corner the edge can be crossed. The risk isn't the single disastrous transgression but the failure to return from it. As one speaker told me, "I'm not really here in a serious way to offend people. . . . I want a humorous exchange, not a violent one. . . . You control the mood by moderating what you say and observing your audience so no one gets too angry. . . . It's a bad speaker if someone gets too riled up."

20. Newmahr (2011: 159–65), interestingly, seeks to extend edgework beyond what she sees as its male-oriented focus in its concern with individual skill in just about safely navigating a hazardous environment and assumed risk, to focus instead on collaborative interactions where "edgeworkers depend on each other for successful boundary negotiation," recognizing the impact of social context on what is experienced as risky, and the importance of "emotional edges"—developing "skills in order to voluntarily negotiate extreme emotional and psychological boundaries."

CHAPTER 9

1. Sedgwick (2003: 141) also comments on the "paranoid trust in exposure" of what will come about through the revelation of what is wrong.

2. They may also be read as what is past, produced by a future that is coming into place. Deleuze and Guattari (2004: 476) use the notion of "reverse causalities" to characterize "an action of the future on the present . . . [where] what does not yet exist is already in action, in a different form." See also Nail 2010.

3. See Foreword, "Our Human Rights Strategy and Programme of Action: 2009–2012" (EHRC, London, November 2009), 1.

4. This followed an official inspection, the report from which commented, "There are major areas of unresolved difficulty where the school's philosophy is in conflict with wider external expectations of pupils' levels of achievement and progress. The most serious difficulty for the school is that it does not agree that identified weaknesses in its provision are weaknesses: such judgements are seen as external impositions at odds with the school's beliefs and values." Ofsted Inspection, conducted March 1–5, 2009, para. 60; http://www.ofsted.gov.uk/inspection-reports /find-inspection-report/provider/ELS/124870/%28type%29/16384%2C32768/%2 8typename%29/Independent%20education (accessed April 8, 2013).

5. Although this clarity may also make particulate sites more vulnerable to criticism and attack, as Summerhill School encountered in their Ofsted inspection in 1999, and subsequent governmental action, see chapter 7.

6. In this way, I go beyond those scholars who treat how the state is expressly imagined in everyday life as an integral dimension of the imagined state but who neglect to consider the contribution that everyday (or activist) imaginings make to the state's actualization (or who see its actualization only as something imagined).

7. Of course, different conceptual lines can impact on each other, but whether or not they do, and what follows from it, will depend (at least in part) on their force—a force that may also seem quite different depending on the place and angle from which it is approached. There is a parallel here with legal pluralism. From the perspective of the state, community rules and norms may appear utterly dependent on the space that the state has carved out for them. While from the perspective of the community concerned, the authority of their norms and rules may come from within—as self-authored and self-authorizing.

REFERENCES

Abensour, Miguel. 1973. "Les Formes De l'Utopie Socialistes-Communistes." PhD diss., University of Paris.

Adam, Barry D., Jan Willem Duyvendak, and André Krouwel, eds. 1999. *The Global Emergence of Gay and Lesbian Politics: National Imprints of a Worldwide Movement.* Philadelphia: Temple University Press.

Adams, Mags, Gemma Moore, Trevor Cox, Ben Croxford, Mohamed Refaee, and Steve Sharples. 2007. "The 24-Hour City: Residents' Sensorial Experiences." *Senses and Society* 2 (2): 201–16.

Agamben, Giorgio. 1998. *Homo Sacer: Sovereign Power and Bare Life.* Stanford: Stanford University Press.

Agnew, Jean-Christophe. 1986. *Worlds Apart: The Market and the Theater in Anglo-American Thought, 1550–1750.* Cambridge: Cambridge University Press.

Ahluwalia, Pal. 2003. "The Wonder of the African Market: Post-colonial Inflections." *Pretexts: Literary and Cultural Studies* 12 (2): 133–44.

Ahmed, Sara. 2004a. "Collective Feelings, Or, the Impressions Left by Others." *Theory, Culture and Society* 21 (2): 25–42.

———. 2004b. "Declarations of Whiteness: The Non-Performativity of Anti-Racism." *Borderlands* 3 (2). Online.

———. 2006. *Queer Phenomenology: Orientations, Objects, Others.* Durham: Duke University Press.

Alaimo, Stacy. 2010. "The Naked Word: The Trans-Corporeal Ethics of the Protesting Body." *Women and Performance: A Journal of Feminist Theory* 20 (1): 15–36.

Alcoff, Linda, and Elizabeth Potter, eds. 1993. *Feminist Epistemologies.* New York: Routledge.

Aldridge, Theresa, and Alan Patterson. 2002. "LETS Get Real: Constraints on the Development of Local Exchange Trading Schemes." *Area* 34 (4): 370–81.

Aldridge, Theresa, Jane Tooke, Roger Lee, Andrew Leyshon, Nigel Thrift, and Colin Williams. 2001. "Recasting Work: The Example of Local Exchange Trading Schemes." *Work, Employment and Society* 15 (3): 565–79.

Alexander, Gregory S. 1998. "Property as Propriety." *Nebraska Law Review* 77: 667–702.

Alexander, Jeffrey C. 2001. "Robust Utopias and Civil Repairs." *International Sociology* 16 (4): 579–91.

Allen, Tony. 2004. *A Summer in the Park: A Journal of Speakers' Corner*. London: Freedom Press.

Anderson, Ben. 2006. "'Transcending without Transcendence': Utopianism and an Ethos of Hope." *Antipode* 38 (4): 691–710.

Anderson, Elijah. 2004. "The Cosmopolitan Canopy." *Annals of the American Academy of Political and Social Science* 595 (1): 14–31.

Anthias, Floya. 2006. "Belongings in a Globalising and Unequal World: Rethinking Translocations." In *The Situated Politics of Belonging*, edited by Nira Yuval-Davis, Kalpana Kannabiran, and Ulrike Vieten, 17–31. London: Sage.

Appadurai, Arjun. 1986. *The Social Life of Things: Commodities in Cultural Perspective*. Cambridge: Cambridge University Press.

Appleton, Matthew. 2000. *A Free Range Childhood: Self Regulation at Summerhill*. Brandon, Vt.: Foundation for Educational Renewal.

Arendt, Hannah. 1958. *The Human Condition*. Chicago: University of Chicago Press.

Arneil, Barbara. 2000. "The Politics of the Breast." *Canadian Journal of Women and the Law* 12: 345–70.

Arnold, Craig Anthony. 2002. "The Reconstitution of Property: Property as a Web of Interests." *Harvard Environmental Law Review* 26: 281.

Bain, Alison, and Catherine Nash. 2006. "Undressing the Researcher: Feminism, Embodiment and Sexuality at a Queer Bathhouse Event." *Area* 38 (1): 99–106.

Bain, Alison, and Catherine Nash. 2007. "The Toronto Women's Bathhouse Raid: Querying Queer Identities in the Courtroom." *Antipode* 39 (1): 17–34.

Baker, John, Kathleen Lynch, Sara Cantillon, and Judy Walsh. 2004. *Equality: From Theory to Action*. Basingstoke, U.K.: Palgrave Macmillan.

Bakhtin, Mikhail. 1968. *Rabelais and His World*. Cambridge: MIT Press.

Bal, Mieke. 2002. *Travelling Concepts in the Humanities: A Rough Guide*. Toronto: University of Toronto Press.

Barcan, Ruth. 2001. "'The Moral Bath of Bodily Unconsciousness': Female Nudism, Bodily Exposure and the Gaze." *Continuum* 15 (3): 303–17.

———. 2004. *Nudity: A Cultural Anatomy*. Oxford: Berg.

Barker, Nicola. 2012. *Not the Marrying Kind: Feminist Critiques of Marriage and the Legal Recognition of Same-Sex Relationships*. Basingstoke, U.K.: Palgrave Macmillan.

Barnes, Marian, and Tula Brannelly. 2008. "Achieving Care and Social Justice for People with Dementia." *Nursing Ethics* 15 (3): 384–95.

Barry, John, and John Proops. 1999. "Seeking Sustainability Discourses with Q Methodology." *Ecological Economics* 28 (3): 337–45.

Barta, Tony. 2008. "Sorry, and Not Sorry, in Australia: How the Apology to the Stolen Generations Buried a History of Genocide." *Journal of Genocide Research* 10 (2): 201–14.

Barthes, Roland. 1977. *Sade, Fourier, Loyola*. London: Cape.

Bauman, Zygmunt. 1993. *Postmodern Ethics*. Oxford: Blackwell.

———. 2003a. *Liquid Love: On the Frailty of Human Bonds*. Cambridge, U.K.: Polity Press.

———. 2003b. "Utopia with No Topos." *History of the Human Sciences* 16 (1): 11–25.

Beasley, Chris, and Carol Bacchi. 2005. "The Political Limits of 'Care' in Re-imagining Interconnection/Community and an Ethical Future." *Australian Feminist Studies* 20 (46): 49–64.

Bedford, Kate. 2009. *Developing Partnerships: Gender, Sexuality, and the Reformed World Bank*. Minneapolis: University of Minnesota Press.

Bell, David. 2007. "The Hospitable City: Social Relations in Commercial Spaces." *Progress in Human Geography* 31 (1): 7–22.

Bell, David, and Ruth Holliday. 2000. "Naked as Nature Intended." *Body and Society* 6 (3–4): 127–40.

Ben-Galim, Dalia, Mary Campbell, and Jane Lewis. 2007. "Equality and Diversity: A New Approach to Gender Equality Policy in the U.K." *International Journal of Law in Context* 3 (1): 19–33.

Benhabib, Seyla. 1992. *Situating the Self: Gender, Community, and Postmodernism in Contemporary Ethics*. London: Polity Press.

Bennett, Jane. 2010. *Vibrant Matter: A Political Ecology of Things*. Durham: Duke University Press.

Benzer, Matthias. 2011. "Social Critique in the Totally Socialized Society." *Philosophy and Social Criticism* 37 (5): 575–603.

Berlant, Lauren, and Michael Warner. 2002. "Sex in Public." In *Publics and Counterpublics*, edited by Michael Warner, 187–208. New York: Zone Books.

Bernstein, J. M. 2001. *Adorno: Disenchantment and Ethics*. Cambridge: Cambridge University Press.

Berubé, Allan. 1996. "The History of Gay Bathhouses." In *Policing Public Sex: Queer Politics and the Future of AIDS Activism*, edited by Dangerous Bedfellows, 187–220. Boston: South End Press.

Besnier, Niko. 2004. "Consumption and Cosmopolitanism: Practicing Modernity at the Second-Hand Marketplace in Nuku'alofa, Tonga." *Anthropological Quarterly* 77 (1): 7–45.

Bey, Hakim. 2003. *T.A.Z.: The Temporary Autonomous Zone, Ontological Anarchy, Poetic Terrorism*. New York: Autonomedia.

Bhatti, Mark, Andrew Church, Amanda Claremont, and Paul Stenner. 2009. "'I Love Being in the Garden': Enchanting Encounters in Everyday Life." *Social and Cultural Geography* 10 (1): 61–76.

Bhavnani, Kum-Kum, and John Foran. 2008. "Feminist Futures: From Dystopia to Eutopia?" *Futures* 40 (4): 319–28.

Binson, Diane, and William Woods. 2003. "A Theoretical Approach to Bathhouse Environments." *Journal of Homosexuality* 44 (3–4): 23–31.

Bird-David, Nurit, and Asaf Darr. 2009. "Commodity, Gift and Mass-Gift: On Gift-Commodity Hybrids in Advanced Mass Consumption Cultures." *Economy and Society* 38 (2): 304–25.

Bloch, Ernst. 1971. *On Karl Marx*. New York: Herder and Herder.

———. 1986. *The Principle of Hope*. Oxford: Blackwell.

Blocher, Joseph. 2008. "Institutions in the Marketplace of Ideas." *Duke Law Journal* 57: 821–90.

Blomley, Nicholas. 2004a. "The Boundaries of Property: Lessons from Beatrix Potter." *Canadian Geographer / Le Géographe Canadien* 48 (2): 91–100.

———. 2004b. *Unsettling the City: Urban Land and the Politics of Property*. London: Routledge.

———. 2008a. "Enclosure, Common Right and the Property of the Poor." *Social and Legal Studies* 17 (3): 311–31.

———. 2008b. "Simplification Is Complicated: Property, Nature, and the Rivers of Law." *Environment and Planning A* 40 (8): 1825–42.

Boellstorff, Tom. 2008. *Coming of Age in Second Life*. Princeton: Princeton University Press.

Bourdieu, Pierre. 2000. *Pascalian Meditations*. Translated by Richard Nice. Palo Alto, Calif.: Stanford University Press.

Bowden, Peta. 1997. *Caring: Gender-Sensitive Ethics*. London: Routledge.

Boyd, Susan B. 1999. "Family, Law and Sexuality: Feminist Engagements." *Social and Legal Studies* 8 (3): 369–90.

Boyne, Roy. 2001. "Cosmopolis and Risk." *Theory, Culture and Society* 18 (4): 47–63.

Braidotti, Rosi. 2010. "On Putting the Active Back into Activism." *New Formations* 68 (1): 42–57.

Brannen, Julia. 2005. "Time and the Negotiation of Work-Family Boundaries: Autonomy or Illusion?" *Time and Society* 14 (1): 113–31.

Brietzke, Paul H. 1997. "How and Why the Marketplace of Ideas Fails." *Valparaiso University Law Review* 31: 951–70.

Brown, Wendy. 1995. *States of Injury: Power and Freedom in Late Modernity*. Princeton: Princeton University Press.

Browne, Kath. 2009. "Naked and Dirty: Rethinking (Not) Attending Festivals." *Journal of Tourism and Cultural Change* 7 (2): 115–32.

Buie, Sarah. 1996. "Market as Mandala: The Erotic Space of Commerce." *Organization* 3 (2): 225–32.

Butler, Judith, et al. 2011. *Occupy! Scenes from Occupied America*. London: Verso.

Caillois, Roger. 1961. *Man, Play, and Games*. Translated by Meyer Barash. New York: Free Press.

Callon, Michel, Cecile Méadel, and Vololona Rabeharisoa. 2002. "The Economy of Qualities." *Economy and Society* 31 (2): 194–217.

Carpenter, Mick. 2009. "The Capabilities Approach and Critical Social Policy: Lessons from the Majority World?" *Critical Social Policy* 29 (3): 351–73.

Carr, Matt. 2010. "Slouching towards Dystopia: The New Military Futurism." *Race and Class* 51 (3): 13–32.

Cetina, Karin Knorr, and Urs Bruegger. 2000. "The Market as an Object of Attachment: Exploring Postsocial Relations in Financial Markets." *Canadian Journal of Sociology / Cahiers Canadiens de Sociologie* 25 (2): 141–68.

———. 2002. "Traders' Engagement with Markets: A Postsocial Relationship." *Theory, Culture and Society* 19 (5–6): 161–85.

Chilton, Paul. 2004. *Analysing Political Discourse: Theory and Practice*. London: Routledge.

Clarke, John, and Janet Newman. 1997. *The Managerial State*. London: Sage.

Classen, Constance. 2005. *The Book of Touch*. Oxford: Berg.

Clement, Grace. 1996. *Care, Autonomy, and Justice: Feminism and the Ethic of Care*. Boulder, Colo.: Westview Press.

Cleminson, Richard. 2004. "Making Sense of the Body: Anarchism, Nudism and Subjective Experience." *Bulletin of Spanish Studies* 81 (6): 697–716.

Cloyes, Kristin. 2002. "Agonizing Care: Care Ethics, Agonistic Feminism and a Political Theory of Care." *Nursing Inquiry* 9 (3): 203–14.

Cockburn, Tom. 2005. "Children and the Feminist Ethic of Care." *Childhood* 12 (1): 71–89.

Cohen, Ed. 2009. *A Body Worth Defending: Immunity, Biopolitics, and the Apotheosis of the Modern Body*. Durham: Duke University Press.

Colebrook, Claire. 2002. *Gilles Deleuze*. London: Routledge.

Coleman, Stephen. 1997. *Stilled Tongues: From Soapbox to Soundbite*. London: Porcupine Press.

Comaroff, John L., and Jean Comaroff. 1992. *Ethnography and the Historical Imagination*. Boulder, Colo.: Westview Press.

Connolly, William E. 2011. *A World of Becoming*. Durham: Duke University Press.

Cook, Deborah. 2005. "From the Actual to the Possible: Nonidentity Thinking." *Constellations* 12 (1): 21–35.

Cook, Joanne, Peter Dwyer, and Louise Waite. 2010. "The Experiences of Accession 8 Migrants in England: Motivations, Work and Agency." *International Migration* 49 (2): 54–79.

Coole, Diana, and Samantha Frost. 2010. *New Materialisms: Ontology, Agency, and Politics*. Durham: Duke University Press.

Cooper, Davina. 1995. *Power in Struggle: Feminism, Sexuality and the State*. New York: New York University Press.

———. 1996. "Institutional Illegality and Disobedience: Local Government Narratives." *Oxford Journal of Legal Studies* 16 (2): 255–74.

———. 1998. *Governing Out of Order: Space, Law and the Politics of Belonging*. London: Rivers Oram Press.

———. 2002. "Imagining the Place of the State: Where Governance and Social Power Meet." In *Handbook of Lesbian and Gay Studies*, edited by Diane Richardson and Steve Seidman, 231–52. London: Sage.

———. 2004. *Challenging Diversity: Rethinking Equality and the Value of Difference*. Cambridge: Cambridge University Press.

———. 2006a. "Active Citizenship and the Governmentality of Local Lesbian and Gay Politics." *Political Geography* 25 (8): 921–43.

———. 2006b. "'Sometimes a Community and Sometimes a Battlefield': From the

Comedic Public Sphere to the Commons of Speakers' Corner." *Environment and Planning D: Society and Space* 24: 753–75.

———. 2007. "'Well, You Go There to Get Off': Visiting Feminist Care Ethics through a Women's Bathhouse." *Feminist Theory* 8 (3): 243–62.

———. 2009. "Caring for Sex and the Power of Attentive Action: Governance, Drama, and Conflict in Building a Queer Feminist Bathhouse." *Signs* 35 (1): 105–30.

———. 2013. "Public Bodies: Conceptualising Active Citizenship and the Embodied State." In *Beyond Citizenship? Feminism and the Transformation of Belonging*, edited by Sasha Roseneil, 112–37. London: Palgrave Macmillan.

Cooper, Davina, and Didi Herman. 2013. "Up Against the Property Logic of Equality Law: Conservative Christian Accommodation Claims and Gay Rights." *Feminist Legal Studies* 21 (1): 61–80.

Cooper, Davina, and Surya Monro. 2003. "Governing from the Margins: Queering the State of Local Government." *Contemporary Politics* 9 (3): 229–55.

Cooper, Robert, and John Law. 1995. "Organization: Distal and Proximal Views." In *Research in the Sociology of Organizations*, edited by S. Bacharach, P. Gagliardi, and B. Mundell, 237–74. Greenwich, Conn.: JAI Press.

Corbin, Alain. 1986. *The Foul and the Fragrant: Odor and the French Social Imagination.* Cambridge: Harvard University Press.

Crewe, Louise, and Nicky Gregson. 1998. "Tales of the Unexpected: Exploring Car Boot Sales as Marginal Spaces of Contemporary Consumption." *Transactions of the Institute of British Geographers* 23 (1): 39–53.

Croall, Jonathan. 1983. *Neill of Summerhill: The Permanent Rebel.* London: Routledge and Kegan Paul.

Crow, Graham, and Graham Allan. 1995. "Community Types, Community Typologies and Community Time." *Time and Society* 4 (3): 147–66.

Curtis, Bruce. 2008. "'I Can Tell by the Way You Smell': Dietetics, Smell, Social Theory." *Senses and Society* 3 (1): 5–22.

Cvetkovich, Ann. 2003. *An Archive of Feelings: Trauma, Sexuality, and Lesbian Public Cultures.* Durham: Duke University Press.

———. 2007. "Public Feelings." *South Atlantic Quarterly* 106 (3): 459–68.

Dahl, Hanne Marlene. 2000. "A Perceptive and Reflective State?" *European Journal of Women's Studies* 7 (4): 475–94.

Daley, Caroline. 2005. "From Bush to Beach: Nudism in Australasia." *Journal of Historical Geography* 31 (1): 149–67.

Dauncey, George. 1988. *After the Crash: The Emergence of the Rainbow Economy.* London: Green Print.

Davies, Margaret. 1999. "Queer Property, Queer Persons: Self-Ownership and Beyond." *Social and Legal Studies* 8 (3): 327–52.

———. 2007. *Property: Meanings, Histories, Theories.* London: Routledge Cavendish.

Dean, Mitchell. 2008. "Governing Society: The Story of Two Monsters." *Journal of Cultural Economy* 1 (1): 25–38.

Deckha, Maneesha. 2011. "Pain as Culture: A Postcolonial Feminist Approach to s/m and Women's Agency." *Sexualities* 14 (2): 129–50.

DeFilippis, James. 1997. "From a Public Re-creation to Private Recreation: The Transformation of Public Space in South Street Seaport." *Journal of Urban Affairs* 19 (4): 405–17.

DeLanda, Manuel. 2006. *A New Philosophy of Society: Assemblage Theory and Social Complexity.* London: Continuum.

Deleuze, Gilles, and Félix Guattari. 1994. *What Is Philosophy?* Translated by Graham Burchell and Hugh Tomlinson. New York: Columbia University Press.

———. 2004. *A Thousand Plateaus: Capitalism and Schizophrenia.* Translated by Brian Massumi. London: Continuum.

Derrida, Jacques. 1992a. "Force of Law: The Mystical Foundation of Authority." In *Deconstruction and the Possibility of Justice,* edited by Drucilla Cornell and Michael Rosenfeld, 3–67. New York: Routledge.

———. 1992b. *Given Time: I. Counterfeit Money.* Translated by Peggy Kamuf. Chicago: University of Chicago Press.

———. 1994. *Specters of Marx: The State of the Debt, the Work of Mourning, and the New International.* Translated by Peggy Kamuf. New York: Routledge.

———. 1995. *Points . . . : Interviews, 1974–1994.* Translated by Elisabeth Weber et al. Stanford: Stanford University Press.

———. 2005. *On Touching—Jean Luc Nancy.* Translated by Christine Irizarry. Stanford: Stanford University Press.

Dickberry, F. 2006. *The Storm of London: A Social Rhapsody.* London: Adamant Media. Originally published 1904.

Dickens, Linda. 2007. "The Road Is Long: Thirty Years of Equality Legislation in Britain." *British Journal of Industrial Relations* 45 (3): 463–94.

Dikeç, Mustafa. 2002. "Pera Peras Poros: Longings for Spaces of Hospitality." *Theory, Culture and Society* 19 (1–2): 227–47.

DiMaggio, Paul, and Walter Powell, 1983. "The Iron Cage Revisited: Institutional Isomorphism and Collective Rationality in Organizational Fields." *American Sociological Review* 48 (2): 147–60.

Dobson, Ross. 1993. *Bringing the Economy Home from the Market.* Montreal: Black Rose Books.

Doherty, Brian. 2004. *This Is Burning Man: The Rise of a New American Underground.* Boston: Little, Brown.

Dolan, Jill. 2005. *Utopia in Performance: Finding Hope at the Theater.* Ann Arbor: University of Michigan Press.

Donovan, Josephine, and Carol J. Adams, eds. 2007. *The Feminist Care Tradition in Animal Ethics: A Reader.* New York: Columbia University Press.

Drakopoulou, Maria. 2000. "The Ethic of Care, Female Subjectivity and Feminist Legal Scholarship." *Feminist Legal Studies* 8 (2): 199–226.

Dube, Saurabh. 2002. "Presence of Europe: An Interview with Dipesh Chakrabarty." *South Atlantic Quarterly* 101 (4): 859–68.

Dumm, Thomas. 1999. "Leaky Sovereignty: Clinton's Impeachment and the Crisis of Infantile Republicanism." *Theory and Event* 2 (4): online.

Dworkin, Ronald. 2000. *Sovereign Virtue: The Theory and Practice of Equality*. Cambridge: Harvard University Press.

Ebert, Teresa L. 1992–93. "Ludic Feminism, the Body, Performance, and Labor: Bringing 'Materialism' Back into Feminist Cultural Studies." *Cultural Critique* 23: 5–50.

Edensor, Tim. 2007. "Sensing the Ruin." *Senses and Society* 2 (2): 217–32.

Engster, Daniel. 2007. *The Heart of Justice: Care Ethics and Political Theory*. Oxford: Oxford University Press.

Escobar, Arturo. 1995. *Encountering Development: The Making and Unmaking of the Third World*. Princeton: Princeton University Press.

Evans, Michael. S. 2009. "Zelizer's Theory of Money and the Case of Local Currencies." *Environment and Planning A* 41 (5): 1026–41.

Featherstone, Mark. 2010. "Event Horizon: Utopia-Dystopia in Bauman's Thought." In *Bauman's Challenge: Sociological Issues for the 21st Century*, edited by Mark Davis and Keith Tester, 127–47. London: Palgrave Macmillan.

Feldman, Allen. 1997. "Violence and Vision: The Prosthetics and Aesthetics of Terror." *Public Culture* 10 (1): 24–60.

Felski, Rita. 1999. "The Invention of Everyday Life." *New Formations* 39: 15–31.

Ferrell, Jeff. 2001. *Tearing Down the Streets: Adventures in Urban Anarchy*. New York: Palgrave.

———. 2005. "The Only Possible Adventure: Edgework and Anarchy." In *Edgework: The Sociology of Risk-Taking*, edited by Stephen Lyng, 75–88. New York: Routledge.

Fisher, Berenice, and Joan Tronto. 1990. "Toward a Feminist Theory of Caring." In *Circles of Care: Work and Identity in Women's Lives*, edited by Emily Abel and Margaret Nelson, 35–62. Albany: State University of New York Press.

Fisher, William F., and Thomas Ponniah. 2003. *Another World Is Possible: Popular Alternatives to Globalization at the World Social Forum*. London: Zed.

Fitting, Peter. 1991. "Utopias beyond Our Ideals: The Dilemma of the Right-Wing Utopia." *Utopian Studies* 2 (1–2): 95–109.

Fligstein, Neil, and Luke Dauter. 2007. "The Sociology of Markets." *Annual Review of Sociology* 33: 105–28.

Forrest, Ray, and Ade Kearns. 2001. "Social Cohesion, Social Capital and the Neighbourhood." *Urban Studies* 38 (12): 2125–43.

Foucault, Michel. 1984. "What Is Enlightenment?" In *The Foucault Reader*, edited by Paul Rabinow, 32–50. New York: Pantheon Books.

———. 1988. *Politics, Philosophy, Culture: Interviews and Other Writings, 1977–1984*, edited by Lawrence D. Kritzman. London: Routledge.

———. 1997. *Ethics: Subjectivity and Truth*. In *The Essential Works of Michel Foucault*, edited by Paul Rabinow. New York: New Press.

Fraser, Nancy. 1989. "Talking about Needs: Interpretive Contests as Political Conflicts in Welfare-State Societies." *Ethics* 99 (2): 291–313.

———. 1990. "Rethinking the Public Sphere: A Contribution to the Critique of Actually Existing Democracy." *Social Text* 25/26: 56–80.

———. 1997. *Justice Interruptus: Critical Reflections on the "Postsocialist" Condition*. New York: Routledge.

Fredman, Sandra. 2011. *Discrimination Law*. 2nd ed. Oxford: Oxford University Press.

Freeman, Richard, and Jo Maybin. 2011. "Documents, Practices and Policy." *Evidence and Policy: A Journal of Research, Debate and Practice* 7 (2): 155–70.

Freyfogle, Eric T. 1995. "Owning and Taking of Sensitive Lands." *UCLA Law Review* 43: 77–138.

Gallant, Chanelle, and Loralee Gillis. 2001. "Pussies Bite Back: The Story of the Women's Bathhouse Raid." *Torquere: Journal of the Canadian Lesbian and Gay Studies Association* 3: 152–67.

Gane, Nicholas. 2009. "Concepts and the New Empiricism." *European Journal of Social Theory* 12 (1): 83–97.

Gardiner, Michael. 1992. "Bakhtin's Carnival: Utopia as Critique." *Utopian Studies* 3 (2): 21–49.

———. 2004. "Everyday Utopianism: Lefebvre and His Critics." *Cultural Studies* 18 (2–3): 228–54.

———. 2006. "Marxism and the Convergence of Utopia and the Everyday." *History of the Human Sciences* 19 (3): 1–32.

Garforth, Lisa. 2009. "No Intentions? Utopian Theory after the Future." *Journal for Cultural Research* 13 (1): 5–27.

Gatens, Moira. 1996. *Imaginary Bodies: Ethics, Power and Corporeality*. London: Routledge.

Geisler, Cheryl. 2001. "Textual Objects: Accounting for the Role of Texts in the Everyday Life of Complex Organizations." *Written Communication* 18 (3): 296–325.

Gell, Alfred. 1999. *The Art of Anthropology: Essay and Diagrams*. London: Athlone Press.

Geoghegan, Vincent. 1997. "Remembering the Future." In *Not Yet: Reconsidering Ernst Bloch*, edited by Jamie Owen Daniel and Tom Moylan, 15–32. London: Verso.

———. 2003. "Hope Lost, Hope Regained." *History of the Human Sciences* 16 (1): 151–57.

Gibson-Graham, J. K. 2006a. *The End of Capitalism (As We Knew It): A Feminist Critique of Political Economy*. Minneapolis: University of Minnesota Press. Originally published 1996.

———. 2006b. *A Postcapitalist Politics*. Minneapolis: University of Minnesota Press.

Giesler, Markus. 2008. "Conflict and Compromise: Drama in Marketplace Evolution." *Journal of Consumer Research* 34 (6): 739–53.

Gill, Nick. 2009. "Presentational State Power: Temporal and Spatial Influences over Asylum Sector Decisionmakers." *Transactions of the Institute of British Geographers* 34 (2): 215–33.

———. 2010. "Tracing Imaginations of the State: The Spatial Consequences of Difference State Concepts among Asylum Activist Organizations." *Antipode* 42 (5): 1048–70.

Gilligan, Carol. 1982. *In a Different Voice: Psychological Theory and Women's Development*. Cambridge: Harvard University Press.

Gilroy, Paul. 1993. *The Black Atlantic: Modernity and Double Consciousness*. Cambridge: Harvard University Press.

Giroux, Henry A. 2008. "Beyond the Biopolitics of Disposability: Rethinking Neoliberalism in the New Gilded Age." *Social Identities* 14 (5): 587–620.

Goffman, Erving. 1963. *Behavior in Public Places*. New York: Free Press.

Goldberg-Hiller, Jonathan. 2012. "Reconciliation and Plasticity in a Postcolonial Hawai'i." *Law, Culture and the Humanities* 8 (3): 485–512.

Goldberg-Hiller, Jonathan, and Noenoe K. Silva. 2011. "Sharks and Pigs: Animating Hawaiian Sovereignty against the Anthropological Machine." *South Atlantic Quarterly* 110 (2): 429–46.

Goldman, Michael. 2006. *Imperial Nature: The World Bank and Struggles for Social Justice in the Age of Globalization*. New Haven: Yale University Press.

Goodin, Robert E. 1985. *Protecting the Vulnerable: A Reanalysis of Our Social Responsibilities*. Chicago: University of Chicago Press.

Gordon, Angus. 1999. "Turning Back: Adolescence, Narrative, and Queer Theory." *GLQ: A Journal of Lesbian and Gay Studies* 5 (1): 1–24.

Gordon, Avery. 1997. *Ghostly Matters: Haunting and the Sociological Imagination*. Minneapolis: University of Minnesota Press.

Gotham, Kevin Fox. 2005. "Tourism from Above and Below: Globalization, Localization and New Orleans's Mardi Gras." *International Journal of Urban and Regional Research* 29 (2): 309–26.

Grabham, Emily. 2009a. "'Flagging' the Skin: Corporeal Nationalism and the Properties of Belonging." *Body and Society* 15 (1): 63–82.

———. 2009b. "Shaking Mr Jones: Law and Touch." *International Journal of Law in Context* 5 (4): 343–53.

Grabham, Emily, Davina Cooper, Jane Krishnadas, and Didi Herman, eds. 2009. *Intersectionality and Beyond: Law, Power and the Politics of Location*. London: Routledge.

Graham, Nicole. 2010. *Lawscape: Property, Environment, Law*. New York: Routledge.

Granovetter, Mark. 1973. "The Strength of Weak Ties." *American Journal of Sociology* 78 (6): 1360–80.

Gray, Kevin. 1991. "Property in Thin Air." *Cambridge Law Journal* 50 (2): 252–307.

Gray, Kevin, and Susan Francis Gray. 1998. "The Idea of Property in Land." In *Land Law: Themes and Perspectives*, edited by Susan Bright and John Dewar, 15–51. Oxford: Oxford University Press.

Gregory, Lee. 2009. "Change Takes Time: Exploring Structural and Development Issues of Time Banking." *International Journal of Community Currency Research* 13: 19–32.

Gregson, Nicky, and Louise Crewe. 1997. "The Bargain, the Knowledge, and the Spectacle: Making Sense of Consumption in the Space of the Car-Boot Sale." *Environment and Planning D* 15 (1): 87–112.

Gribble, David. 1998. *Real Education: Varieties of Freedom*. Bristol, U.K.: Libertarian Education.

Griffiths, John. 1986. "What Is Legal Pluralism?" *Legal Pluralism and Unofficial Law* 24: 1–56.

Gross, David. 1985. "Temporality and the Modern State." *Theory and Society* 14 (1): 53–82.

Grossberg, Lawrence. 2010. *Cultural Studies in the Future Tense.* Durham: Duke University Press.

Grosz, Elizabeth. 1994. *Volatile Bodies: Toward a Corporeal Feminism.* Bloomington: Indiana University Press.

———. 2005. *Time Travels: Feminism, Nature, Power.* Durham: Duke University Press.

Grundy, John, and Miriam Smith. 2005. "The Politics of Multiscalar Citizenship: The Case of Lesbian and Gay Organizing in Canada." *Citizenship Studies* 9 (4): 389–404.

Guiraudon, Virginie, and Gallya Lahav. 2000. "A Reappraisal of the State Sovereignty Debate: The Case of Migration Control." *Comparative Political Studies* 33 (2): 163–95.

Guthman, Julie. 2003. "Fast Food / Organic Food: Reflexive Tastes and the Making of 'Yuppie Chow.'" *Social and Cultural Geography* 4 (1): 45–58.

Hacking, Ian. 2002. "Inaugural Lecture: Chair of Philosophy and History of Scientific Concepts at the Collège de France, 16 January 2001." *Economy and Society* 31 (1): 1–14.

Hall, C. Michael, Liz Sharples, Brock Cambourne, and Niki Macionis, eds. 2000. *Wine Tourism around the World: Development, Management and Markets.* Oxford: Butterworth Heinemann.

Hall, Stuart. 2003. "Marx's Notes on Method: A 'Reading' of the 1857 Introduction." *Cultural Studies* 17 (2): 113–49.

Halley, Janet. 2008. *Split Decisions: How and Why to Take a Break from Feminism.* Princeton: Princeton University Press.

Hallward, Peter. 2006. *Out of This World: Deleuze and the Philosophy of Creation.* London: Verso.

Hammers, Corie. 2008a. "Bodies That Speak and the Promise of Queer: Looking to Two Lesbian/Queer Bathhouses for a Third Way." *Journal of Gender Studies* 17 (2): 147–64.

———. 2008b. "Making Space for an Agentic Sexuality? The Examination of a Lesbian/Queer Bathhouse." *Sexualities* 11 (5): 547–72.

———. 2009a. "An Examination of Lesbian/Queer Bathhouse Culture and the Social Organization of (Im)Personal Sex." *Journal of Contemporary Ethnography* 38 (3): 308–35.

———. 2009b. "Space, Agency, and the Transfiguring of Lesbian/Queer Desire." *Journal of Homosexuality* 56 (6): 757–85.

Hansen, Thomas Blom, and Finn Stepputat. 2001. "Introduction: States of Imagination." In *Ethnographic Explorations of the Postcolonial State,* edited by Thomas Blom Hansen and Finn Stepputat, 1–41. Durham: Duke University Press.

Harding, Rosie. 2011. *Regulating Sexuality: Legal Consciousness in Lesbian and Gay Lives.* London: Routledge.

Harding, Sandra, ed. 2004. *The Feminist Standpoint Theory Reader: Intellectual and Political Controversies.* New York: Routledge.

Harris, Cheryl I. 1993. "Whiteness as Property." *Harvard Law Review* 106: 1707–91.

Harris, J. W. 1996. "Who Owns My Body." *Oxford Journal of Legal Studies* 16 (1): 55–84.

Hartley, John, and Joshua Green. 2006. "The Public Sphere on the Beach." *European Journal of Cultural Studies* 9 (3): 341–62.

Hartman, William, Marilyn Fithian, and Donald Johnson. 1970. *Nudist Society: An Authoritative, Complete Study of Nudism in America*. New York: Crown.

Hartsock, Nancy. 1997. "Comment on Hekman's 'Truth and Method: Feminist Standpoint Theory Revisited': Truth or Justice?" *Signs* 22 (2): 367–74.

Held, Virginia. 2006. *The Ethics of Care: Personal, Political, Global*. Oxford: Oxford University Press. Online edition.

Hennessy, Rosemary. 2000. *Profit and Pleasure: Sexual Identities in Late Capitalism*. New York: Routledge.

Henricks, Thomas S. 2006. *Play Reconsidered: Sociological Perspectives on Human Expression*. Urbana: University of Illinois Press.

Hepple, Bob. 2010. "The New Single Equality Act in Britain." *Equalities Rights Review* 5: 11–24.

———. 2011. "Enforcing Equality Law: Two Steps Forward and Two Steps Backwards for Reflexive Regulation." *Industrial Law Journal* 40 (4): 315–35.

Herman, Didi. 1994. *Rights of Passage: Struggles for Lesbian and Gay Legal Equality*. Toronto: University of Toronto Press.

———. 1997. *The Antigay Agenda: Orthodox Vision and the Christian Right*. Chicago: University of Chicago Press.

———. 2011. *An Unfortunate Coincidence: Jews, Jewishness and English Law*. Oxford: Oxford University Press.

Hetherington, Kevin. 1997. *The Badlands of Modernity: Heterotopia and Social Ordering*. London: Routledge.

———. 2003. "Spatial Textures: Place, Touch, and Praesentia." *Environment and Planning A* 35 (11): 1933–44.

Highmore, Ben. 2002. *The Everyday Life Reader*. London: Routledge.

Ho, Ming-sho, and Jane Hindley. 2011. "The Humanist Challenge in Taiwan's Education: Liberation, Social Justice and Ecology." *Capitalism Nature Socialism* 22 (1): 76–94.

Holmes, Jacqueline Schoemaker. 2006. "Bare Bodies, Beaches, and Boundaries: Abjected Outsiders and Rearticulation at the Nude Beach." *Sexuality and Culture* 10 (4): 29–53.

hooks, bell. 1991. *Yearning: Race, Gender, and Cultural Politics*. London: Turnaround.

Hope, Wayne. 2009. "Conflicting Temporalities: State, Nation, Economy and Democracy under Global Capitalism." *Time and Society* 18 (1): 62–85.

Howes, David, and Marc Lalonde. 1991. "The History of Sensibilities: Of the Standard of Taste in Mid-Eighteenth Century England and the Circulation of Smells in Post-Revolutionary France." *Dialectical Anthropology* 16 (2): 125–35.

Hughes, Bill, Linda McKie, Debra Hopkins, and Nick Watson. 2005. "Love's Labours Lost? Feminism, the Disabled People's Movement and an Ethic of Care." *Sociology* 39 (2): 259–75.

Hughes, Howard, Juan Carlos Monterrubio, and Amanda Miller. 2010. "'Gay' Tourists and Host Community Attitudes." *International Journal of Tourism Research* 12 (6): 774–86.

Huizinga, Johan. 1970. *Homo Ludens: A Study of the Play Element in Culture*. London: Temple Smith.

———. 1993. "The Nature of Play." *Philosophic Inquiry in Sport* 5–7.

Hume, David. 1965. *Of the Standard of Taste, and Other Essays*, edited by John W. Lenz. Indianapolis: Bobbs-Merrill. Originally published 1757.

Humphrey, Chris. 2000. "Bakhtin and the Study of Popular Culture: Re-thinking Carnival as a Historical and Analytical Concept." In *Materializing Bakhtin: The Bakhtin Circle and Social Theory*, edited by Craig Brandist and Galin Tihanov, 164–72. Basingstoke, U.K.: Palgrave.

Hunter, Shona. 2008. "Living Documents: A Feminist Psychosocial Approach to the Relational Politics of Policy Documentation." *Critical Social Policy*, 28 (4): 506–28.

Hyde, Lewis. 1979. *The Gift: Imagination and the Erotic Life of Property*. New York: Random House.

Ingber, Stanley. 1984. "The Marketplace of Ideas: A Legitimizing Myth." *Duke Law Journal* 1984 (1): 1–91.

Irigaray, Luce. 1985. *This Sex Which Is Not One*. Translated by Catherine Porter. Ithaca: Cornell University Press.

Jacobs, Jane. 1962. *The Death and Life of Great American Cities*. London: Jonathan Cape.

Jacoby, Russell. 2005. *Picture Imperfect: Utopian Thought for an Anti-Utopian Age*. New York: Columbia University Press.

Jameson, Fredric. 1977. "Of Islands and Trenches: Naturalization and the Production of Utopian Discourse." *Diacritics* 7 (2): 2–21.

———. 1991. *Postmodernism, Or, the Cultural Logic of Late Capitalism*. Durham: Duke University Press.

Jeffries, Matthew. 2006. "'For a Genuine and Noble Nakedness'? German Naturism in the Third Reich." *German History* 24 (1): 62–84.

Jessop, Bob. 1990. *State Theory: Putting the Capitalist State in its Place*. University Park: Pennsylvania State University Press.

Jessop, Sharon. 2009. "Children's Participation: An Arendtian Criticism." *Educational Philosophy and Theory* 1–18. Online.

Jones, Martin, and Bob Jessop. 2010. "Thinking State/Space Incompossibly." *Antipode* 42 (5): 1119–49.

Josipovici, Gabriel. 1996. *Touch*. New Haven: Yale University Press.

Kanter, Rosabeth Moss. 1972. *Commitment and Community: Communes and Utopias in Sociological Perspective*. Cambridge: Harvard University Press.

———, ed. 1973a. *Communes: Creating and Managing the Collective Life*. New York: Harper and Row.

———. 1973b. "Getting It All Together: Group Issues in Contemporary Communes." In *Communes: Creating and Managing the Collective Life*, edited by Rosabeth Moss Kanter, 400–407. New York: Harper and Row.

Keenan, Sarah. 2010. "Subversive Property: Reshaping Malleable Spaces of Belonging." *Social and Legal Studies* 19 (4): 423–39.

Kenway, Christopher. 1998. "Nudism, Health, and Modernity: The Natural Cure as
Proposed by the German Physical Culture Movement 1900–1914." *Nineteenth Century Prose* 25 (1): 102–15.

King, Roger J. H. 1991. "Caring about Nature: Feminist Ethics and the Environment."
Hypatia 6 (1): 75–89.

Kinsman, Gary. 1987. *The Regulation of Desire: Sexuality in Canada.* Montreal: Black
Rose Books.

Kittay, Eva F. 1999. *Love's Labor.* London: Routledge.

Kleinhans, Martha-Marie, and Roderick Macdonald. 1997. "What Is a *Critical* Legal
Pluralism?" *Canadian Journal of Law and Society* 12 (2): 25–46.

Knox, Paul L. 2005. "Creating Ordinary Places: Slow Cities in a Fast World." *Journal
of Urban Design* 10 (1): 1–11.

Koehn, Daryl. 1998. *Rethinking Feminist Ethics: Care, Trust and Empathy.* London:
Routledge.

Korn, Claire V. 1990. *Alternative American Schools: Ideals in Action.* Albany: State University of New York Press.

Kraftl, Peter. 2007. "Utopia, Performativity, and the Unhomely." *Environment and
Planning D: Society and Space* 25 (1): 120–43.

Kumar, Krishan. 1987. *Utopia and Anti-Utopia in Modern Times.* Oxford: Blackwell.

Lamble, Sarah. 2009. "Unknowable Bodies, Unthinkable Sexualities: Lesbian and
Transgender Legal Invisibility in the Toronto Women's Bathhouse Raid." *Social and
Legal Studies* 18 (1): 111–30.

———. 2012. "Epistemologies of Possibility: Social Movements, Knowledge Production and Political Transformation." PhD diss., University of Kent.

Langman, Lauren. 2002. "Suppose They Gave a Culture War and No One Came."
American Behavioral Scientist 46 (4): 501–34.

Lansley, Stewart, Sue Goss, and Christian Wolmar. 1989. *Councils in Conflict: The Rise
and Fall of the Municipal Left.* Basingstoke, U.K.: Macmillan.

Latour, Bruno. 2005. *Reassembling the Social: An Introduction to Actor-Network Theory.*
Oxford: Oxford University Press.

Lawrence, Charles, III. 1990. "If He Hollers Let Him Go: Regulating Racist Speech
on Campus." *Duke Law Journal* 431: 483.

Leccardi, Carmen. 1996. "Rethinking Social Time: Feminist Perspectives." *Time and
Society* 5 (2): 169–86.

Leckey, Robert. 2010. "Filiation and the Translation of Legal Concepts." *Legal Engi-
neering and Comparative Law* 2: 123–41.

Lee, Roger, Andrew Leyshon, Theresa Aldridge, Jane Tooke, Colin Williams, and
Nigel Thrift. 2004. "Making Geographies and Histories? Constructing Local Cir-
cuits of Value." *Environment and Planning D: Society and Space* 22 (4): 595–617.

Leitch, Alison. 2003. "Slow Food and the Politics of Pork Fat: Italian Food and European Identity." *Ethnos* 68 (4): 437–62.

Levitas, Ruth. 1990. *The Concept of Utopia.* London: Philip Allan.

———. 1993. "The Future of Thinking about the Future." In *Mapping the Futures: Local Cultures, Global Change,* edited by Jon Bird, Barry Curtis, Tim Putnam, George Robertson, and Lisa Tickner, 256–65. London: Routledge.

———. 1997. "Educated Hope: Ernst Bloch on Abstract and Concrete Utopia." In *Not Yet: Reconsidering Ernst Bloch,* edited by Jamie Owen Daniel and Tom Moylan, 65–79. London: Verso.

———. 2005. "The Imaginary Reconstitution of Society, Or, Why Sociologists and Others Should Take Utopia More Seriously." Inaugural lecture, University of Bristol, October.

———. 2007. "Looking for the Blue: The Necessity of Utopia." *Journal of Political Ideologies* 12 (3): 289–306.

———. 2010. "Back to the Future: Wells, Sociology, Utopia and Method." *Sociological Review* 58 (4): 530–47.

———. 2013. *Utopia as Method: The Imaginary Reconstitution of Society.* London: Palgrave Macmillan.

Lewis, Gail. 2005. "Welcome to the Margins: Diversity, Tolerance, and Policies of Exclusion." *Ethnic and Racial Studies* 28 (3): 536–58.

Locke, John. 1988. *Two Treatises of Government.* Cambridge: Cambridge University Press. Originally published 1821.

Lofland, Lyn. 1998. *The Public Realm: Exploring the City's Quintessential Social Territory.* New York: Aldine de Gruyter.

Lorimer, Hayden. 2005. "Cultural Geography: The Busyness of Being 'More-Than-Representational.'" *Progress in Human Geography* 29 (1): 83–94.

Lyng, Stephen. 2005a. "Edgework and the Risk-Taking Experience." In *Edgework: The Sociology of Risk-Taking,* edited by Stephen Lyng, 3–16. New York: Routledge.

———. 2005b. "Sociology at the Edge: Social Theory and Voluntary Risk Taking." In *Edgework: The Sociology of Risk-Taking,* edited by Stephen Lyng, 17–50. New York: Routledge.

Mabbett, Deborah. 2008. "Aspirational Legalism and the Role of the Equality and Human Rights Commission in Equality Policy." *Political Quarterly* 79 (1): 45–52.

Macaulay, Stewart. 2003. "The Real and the Paper Deal: Empirical Pictures of Relationships, Complexity and the Urge for Transparent Simple Rules." In *Implicit Dimensions of Contract: Discrete, Relational and Network Contracts,* edited by David Campbell, Hugh Colins, and John Wightman, 51–102. Oxford: Hart.

MacCormick, Neil. 1993. "Beyond the Sovereign State." *Modern Law Review* 56 (1): 1–18.

Macdonald, Roderick, and David Sandomierski. 2006. "Against Nomopolies." *Northern Ireland Legal Quarterly* 57 (4): 610–33.

Maher, JaneMaree. 2009. "Accumulating Care: Mothers beyond the Conflicting Temporalities of Caring and Work." *Time and Society* 18 (2–3): 231–45.

Manley, Catherine, and Theresa Aldridge. 2000. "Can LETS Make It Better? A Stirling Example." *A Life in the Day* 4 (4): 3–10.

Manning, Erin. 2007. *Politics of Touch: Sense, Movement, Sovereignty.* Minneapolis: University of Minnesota Press.

Martín Alcoff, Linda, and Alireza Shomali. 2010. "Adorno's Dialectical Realism." *Symposium: Canadian Journal of Continental Philosophy* 14 (2): 45–65.

Marx, Karl. 2001. *The Civil War in France.* London: Electric Book Company. Originally published 1871.

Massey, Doreen. 2005. *For Space.* London: Sage.

Massumi, Brian. 2002. *Parables for the Virtual: Movement, Affect, Sensation.* Durham: Duke University Press.

Matsuda, Mari J., Charles Lawrence, Richard Delgado, and Kimberle Crenshaw. 1993. *Words That Wound: Critical Race Theory, Assaultive Speech, and the First Amendment.* Boulder, Colo.: Westview Press.

Maurer, Bill. 2003. "Comment: Got Language? Law, Property, and the Anthropological Imagination." *American Anthropologist* 105 (4): 775–81.

May, Jon, and Nigel J. Thrift. 2001. *Timespace: Geographies of Temporality.* London: Routledge.

May, Todd. 2010. *Contemporary Political Movements and the Thought of Jacques Rancière: Equality in Action.* Edinburgh: Edinburgh University Press.

Mbembe, Achille. 2003. "Necropolitics." *Public Culture* 15 (1): 11–40.

McCaughey, Martha, and Christina French. 2001. "Women's Sex-Toy Parties: Technology, Orgasm, and Commodification." *Sexuality and Culture* 5 (3): 77–96.

McIlvenny, Paul. 1996a. "Heckling in Hyde Park: Verbal Audience Participation in Popular Public Discourse." *Language in Society* 25 (1): 27–60.

———. 1996b. "Popular Public Discourse at Speakers' Corner: Negotiating Cultural Identities in Interaction." *Discourse and Society* 7 (1): 7–37.

McLellan, Josie. 2007. "State Socialist Bodies: East German Nudism from Ban to Boom." *Journal of Modern History* 79 (1): 48–79.

———. 2009. "Visual Dangers and Delights: Nude Photography in East Germany." *Past and Present* 205 (1): 143–74.

McRuer, Robert. 2006. *Crip Theory: Cultural Signs of Queerness and Disability.* New York: New York University Press.

Meacham, Standish. 1999. *Regaining Paradise: Englishness and the Early Garden City Movement.* New Haven: Yale University Press.

Merrill, Frances, and Mason Merrill. 1931. *Among the Nudists.* London: Noel Douglas.

Merry, Sally Engle. 1988. "Legal Pluralism." *Law and Society Review* 22 (5): 869–96.

Metcalf, Bill, ed. 1995. *From Utopian Dreaming to Communal Reality: Cooperative Lifestyles in Australia.* Sydney: University of New South Wales Press.

Miller, Tim C., and Dan N. Stone. 2009. "Public Speaking Apprehension (PSA), Motivation and Affect among Accounting Majors: A Proof-of-Concept Intervention." *Issues in Accounting Education* 24 (2): 265–98.

Misri, Deepti. 2011. "'Are You a Man?' Performing Naked Protest in India." *Signs* 36 (3): 603–25.

Mitchell, Timothy. 1991. "The Limits of the State: Beyond Statist Approaches and Their Critics." *American Political Science Review* 85 (1): 77–96.

Möhring, Maren. 2005. "Working Out the Body's Boundaries: Physiological, Aesthetic, and Psychic Dimensions of the Skin in German Nudism, 1890–1930." In *Body Parts: Critical Explorations in Corporeality*, edited by Christopher Forth and Ivan Crozier, 229–46. Lanham, Md.: Lexington Books.

Moore, Geoff. 2004. "The Fair Trade Movement: Parameters, Issues and Future Research." *Journal of Business Ethics* 53 (1): 73–86.

Morris, William. 2003. *News from Nowhere, Or, an Epoch of Rest: Being Some Chapters from a Utopian Romance*. Oxford: Oxford University Press. Originally published 1890.

Moylan, Tom. 1986. *Demand the Impossible: Science Fiction and the Utopian Imagination*. New York: Methuen.

———. 2000. *Scraps of the Untainted Sky: Science Fiction, Utopia, Dystopia*. Boulder, Colo.: Westview Press.

Muñoz, José E. 2009. *Cruising Utopia: The Then and There of Queer Futurity*. New York: New York University Press.

Nail, Thomas. 2010. "Constructivism and the Future Anterior of Radical Politics." *Anarchist Developments in Cultural Studies* 1: 73–94.

Nash, Catherine J. 2011. "Trans Experiences in Lesbian and Queer Space." *Canadian Geographer / Le Géographe Canadien* 55 (2): 192–207.

Nash, Catherine J., and Alison Bain. 2007. "'Reclaiming Raunch': Spatializing Queer Identities at Toronto Women's Bathhouse Events." *Journal of Social and Cultural Geography* 8 (1): 47–62.

Neill, A. S. 1945. *Hearts Not Heads in the School*. London: H. Jenkins.

———. 1948. *That Dreadful School*. London: H. Jenkins.

———. 1967. *Talking of Summerhill*. London: Gollancz.

———. 1968. *Summerhill*. Harmondsworth, U.K.: Pelican.

Nelson, Michelle, Mark Rademacher, and Hye-Jin Paek. 2007. "Downshifting Consumer = Upshifting Citizen? An Examination of a Local Freecycle Community." *Annals of the American Academy of Political and Social Science* 611 (1): 141–56.

Newmahr, Staci. 2011. *Playing on the Edge: Sadomasochism, Risk, and Intimacy*. Bloomington: Indiana University Press.

Newman, Janet. 2001. *Modernising Governance: New Labour, Policy and Society*. London: Sage.

———. 2007. "The 'Double Dynamics' of Activation: Institutions, Citizens and the Remaking of Welfare Governance." *International Journal of Sociology and Social Policy* 27 (9–10): 364–75.

Newman, Janet, and John Clarke. 2009. *Publics, Politics and Power: Remaking the Public in Public Services*. London: Sage.

Noddings, Nel. 1984. *Caring: A Feminine Approach to Ethics and Moral Education*. Berkeley: University of California Press.

———. 2002. *Starting at Home: Caring and Social Policy*. Berkeley: University of California Press.

Nolan, James. 1998. *The Therapeutic State: Justifying Government at Century's End*. New York: New York University Press.

North, Peter. 1999. "Explorations in Heterotopia: Local Exchange Trading Schemes (LETS) and the Micropolitics of Money and Livelihood." *Environment and Planning D: Society and Space* 17 (1): 69–86.

———. 2006. *Alternative Currency Movements as a Challenge to Globalization? A Case-Study of Manchester's Local Currency Networks*. Aldershot, U.K.: Ashgate.

———. 2007. *Money and Liberation: The Micropolitics of Alternative Currency Movements*. Minneapolis: University of Minnesota Press.

Oakeshott, Michael. 1962. *Rationalism in Politics and Other Essays*. New York: Methuen.

———. 1990. *On Human Conduct*. Oxford: Clarendon Press.

Obrador-Pons, Pau. 2007. "A Haptic Geography of the Beach: Naked Bodies, Vision and Touch." *Social and Cultural Geography* 8 (1): 123–41.

———. 2009. "Building Castles in the Sand: Repositioning Touch on the Beach." *Senses and Society* 4 (2): 195–210.

O'Cinneide, Colm. 2007. "The Commission for Equality and Human Rights: A New Institution for New and Uncertain Times." *Industrial Law Journal* 36 (2): 141–62.

Oldenburg, Ray. 1989. *The Great Good Place: Cafes, Coffee Shops, Community Centers, Beauty Parlors, General Stores, Bars, Hangouts, and How They Get You through the Day*. New York: Paragon House.

Pacione, Michael. 1997. "Local Exchange Trading Systems as a Response to the Globalisation of Capitalism." *Urban Studies* 34 (8): 1179–97.

Painter, Joe. 2006. "Prosaic Geographies of Stateness." *Political Geography* 25 (7): 752–74.

Pallasmaa, Juhani. 2000. "Hapticity and Time: Notes on Fragile Architecture." *Architectural Review* 207 (1239): 78–84.

Parkins, Wendy. 2004. "Out of Time: Fast Subjects and Slow Living." *Time and Society* 13 (2–3): 363–82.

Parmelee, Maurice. 1929. *Nudism in Modern Life*. London: Noel Douglas.

Paterson, Mark. 2007. *The Senses of Touch: Haptics, Affects and Technologies*. Oxford: Berg.

Patton, Paul. 2010. *Deleuzian Concepts: Philosophy, Colonization, Politics*. Stanford: Stanford University Press.

Peacock, Mark. 2000. "Local Exchange Trading Systems: A Solution to the Employment Dilemma?" *Annals of Public and Cooperative Economics* 71 (1): 55–78.

Peeters, Evert. 2006. "Authenticity and Asceticism: Discourse and Performance in Nude Culture and Health Reform in Belgium, 1920–1940." *Journal of the History of Sexuality* 15 (3): 432–61.

Peñalver, Eduardo M., and Sonia Katyal. 2010. *Property Outlaws: How Squatters, Pirates, and Protesters Improve the Law of Ownership*. New Haven: Yale University Press.

Penner, James. 1996. "The 'Bundle of Rights' Picture of Property." *UCLA Law Review* 43: 711–820.

———. 1997. *The Idea of Property Law*. Oxford: Clarendon Press.

Peters, John D. 2005. *Courting the Abyss: Free Speech and the Liberal Tradition*. Chicago: University of Chicago Press.

Petrini, Carlo. 2001. *Slow Food: The Case for Taste*. New York: Columbia University Press.

Phillips, Anne. 1999. *Which Equalities Matter?* Cambridge, U.K.: Polity Press.

Piercy, Marge. 1976. *A Woman on the Edge of Time*. New York: Alfred A. Knopf.

Pietrykowski, Bruce. 2004. "You Are What You Eat: The Social Economy of the Slow Food Movement." *Review of Social Economy* 62 (3): 307–21.

Pinder, David. 2002. "In Defence of Utopian Urbanism: Imagining Cities after the 'End of Utopia.'" *Geografiska Annaler: Series B, Human Geography* 84 (3–4): 229–41.

Popenoe, Joshua. 1970. *Inside Summerhill*. New York: Hart.

Pratt, Mary Louise. 1991. "Arts of the Contact Zone." *Profession* 1991: 33–40.

———. 1992. *Imperial Eyes: Travel Writing and Transculturation*. New York: Routledge.

Purdue, Derrick, Jörge Dürrschmidt, Peter Jowers, and Richard O'Doherty. 1997. "DIY Culture and Extended Milieux: LETS, Veggie Boxes and Festivals." *Sociological Review* 45 (4): 645–67.

Raddon, Mary-Beth. 2003. *Community and Money: Men and Women Making Change*. Montreal: Black Rose Books.

Radin, Margaret Jane. 1993. *Reinterpreting Property*. Chicago: University of Chicago Press.

———. 1994. "What, If Anything, Is Wrong with Baby Selling." *Pacific Law Journal* 26: 135–45.

Raghuram, Parvati, Clare Madge, and Pat Noxolo. 2009. "Rethinking Responsibility and Care for a Postcolonial World." *Geoforum* 40 (1): 5–13.

Rai, Shirin. 1996. "Women and the State in the Third World." In *Women and Politics in the Third World*, edited by Haleh Afshar, 26–40. London: Routledge.

Rancière, Jacques. 1995. *On the Shores of Politics*. London: Routledge.

Rau, Henrike. 2002. "Time Divided—Time United? Temporal Aspects of German Unification." *Time and Society* 11 (2–3): 271–94.

Ravenscroft, Neil, and Paul Gilchrist. 2009. "Spaces of Transgression: Governance, Discipline and Reworking the Carnivalesque." *Leisure Studies* 28 (1): 35–49.

Rawls, John. 1996. *Political Liberalism*. New York: Columbia University Press.

Reader, Soran, and Gillian Brock. 2004. "Needs, Moral Demands and Moral Theory." *Utilitas* 16 (3): 251–66.

Rhodes, R. A. W. 1994. "The Hollowing Out of the State: The Changing Nature of the Public Service in Britain." *Political Quarterly* 65 (2): 138–51.

Richardson, Diane, and Surya Monro. 2012. *Sexuality, Equality and Diversity*. Basingstoke, U.K.: Palgrave Macmillan.

Ricoeur, Paul. 1986. *Lectures on Ideology and Utopia*. New York: Columbia University Press.

Rifkin, Jeremy. 1987. *Time Wars: The Primary Conflict in Human History*. New York: Henry Holt.

Roberts, John. 2000. "The Enigma of Free Speech: Speakers' Corner, the Geography of Governance and a Crisis of 'Rationality.'" *Social and Legal Studies* 9 (2): 271–92.

———. 2001. "Spatial Governance and Working Class Public Spheres: The Case of a Chartist Demonstration at Hyde Park." *Journal of Historical Sociology* 14 (3): 308–36.

———. 2008. "Expressive Free Speech, the State and the Public Sphere: A Bakhtinian-Deleuzian Analysis of 'Public Address' at Hyde Park." *Social Movement Studies* 7 (2): 101–19.

Robertson, James. 2005. *The New Economics of Sustainable Development—A Briefing for Policy Makers*. Originally published for the European Commission, 1999. http://www.jamesrobertson.com/book/neweconomicsofsustainabledevelopment.pdf

Robinson, Fiona. 1999. *Globalizing Care: Ethics, Feminist Theory, and International Relations*. Boulder, Colo.: Westview Press.

Robinson, Kim Stanley. 1993. *Red Mars*. New York: Spectra.

Roediger, David. 1999. "The Pursuit of Whiteness: Property, Terror, and Expansion, 1790–1860." *Journal of the Early Republic* 19 (4): 579–600.

Rose, Carol M. 1998. "The Several Futures of Property: Of Cyberspace and Folk Tales, Emission Trades and Ecosystems." *Minnesota Law Review* 83: 129–82.

Rose, Nikolas. 1996. "Governing Advanced Liberal Democracies." In *Foucault and Political Reason*, edited by Andrew Barry, Thomas Osborne, and Nikolas Rose, 37–64. London: UCL Press.

Roseneil, Sasha. 1995. *Disarming Patriarchy: Feminism and Political Action at Greenham*. Buckingham, U.K.: Open University Press.

Ross, Becki. 1995. *The House That Jill Built: A Lesbian Nation in Formation*. Toronto: University of Toronto Press.

Ross, Chad. 2005. *Naked Germany: Health, Race and the Nation*. Oxford: Berg.

Rossouw, Gedeon J., and Leon J. van Vuuren. 2003. "Modes of Managing Morality: A Descriptive Model of Strategies for Managing Ethics." *Journal of Business Ethics* 46 (4): 389–402.

Roy, Srirupa. 2006. "Seeing Like a State: National Commemorations and the Public Sphere in India and Turkey." *Comparative Study of Society and History* 48 (1): 200–232.

Ruddick, Sara. 1989. *Maternal Thinking: Toward a Politics of Peace*. Boston: Beacon Press.

Saldanha, Arun. 2005. "Trance and Visibility at Dawn: Racial Dynamics in Goa's Rave Scene." *Social and Cultural Geography* 6 (5): 707–21.

Salzani, Carlo. 2012. "*Quodlibet*: Giorgio Agamben's Anti-Utopia." *Utopian Studies* 23 (1): 212–37.

Santos, Boaventura de Sousa. 2006. *The Rise of the Global Left: The World Social Forum and Beyond*. London: Zed.

Sargisson, Lucy. 2000. *Utopian Bodies and the Politics of Transgression*. London: Routledge.

———. 2007. "The Curious Relationship between Politics and Utopia." In *Utopia*

Method Vision: The Use Value of Social Dreaming, edited by Tom Moylan and Raffaella Baccolini, 25–46. Bern, Switzerland: Peter Lang.

———. 2010. "Friends Have All Things in Common: Utopian Property Relations." *British Journal of Politics and International Relations* 12 (1): 22–36.

———. 2012. *Fool's Gold? Utopianism in the Twenty-First Century*. Basingstoke, U.K.: Palgrave Macmillan.

Sargisson, Lucy, and Lyman Tower Sargent. 2004. *Living in Utopia: New Zealand's Intentional Communities*. Aldershot, U.K.: Ashgate.

Schechner, Richard. 1985. *Between Theatre and Anthropology*. Philadelphia: University of Pennsylvania Press.

Schrank, Sarah. 2012. "Naked Houses: The Architecture of Nudism and the Rethinking of the American Suburbs." *Journal of Urban History* 38 (4): 635–61.

Schroeder, Jeanne Lorraine. 2004. *The Triumph of Venus: The Erotics of the Market*. Berkeley: University of California Press.

Scott, David. 2003. *Behind the G-String*. Jefferson, N.C.: McFarland.

Scott, James. 1998. *Seeing Like a State: How Certain Schemes to Improve the Human Condition Have Failed*. New Haven: Yale University Press.

Sedgwick, Eve Kosofsky. 2003. *Touching Feeling: Affect, Pedagogy, Performativity*. Durham: Duke University Press.

Segefjord, Bjarne. 1970. *Summerhill Diary*. London: Gollancz.

Sennett, Richard. 1992. *The Fall of Public Man*. New York: W. W. Norton.

Sevenhuijsen, Selma. 1998. *Citizenship and the Ethics of Care*. London: Routledge.

———. 2003. "The Place of Care: The Relevance of the Feminist Ethic of Care for Social Policy." *Feminist Theory* 4 (2): 179–97.

Seyfang, Gill. 2001a. "Community Currencies: Small Change for a Green Economy." *Environment and Planning A* 33 (6): 975–96.

———. 2001b. "Working for the Fenland Dollar: An Evaluation of Local Exchange Trading Schemes as an Informal Employment Strategy to Tackle Social Exclusion." *Work, Employment and Society* 15 (3): 581–93.

———. 2004. "Time Banks: Rewarding Community Self-Help in the Inner City?" *Community Development Journal* 39 (1): 62–71.

Seyfang, Gill, and Karen Smith. 2002. *The Time of Our Lives: Using Time Banking for Neighbourhood Renewal and Community Capacity Building*. London: New Economics Foundation.

Shephard, Liz, ed. 1997. LETS *Info Pack*. 8th ed. London: LETSlink UK.

Sherry, John F., Jr. 1990. "A Sociocultural Analysis of a Midwestern American Flea Market." *Journal of Consumer Research* 17 (1): 13–30.

Shildrick, Margrit. 2008. "Corporeal Cuts: Surgery and the Psycho-Social." *Body and Society* 14 (1): 31–46.

Shklar, Judith N. 1994. "What Is the Use of Utopia?" In *Heterotopia: Postmodern Utopia and the Body Politic*, edited by Tobin Siebers, 40–57. Ann Arbor: University of Michigan Press.

Shrum, Wesley, and John Kilburn. 1996. "Ritual Disrobement at Mardi Gras: Ceremonial Exchange and Moral Order." *Social Forces* 75 (2): 423–58.

Silk, John. 2004. "Caring at a Distance: Gift Theory, Aid Chains and Social Movements." *Social and Cultural Geography* 5 (2): 229–51.

Skinner, B. F. 1976. *Walden Two*. New York: Macmillan.

Śliwa, Martyna, and Kathleen Riach. 2012. "Making Scents of Transition: Smellscapes and the Everyday in 'Old' and 'New' Urban Poland." *Urban Studies* 49 (1): 23–41.

Smart, Alan. 1993. "Gifts, Bribes, and Guanxi: A Reconsideration of Bourdieu's Social Capital." *Cultural Anthropology* 8 (3): 388–408.

Smets, Peer, and Saskia ten Kate. 2008. "Let's Meet! Let's Exchange! LETS as an Instrument for Linking Asylum Seekers and the Host Community in the Netherlands." *Journal of Refugee Studies* 21 (3): 326–46.

Smith, H. W. 1980. "A Modest Test of Cross-Cultural Differences in Sexual Modesty, Embarrassment and Self-Disclosure." *Qualitative Sociology* 3 (3): 223–41.

Smith, Miriam C. 1999. *Lesbian and Gay Rights in Canada: Social Movements and Equality-Seeking, 1971–1995*. Toronto: University of Toronto Press.

Smith, Susan J. 1993. "Bounding the Borders: Claiming Space and Making Place in Rural Scotland." *Transactions of the Institute of British Geographers* 18 (3): 291–308.

Somerville, Margaret, and Tony Perkins. 2003. "Border Work in the Contact Zone: Thinking Indigenous–non-Indigenous Collaboration Spatially." *Journal of Intercultural Studies* 24 (3): 253–66.

Spencer, Sarah. 2008. "Equality and Human Rights Commission: A Decade in the Making." *Political Quarterly* 79 (1): 6–16.

Squires, Judith, and Mark Wickham-Jones. 2002. "Mainstreaming in Westminster and Whitehall: From Labour's Ministry for Women to the Women and Equality Unit." *Parliamentary Affairs* 55 (1): 57–70.

Srivastava, Sarita. 2005. "You're Calling Me a Racist? The Moral and Emotional Regulation of Antiracism and Feminism." *Signs* 31 (1): 29–62.

Staeheli, Lynn A., and Don Mitchell. 2008. *The People's Property? Power, Politics, and the Public*. New York: Routledge.

Stevens, Quentin. 2007. *The Ludic City: Exploring the Potential of Public Spaces*. London: Routledge.

Stillerman, Joel. 2006. "The Politics of Space and Culture in Santiago, Chile's Street Markets." *Qualitative Sociology* 29 (4): 507–30.

Strathern, Marilyn. 2004. "Losing (Out on) Intellectual Resources." In *Law, Anthropology, and the Constitution of the Social*, edited by Alain Pottage and Martha Mundy, 201–33. Cambridge: Cambridge University Press.

———. 2010. "Sharing, Stealing and Borrowing Simultaneously." In *Ownership and Appropriation*, edited by Veronica Strang and Mark Busse, 23–42. Oxford: Berg.

Stronach, Ian, and Heather Piper. 2008. "Can Liberal Education Make a Comeback? The Case of 'Relational Touch' at Summerhill School." *American Educational Research Journal* 45 (1): 6–37.

Styles, Joseph. 1979. "Outsider/Insider: Researching Gay Baths." *Urban Life* 8 (2): 139–52.

Sutton, Barbara. 2007. "Naked Protest: Memories of Bodies and Resistance at the World Social Forum." *Journal of International Women's Studies* 8 (3): 139–48.

Suvin, Darko. 1979. *Metamorphoses of Science Fiction*. New Haven: Yale University Press.

Tamanaha, Brian. 1993. "The Folly of the 'Social Scientific' Concept of Legal Pluralism." *Journal of Law and Society* 20 (2): 192–217.

Tattelman, Ira. 1999. "Speaking to the Gay Bathhouse: Communicating in Sexually Charged Spaces." In *Public Sex/Gay Space*, edited by William Leap, 71–94. New York: Columbia University Press.

———. 2000. "Presenting a Queer (Bath)House." In *Queer Frontiers: Millennial Geographies, Genders, and Generations*, edited by Joseph Boone, Martin Dupuis, Martin Meeker, Karin Quimby, Cindy Sarver, Debra Silverman, and Rosemary Weatherston, 222–58. Madison: University of Wisconsin Press.

Taylor, Antony. 1995. "'Commons Stealers,' 'Land-Grabbers' and 'Jerry Builders': Space, Popular Radicalism and the Politics of Public Access in London, 1848–1880." *International Review of Social History* 40 (3): 383–408.

Tewksbury, Richard. 2002. "Bathhouse Intercourse: Structural and Behavioral Aspects of an Erotic Oasis." *Deviant Behavior* 23 (1): 75–112.

Thomas, Keith. 2005. "Magical Healing: The King's Touch." In *The Book of Touch*, edited by Constance Classen, 354–62. Oxford: Berg.

Thompson, E. P. 1977. *William Morris: Romantic to Revolutionary*. Rev. ed. London: Merlin Press.

Thompson, Hunter. 2005. *Fear and Loathing in Las Vegas*. London: Harper Perennial. Originally published 1972.

Thrift, Nigel J. 2008. *Non-Representational Theory: Space, Politics, Affect*. London: Routledge.

Tiemann, Thomas K. 2008. "Grower-Only Farmers' Markets: Public Spaces and Third Places." *Journal of Popular Culture* 41 (3): 467–87.

Tietze, Susanne, and Gillian Musson. 2002. "When 'Work' Meets 'Home': Temporal Flexibility as Lived Experience." *Time and Society* 11 (2–3): 315–34.

Tronto, Joan. 1993. *Moral Boundaries*. New York: Routledge.

Tsing, Anna Lowenhaupt. 2005. *Friction: An Ethnography of Global Connection*. Princeton: Princeton University Press.

Twitchell, James B. 1992. *Carnival Culture: The Trashing of Taste in America*. New York: Columbia University Press.

Underkuffler, Laura S. 2003. *The Idea of Property: Its Meaning and Power*. Oxford: Oxford University Press.

Valverde, Mariana. 1999. "Derrida's Justice and Foucault's Freedom: Ethics, History, and Social Movements." *Law and Social Inquiry* 24 (3): 655–76.

Valverde, Mariana, and Miomir Cirak. 2003. "Governing Bodies, Creating Gay Spaces: Policing and Security Issues in 'Gay' Downtown Toronto." *British Journal of Criminology* 43 (1): 102–21.

Vincent, Susan. 2003. "Preserving Domesticity: Reading Tupperware in Women's Changing Domestic, Social and Economic Roles." *Canadian Review of Sociology and Anthropology* 40 (2): 171–96.

Voskuil, Lynn. 2002. "Feeling Public: Sensation Theater, Commodity Culture, and the Victorian Public Sphere." *Victorian Studies* 44 (2): 245–74.

Waldron, Jeremy. 1996. "Rights and Needs: The Myth of Disjunction." In *Legal Rights: Historical and Philosophical Perspectives*, edited by Austin Sarat and Thomas R. Kearns, 87–109. Ann Arbor: University of Michigan Press.

Warner, Michael. 2002. *Publics and Counterpublics*. New York: Zone Books.

Warner, Tom. 2002. *Never Going Back: A History of Queer Activism in Canada*. Toronto: University of Toronto Press.

Warren, Howard. 1933. "Social Nudism and the Body Taboo." *Psychological Review* 40 (2): 160–83.

Watson, Irene. 1998. "Naked Peoples: Rules and Regulations." *Law Text Culture* 4 (1): 1–17.

Watson, Sophie. 2009. "The Magic of the Marketplace: Sociality in a Neglected Public Space." *Urban Studies* 46 (8): 1577–91.

Wegner, Phillip. 2002. *Imaginary Communities: Utopia, the Nation, and the Spatial Histories of Modernity*. Berkeley: University of California Press.

Weinberg, Martin. 1965. "Sexual Modesty, Social Meanings, and the Nudist Camp." *Social Problems* 12 (3): 311–18.

Weinberg, Martin, and Colin J. Williams. 1979. "Gay Baths and the Social Organization of Impersonal Sex." In *Gay Men: The Sociology of Homosexuality*, edited by Martin Levine, 164–81. New York: Harper and Row.

Wells, H. G. 2005. *A Modern Utopia*, edited by Gregory Claeys and Patrick Parrinder. London: Penguin Books. Originally published 1905.

White, Harrison C. 1981. "Where Do Markets Come From?" *American Journal of Sociology* 87 (3): 517–47.

———. 2002. *Markets from Networks: Socioeconomic Models of Production*. Princeton: Princeton University Press.

White, Julie A., and Joan C. Tronto. 2004. "Political Practices of Care: Needs and Rights." *Ratio Juris* 17 (4): 425–53.

Whyte, Jessica. 2010. "'A New Use of the Self': Giorgio Agamben on the Coming Community." *Theory & Event* 13 (1). Project MUSE, available at http://muse.jhu.edu/.

Wigfield, Andrea, and Royce Turner. 2010. *Good Relations Measurement Framework*. London: Equality and Human Rights Commission.

Williams, Colin C. 1996a. "Informal Sector Responses to Unemployment: An Evaluation of the Potential of Local Exchange Trading Systems (LETS)." *Work, Employment and Society* 10 (2): 341–59.

———. 1996b. "Local Exchange and Trading Systems: A New Source of Work and Credit for the Poor and Unemployed?" *Environment and Planning A* 28 (8): 1395–415.

Williams, Colin C., Theresa Aldridge, Roger Lee, Andrew Leyshon, Nigel Thrift, and Jane Tooke. 2001. "Bridges into Work? An Evaluation of Local Exchange and Trading Schemes (LETS)." *Policy Studies* 22 (2): 119–32.

Williams, Colin C., Theresa Aldridge, and Jane Tooke. 2003. "Alternative Exchange

Spaces." In *Alternative Economic Spaces*, edited by Andrew Leyshon, Roger Lee, and Colin Williams, 151–67. London: Sage.

Williams, Colin C., and Jan Windebank. 2001a. "Beyond Social Inclusion through Employment: Harnessing Mutual Aid as a Complementary Social Inclusion Policy." *Policy and Politics* 29 (1): 15–27.

Williams, Colin C., and Jan Windebank. 2001b. "Reconceptualising Paid Informal Exchange: Some Lessons from English Cities." *Environment and Planning A* 33 (1): 121–40.

Woodall, Ellen. 2002. "The American Nudist Movement: From Cooperative to Capital, the Song Remains the Same." *Journal of Popular Culture* 36 (2): 264–84.

Worley, Claire. 2005. "'It's Not about Race. It's about the Community': New Labour and 'Community Cohesion.'" *Critical Social Policy* 25 (4): 483–96.

Wright, Erik O. 2011. "Real Utopias." *Contexts* 10 (2): 36–42.

Wyschogrod, Edith. 1981. "Empathy and Sympathy as Tactile Encounter." *Journal of Medicine and Philosophy* 6 (1): 25–44.

Young, Iris M. 1990. *Justice and the Politics of Difference*. Princeton: Princeton University Press.

———. 1997. "Asymmetrical Reciprocity: On Moral Respect, Wonder, and Enlarged Thought." *Constellations* 3 (3): 340–63.

Yuval-Davis, Nira. 2006. "Belonging and the Politics of Belonging." *Patterns of Prejudice* 40 (3): 197–214.

Zerilli, Linda. 1995. "The Arendtian Body." In *Feminist Interpretations of Hannah Arendt*, edited by Bonnie Honig, 167–93. University Park, Penn.: Pennsylvania State University Press.

———. 2005. "'We Feel our Freedom': Imagination and Judgment in the Thought of Hannah Arendt." *Political Theory* 33 (2): 158–88.

Zukin, Sharon. 1995. *The Cultures of Cities*. Malden, Mass.: Blackwell.

INDEX

Care (*continued*)
122; inequality and, 111; limits of, 127; at marketplace, 199; needs and, 112; as normative concept, 101; racism and, 111; responsibility and, 113; of self, 107, 116–17; time and, 114; vulnerability and, 114–15. *See also* Feminist care ethics

Caring, 123–24

Carnival, 202–5

Casting equality, 51–53, 57–58, 67; as everyday utopia, 47–48; state power and, 237n46. *See also* Equality

Casual sex, 123, 125. *See also* Bathhouse; Toronto Women's and Trans Bathhouse

Chakrabarty, Dipesh, 27

Children, 177, 181–82

Circulatory publics, 88–90, 241n34. *See also* Publics

City space, 96–97

Class: LETS, 143–45; nudism, 83–84; Speakers' Corner, 192–93

Cloud, John, 82

Cloyes, Kristin, 110–11, 115

Coldin, Brian, 74

Coleman, Stephen, 191, 192

Collective identity, 174

Community: through adjudication, 174; boundaries of, 179–80; life, 173; ownership by, 175; property, 159

Community labor: challenges facing, 145–46; design of, 146–48; dimensions of, 137–39; failure of, 153; as inspiring, 153; virtuous cycle, 140. *See also* LETS

Community time, 135, 140–43, 148. *See also* Temporalities

Concepts: actualized, 35; approach toward, 11–15; as colonizing, 126–27; dominant social relations and, 27–30; as dynamic, 36–37; future oriented, 219; histories of, 27; as idealized, 29, 126–27; as ideas, 26–27; as imagined, 35; legitimizing status quo, 28; as lenses, 46, 48–49; materialist approach, 12, 25, 127; more-than-

linguistic, 41; as multiply articulated, 187–88; nonmanifestation, 37, 153–54; potential and, 38, 77–78, 220; recognition of, 41–44, 156; unuttered, 76. *See also* Normative concepts

Conceptual lines, 18, 37, 39, 187–88; creation of new ones, 14; destabilizing of, 43; of equality, 78; force of, 226–27; of marketplace, 199, 207; through nudism, 93; past and, 222–23; as plural, 225; present and, 224–25; of property, 182, 184; as queer, 13; recognition of, 227; social practice and, 221; as stable, 224–25; of state, 68

Concrete utopias, 3–4

Connolly, William, 36–37

Contact zones, 208–10

Contagion, 89–90

Crewe, Louise, 196

Critical distance, 9, 226

Critical proximity, 7, 9, 69, 151, 226

Currency. *See* LETS

Cvetkovich, Ann, 63

Daley, Caroline, 96

Darr, Asaf, 147

Dean, Mitchell, 187

Defamiliarization, 5, 9

Deleuze, Gilles, 26, 249n2

Derrida, Jacques, 37, 197, 243n14

Desire: education of, 81, 103–4

Dickberry, F., 73

Disability, 55, 82–83, 109

Dominion, 167

Dumm, Thomas, 237n45

Dystopia, 30–31

Ealing Council, 63

Economy: equality and, 58; transactions, 147. *See also* LETS; Marketplace

Edgework, 210–13

Emotion. *See* Feeling

Engster, Daniel, 112–13, 117

Epistemology: from margins, 32; utopian 32–34. *See also* Concepts; Conceptual lines; Utopian

Equality: comparison and, 93; concept

Henricks, Thomas, 200–201
Hepple, Bob, 56
Hetherington, Kevin, 40, 41, 51
Holmes, Oliver Wendell, 193
hooks, bell, 32
Hope, Wayne, 245n17
Huizinga, Johan, 199, 211
Humphrey, Chris, 202
Hyde Park, 192, 210
Hygiene: at bathhouse, 106–7; nudism
and, 89–90

Idealized concepts, 28–29, 126–27, 221.
See also Concepts; Normative con-
cepts
Imagining, 12, 35; within actualization,
38; movement from, 219; power of,
39. *See also* Concepts
Ineffable, 40–41, 76, 124. *See also*
Sensation
Inequality: care and, 111; knowledge of,
60; plural, 64; state understanding of,
63. *See also* Equality
Institute for Community Cohesion, 57
Intimate life, 167–68

Jacobs, Jane, 177
Jacoby, Russell, 229n5, 233n14
Jameson, Fredric, 33, 187, 229n8
Jordan, Jill, 130, 148
Josipovici, Gabriel, 50

Kanter, Rosabeth Moss, 179
Keenan, Sarah, 40, 162, 169

Labor market: norms, 147; time, 135, 143–
45. *See also* LETS; Temporalities
Lahav, Gallya, 68
Langdon-Davies, John, 81
Latour, Bruno, 39–40
Leccardi, Carmen, 151
Legal pluralism, 27–28, 136; property
and, 164, 166. *See also* Norms; Rules
LETS (Local Exchange Trading Schemes),
1; challenges faced, 134–35, 145–46;
community building, 139; contribu-
tion of, 134; currency, 130, 132; de-

cline, 133, 149; as everyday utopia,
130; future and, 141; as gift, 140; labor
market and, 143–45; legitimate expectations, 150; member reputations,
150; norm-making, 149; operation
of, 131–32; organizational involvement in, 132; origins of, 131; past and,
141; pricing, 148; proximity to mainstream, 143, 150–52; rhythms, 141,
152; schemes, 132–33; services available, 143; sociability, 137–38, 153; sociality, 141, 152; systems, 132–33; temporalities, 140, 144–45, 147, 151; time
problems, 135; trader autonomy, 148,
150; virtuous cycle, 150, 153–54
Levitas, Ruth, 3, 33, 41, 60, 98, 218, 231n1
Liking: physical display of, 172; property
and, 169–70. *See also* Feeling
Linton, Michael, 131, 132
Lyng, Stephen, 211

MacCormick, Neil, 68
Maher, JaneMaree, 143–44
Manning, Erin, 50
Market: competition and, 194, 248n9;
as concept, 197–99; critique of, 187,
194–95; gift and, 196–97; parody of,
215; play and, 200, 204, 206, 213–15
Marketplace: carnival and, 202–5; di-
versity and, 198; of ideas, 193–96;
payment lacking, 196–98; selection
and, 198; as sociable, 195–96; tast-
ing and, 207–8; tension and, 199;
worth and, 204–5
Marx, Karl, 219
Massey, Doreen, 26, 184–85
Massumi, Brian, 59
May, Todd, 77
Mbembe, Achille, 30, 234n6
Mediations, 39–40; of nudism, 91
Merrill, Frances and Mason, 81, 83, 89
Merry, Sally Engle, 136
Metcalf, Bill, 155
Morality, 121–22
More-than-linguistic concepts. *See*
Ineffable
Morris, William, 42, 196

Property (*continued*)
164–65, 177; sharing and, 170; simplification and, 165–66; stewardship, 176–77; in vote, 164
Proprioception, 50, 94–95
Protected characteristics, 51–52, 56. *See also* Equality
Public appearance, 93–95. *See also* Publics
Public nakedness, 77, 80–81, 89, 93–95
Public norms. *See* Norms
Public nudism. *See* Nudism
Publics: appearing in, 93–95; circulatory, 88–90, 241n34; orientational, 90–93; place, 95–97; sphere, 88
Pussy Palace, 1–2, 103. *See also* Toronto Women's and Trans Bathhouse

Queer, 42–43; equality and, 87

Racism: care and, 111; feminism and, 110; nudism and, 82–84; Toronto Women's and Trans Bathhouse and, 109–11
Radin, Margaret Jane, 162, 171, 183
Rancière, Jacques, 77
Ravenscroft, Neil, 202–3
Rawls, John, 28
Readhead, Zoe, 157, 164, 168, 171, 177; future and, 224; as guardian, 176; as owner, 174, 175; school reputation and, 181–82
Recognition, 41–44; as plural, 164; property and, 163–65
Rees, Jonathan, 47–48
Relationship trading, 130
Risk: play and, 211–12; sex and, 115
Roberts, John, 191–92
Robinson, Kim Stanley, 36
Rose, Carol, 179
Roseneil, Sasha, 12
Rules: within associational nudism, 82, 93; bathhouse, 104, 122; ethics and, 122; at Speakers' Corner, 195–96; at Summerhill, 180. *See also* Norms

Sargent, Lyman Tower, 7
Sargisson, Lucy, 7

Scott, David, 89
Seclusion, 168–69
Sedgwick, Eve Kosofsky, 217
Selfhood, 171
Sennett, Richard, 203
Sensation, 41; of bathhouse emissions, 119; of being naked, 89. *See also* Feeling; Tasting; Touch
Senses of Touch, The, 49
Sevenhuijsen, Selma, 120
Sex: after-care, 108; agreements, 115; anonymous, 107; as needs, 117–18; risk and, 115. *See also* Bathhouse; Toronto Women's and Trans Bathhouse
Sexual agency, 103–4
Sexual education, 103
Shared space nudism, 79–80. *See also* Nudism
Shephard, Liz, 152
Slow food, 10
Social capital, 139
Social marginality, 190
Sociality: through trade, 152; in work, 146–47. *See also* Community labor
Somerville, Margaret, 209
Southall Black Sisters, 63
Speakers' Corner, 2; as carnival, 203; as contact zone, 208–10; edgework, 210–13; as everyday utopia, 189–90; location, 188–89; as marketplace, 195; masculinity of, 190; origins, 191–92; risky play and, 211–12; tasting at, 206–7; tension at, 199; as third place, 208, 209; users, 191
Srivastava, Sarita, 110, 124
State: apology, 61–62; as assemblage, 66; boundaries of, 237n47; coercive touch, 46; as concept, 65–66; feeling, 63–64, 69; identities, 66–70; imagining of, 38, 67; senses and, 45–46, 70–71; thinned out, 68–70; touch, 46, 48, 71; as touched, 61–63; as utopia, 47
Stevens, Quentin, 211
Stewardship, 176–77. *See also* Property
St-Pierre, Dave, 73

Strangers: sex, 107–8; Speakers' Corner, 189, 209–10; trading and, 138. *See also* Visitors

Strathern, Marilyn, 181

Stronach, Ian, 171

Styles, Joseph, 128

Summerhill, 156–57; authentic self and, 171; belonging, 173; democracy at, 224; as everyday utopia, 157; as family, 173; governance of, 177–78; as home, 157; laws, 165, 181; legal dispute, 176; ownership, 165, 174–75; physical contact at, 172; property, 159, 164–65, 182–83; visitors, 179–80

Suvin, Darko, 24

Tamanaha, Brian, 27

Tasting, 205–8. *See also* Sensation; Touch

Tattelman, Ira, 113, 128

Taylor, Antony, 192

Temporalities: capitalist, 140–41; LETS narratives, 141, 144–45; normative, 94–95, 135–37, 146–48; plural, 151–52. *See also* Future; Past; Present

Thompson, Hunter, 211

Tiemann, Thomas, 196

Tietze, Susanne, 143–44

Time. *See* Temporalities

Toronto Women's and Trans Bathhouse, 7, 103–5; accounts of racism, 109–111; ethics, 120–25; name change, 242n2; politics, 109; stranger sex at, 107–8; vulnerability, 114–16. *See also* Bathhouse; Care; Feminist care ethics

Touch, 49–51; as affect, 50; of disadvantaged, 56; effects of, 71; equality and, 92; as governmental technology, 54; idioms, 46, 53–54, 57; as knowledge, 48, 51; lack of, 58; as lens, 48–49; as light, 55; play and, 210; proximity and, 55; as reciprocating, 50; felt by state, 61–63; at Summerhill, 172. *See also* Sensation

Touch-chains, 55

Touching-feeling state, 65

Trading: sociability norms, 137–38; sociality and, 244n6, 245n14; strangers and, 138. *See also* LETS; Market; Marketplace

Trans discrimination, 106, 109

Tronto, Joan, 112, 117

Tsing, Anna Lowenhaupt, 199, 209

Tunick, Spencer, 84, 89

Unutterable. *See* Ineffable

Urban nudism, 96–97

Utopia: actualization of, 25; as blueprint, 4; change and, 31, 34; concept of, 36; critique and, 5, 18–19, 32–33; as failure, 4; imperfection and, 7; as impossible, 5–6; visitor to, 15–16; as world-building, 33

Utopian: as academic field, 3–7, 33–34, 37, 44, 217–18; as attitude, 34, 220–21; conceptualizing 37, 156; epistemology, 32–34; norms, 189–90; objects, 3; orientation, 3, 5; property and, 183–84; work performed by, 24–25

Variegated social, 158

Visitors, at intentional communities, 179; misrecognition, 42; for research, 15–16, 19; at Summerhill, 179–80; in utopia, 15, 42

Warner, Michael, 88, 93

Webb, Terri Sue, 77

Weinberg, Martin, 113

Welch, Andrew, 77

Wells, H. G., 7

Williams, Colin C., 131, 139, 143

Williams, Colin J., 113

Windebank, Jan, 139

Woman on the Edge of Time, 42

Work/home boundaries, 143–44

World naked bike ride, 73, 80, 94

Wyschogrod, Edith, 50

Zerilli, Linda, 35

Made in the USA
Lexington, KY
14 July 2018